Understanding
The Odyssey

Understanding
The Odyssey

A STUDENT CASEBOOK TO
ISSUES, SOURCES, AND
HISTORIC DOCUMENTS

Claudia Durst Johnson
and Vernon Johnson

The Greenwood Press
"Literature in Context" Series
Claudia Durst Johnson, Series Editor

GREENWOOD PRESS
Westport, Connecticut • London

The Greenwood Press "Literature in Context" Series
Student Casebooks to Issues, Sources, and Historical Documents

The Adventures of Huckleberry Finn
by Claudia Durst Johnson

Animal Farm
by John Rodden

Anne Frank's *The Diary of a Young Girl*
by Hedda Rosner Kopf

The Call of the Wild
by Claudia Durst Johnson

The Catcher in the Rye
by Sanford and Ann Pinsker

The Crucible
by Claudia Durst Johnson
and Vernon E. Johnson

Death of a Salesman
by Brenda Murphy and
Susan C. W. Abbotson

The Grapes of Wrath
by Claudia Durst Johnson

Great Expectations
by George Newlin

The Great Gatsby
by Dalton Gross and MaryJean Gross

Hamlet by Richard Corum

I Know Why the Caged Bird Sings
by Joanne Megna-Wallace

Jamaica Kincaid's *Annie John*
by Deborah Mistron

Jane Eyre
by Debra Teachman

The Literature of World War II
by James H. Meredith

Lord of the Flies
by Kirstin Olsen

Macbeth
by Faith Nostbakken

The Merchant of Venice
by Jay L. Halio

O Pioneers! and *My Antonia*
by Sheryl L. Meyering

Of Mice and Men, The Red Pony, and *The Pearl*
by Claudia Durst Johnson

The Old Man and the Sea
by Patricia Dunlavy Valenti

Othello
by Faith Nostbakken

Pride and Prejudice
by Debra Teachman

A Raisin in the Sun
by Lynn Domina

The Red Badge of Courage
by Claudia Durst Johnson

Richard Wright's *Black Boy*
by Robert Felgar

Romeo and Juliet
by Alan Hager

The Scarlet Letter
by Claudia Durst Johnson

A Separate Peace
by Hallman Bell Bryant

Shakespeare's *Julius Caesar*
by Thomas Derrick

A Tale of Two Cities
by George Newlin

Things Fall Apart
by Kalu Ogbaa

To Kill a Mockingbird
by Claudia Durst Johnson

Zora Neale Hurston's *Their Eyes Were Watching God*
by Neal A. Lester

Library of Congress Cataloging-in-Publication Data

Johnson, Claudia D.
  Understanding the Odyssey : a student casebook to issues, sources, and historic documents / Claudia Durst Johnson and Vernon Johnson.
      p.   cm.—(The Greenwood Press "literature in context" series, ISSN 1074–598X)
  Includes bibliographical references and index.
  ISBN 0–313–30881–0 (alk. paper)
  1. Homer. Odyssey. 2. Odysseus (Greek mythology) in literature. 3. Epic poetry, Greek—History and criticism. I. Johnson, Vernon E. (Vernon Elso), 1921–
II. Title. III. Series.

PA4167 .J635 2003
883′.01—dc21   2002028440

British Library Cataloging in Publication Data is available.

Copyright © 2003 by Claudia Durst Johnson and Vernon Johnson

All rights reserved. No portion of this book may be reproduced, by any process or technique, without the express written consent of the publisher.

Library of Congress Catalog Card Number: 2002028440
ISBN: 0–313–30881–0
ISSN: 1074–598X

First published in 2003

Greenwood Press, 88 Post Road West, Westport, CT 06881
An imprint of Greenwood Publishing Group, Inc.
www.greenwood.com

Printed in the United States of America

The paper used in this book complies with the Permanent Paper Standard issued by the National Information Standards Organization (Z39.48–1984).

10 9 8 7 6 5 4 3 2 1

Every reasonable effort has been made to trace the owners of copyright materials in this book, but in some instances this has proven impossible. The author and publisher will be glad to receive information leading to more complete acknowledgments in subsequent printings of the book, and in the meantime extend their apologies for any omissions.

Copyright Acknowledgments

James F. Clarity, "Arsonists Burn 10 Catholic Churches in Ulster," *New York Times*, 3 July 1998. Copyright © 2001 by the New York Times Co. Reprinted by permission.
James F. Clarity, "Ulster Foes Suspend a Last-Ditch Effort to Avoid a Clash After Slight Progress," *New York Times*, 12 July 1998. Copyright © 2001 by the New York Times Co. Reprinted by permission.
James F. Clarity, "Three Catholic Brothers Killed in Fire, Stunning Ulster and Raising Fears," *New York Times*, 13 July 1998. Copyright © 2001 by the New York Times Co. Reprinted by permission.
Serge Schmemann, "Israel Strikes Hard at Gaza Strip," *New York Times*, 7 March 2002. Copyright © 2001 by the New York Times Co. Reprinted by permission.
James Bennet, "For Fatah, Only a War Can Bring Peace to the Mideast," *New York Times*, 7 March 2002. Copyright © 2001 by the New York Times Co. Reprinted by permission.
"The War Against America. An Unfathomable Attack," *New York Times*, 12 September 2001. Copyright © 2001 by the New York Times Co. Reprinted by permission.
Eric Schmitt and Thom Shanker, "Administration Considers Broader, More Powerful Options for Potential Retaliation," *New York Times*, 13 September 2001. Copyright © 2001 by the New York Times Co. Reprinted by permission.
Blaine Harden, "For Many, Sorrow Turns to Anger and Talk of Vengeance," *New York Times*, 14 September 2001. Copyright © 2001 by the New York Times Co. Reprinted by permission.
Jane Fritsch, "Rescue Workers Rush In, But Many Do Not Return," *New York Times*, 12 September 2001. Copyright © 2001 by the New York Times Co. Reprinted by permission.
Martin Snapp, "It's a Hero's Welcome for FDNY Firefighter," *The (Richmond, CA) Journal*, 8 March 2002. Reprinted with permission.
Martin Snapp, "Mark Bingham Remembered," The (Richmond, CA) Journal, 8 March 2002. Reprinted with permission.

Contents

Introduction   xiii

1. A Literary Analysis of Homer's *The Odyssey*: Transformation and Return   1

2. Greek Mythology and Homer   15

    FROM:
    Thomas Bulfinch, *The Age of Fable* (1898)   28

    FROM:
    Herodotus, *The Histories,* Book II, trans. Henry Cary (1854)   30

    FROM:
    Hesiod, *Theogony, in Hesiod: The Homeric Hymns and Homerica*, trans. Hugh G. Evelyn-White (1914)   32

    FROM:
    Alexander S. Murray, *Manual of Mythology* (1888)   37

    FROM:
    Pausanias, *Guide to Greece*, Book VIII, trans. W.H.S. Jones (1933)   43

    FROM:
    Plato, *The Republic*, Books II and III, in *The Dialogues of Plato*, trans. Benjamin Jowett (1871)   45

3. The Geography of *The Odyssey*   55

    FROM:
    Max Cary, *The Geographic Background of Greek and
    Roman History* (1949)   63

    FROM:
    Strabo, *The Geography of Strabo*, vol. 3, trans. Horace Leonard
    Jones (1917)   65

    FROM:
    Thucydides, *The Histories*, vol. 1, trans. Benjamin Jowett (1900)   67

    FROM:
    Tim Severin, *The Ulysses Voyage* (1987)   68

4. Archaeological Excavations Pertinent to Homer's Epics   71

    FROM:
    Sir Arthur Evans, *The Palace of Minos,* vol. 2, (1928)   77

    FROM:
    Henry (Heinrich) Schliemann, *Mycenae* (1880)   80

    FROM:
    Chrestos Tsountas, *The Mycenaean Age* (1897)   83

5. The Historical Context of *The Odyssey*   87

    FROM:
    Thucydides, The Histories, vol. 1, trans. Benjamin Jowett (1900)   97

    FROM:
    Charles Freeman, *The Greek Achievement* (1999)   99

    FROM:
    John Bagnell Bury, *A History of Greece* (1927)   100

    FROM:
    Robin Osborne, *Greece in the Making* (1996)   102

6. The Trojan War of Myth and Legend   107

    FROM:
    Herodotus, *The History of Herodotus,* trans. George
    Rawlinson (1928)   118

	FROM: *Thucydides, The Histories,* vol. 1, trans. Benjamin Jowett (1900)	122
	FROM: John Bagnell Bury, *A History of Greece* (1927)	124
	FROM: Carl W. Blegen, *Troy and the Trojans* (1963)	126
7.	Supporting Players in *The Odyssey:* The Underclasses	131
	FROM: Hesiod, *Works and Days,* in *Hesiod,* trans. Hugh G. Evelyn-White (1914)	136
	FROM: Michael Wood, *In Search of the Trojan War* (1985)	138
	FROM: Aristotle, *Politics (1944),* trans. Harris Rackham	139
8.	Modern Applications: The Problem of Revenge	143
	FROM: Aeschylus, *The Eumenides,* trans. Philip Vellacott (1956)	151
	FROM: James F. Clarity, "Arsonists Burn 10 Catholic Churches in Ulster," *New York Times* (July 3, 1998)	153
	FROM: James F. Clarity, "Ulster Foes Suspend a Last-Ditch Effort to Avoid a Clash After Slight Progress," *New York Times* (July 12, 1998)	154
	FROM: James F. Clarity, "Three Catholic Brothers Killed in Fire, Stunning Ulster and Raising Fears," *New York Times* (July 13, 1998)	155
	FROM: Serge Schmemann, "Israel Strikes Hard at Gaza Strip," *New York Times* (March 7, 2002)	157
	FROM: James Bennet, "For Fatah, Only a War Can Bring Peace to the Mideast," *New York Times* (March 7, 2002)	157

FROM:
"The War Against America. An Unfathomable Attack,"
New York Times (September 12, 2001)   159

FROM:
Eric Schmitt and Thom Shanker, "Administration Considers Broader, More Powerful Options for Potential Retaliation,"
New York Times (September 13, 2001)   160

FROM:
Blaine Harden, "For Many, Sorrow Turns to Anger and Talk of Vengeance," *New York Times* (September 14, 2001)   161

9. Contemporary Applications: The Athlete and Athletics   165

FROM:
Richard Schaap, *An Illustrated History of the Olympics* (1963)   172

FROM:
"Gold Medal for Jesse Owens," Hearings Before the Subcommittee on Consumer Affairs and Coinage, 100th Congress, July 12, 1988 (1988)   175

FROM:
Janet C. Harris, *Athletes and the American Hero Dilemma* (1994)   179

10. Modern Applications: The Evolution of the Heroic Ideal   183

FROM:
Sergeant York: His Own Life Story and War Diary, ed. Tom Skeyhill (1928)   192

FROM:
Official Narrative for Medal of Honor Recipient Murphy, Audie L.; Committee on Veterans' Affairs, U.S. Senate, Medal of Honor Recipients (1973)   203

FROM:
Hugh Thompson Jr., testimony, in *Report of the Department of the Army Review of the Preliminary Investigation into the My Lai Incident* (1970)   207

FROM:
The Soldier's Medal for Heroism Awarded to Hugh C.
Thompson, Jr. (1998)   209

FROM:
Jane Fritsch, "Rescue Workers Rush In, but Many Do Not
Return," *New York Times* (September 12, 2001)   212

FROM:
Martin Snapp, "It's a Hero's Welcome for FDNY
Firefighter," *The Journal (Richmond, CA),* (March 8, 2002)   213

FROM:
Martin Snapp, "Mark Bingham Remembered," *The
Journal* (Richmond, CA), (March 8, 2002)   215

Index   219

Introduction

Homer's epic, *The Odyssey*, composed in Greece around the eighth century B.C., has resonated throughout the Western world for over 2,700 years, as few other works of literature have. Its title long ago became synonymous with the adventure-filled journey of a single hero, whether real or fictional, profound or mundane. Few literary odysseys or journeys have failed to draw on the ancient story of Odysseus, literally or metaphorically depicting engaging giants and monsters, the resisting of sirens and other temptresses, or a descent to the land of the dead.

It is difficult to overstate the influence of *The Odyssey*. The Greeks gave Homer the stature of a god and treated his works as sacred texts. Homer was the primary source for playwrights of classical Greece in the fifth century B.C., one of the two or three most illustrious periods of Western drama. Alexander the Great was just the first of many larger-than-life soldiers inspired by the warriors in Homer's epics. Homer's influence is also to be found in classical literary masterpieces of other countries: Virgil's *Aenead*, Dante's *Divine Comedy*, Cervantes' *Don Quixote*, Shakespeare's *Troilus and Cressida*, John Milton's *Paradise Lost*, and even in Mark Twain's antiheroic saga, *Adventures of Huckleberry Finn*. In the twentieth-century novel *Ulysses*, regarded as one of the most important works of fiction in modern English, the Irish novelist James Joyce takes his title, incidents, and themes from Homer's classic, transporting and translating them to modern-day Dublin. Charles Frazier's 1997 publishing phenomenon, the novel *Cold Mountain*, which sold 2.8 million copies, was also the story of a returning warrior, this time a wounded Confederate soldier in the American Civil War, whose journey back home to the woman he loves is very much in the vein of Homer's *The Odyssey*.

A remarkable illustration of the enduring power of *The Odyssey* can be observed as recently as the turn of the twenty-first century, when Hollywood's Universal Studios released a popular film, *Oh Brother, Where Art Thou?*, described as a comedic rendering of *The Odyssey*, this time set in the state of Mississippi in 1937. The major character, wily like Odysseus, is named Ulysses Everett McGill. Just as Homer's Odysseus journeys to rejoin his wife Penelope, so McGill is going home, after his imprisonment in the penitentiary, to his wife, named Penny. Like Homer's Penelope, Penny has attracted suitors in McGill's absence. A riverside baptism has the same narcotic effect on McGill's companions as the Land of the Lotus Eaters has on Odysseus' men. They also are tempted by sirens, and encounter a one-eyed villain (like Odysseus' Cyclopes) and a politician named Homer Stokes.

Homer has not only been an original source of inspiration for writers, painters, sculptors, and filmmakers, he is our first source of information about the mythology, history, and culture of ancient Greece.

The Odyssey is classified as an epic, a long poem delineating the mythic stories and, through them, the values of a nation at its inception. The epic follows a single hero whose presence unifies the numerous episodic challenges typical of the work. The larger-than-life central characters of epics take on colossal challenges: escaping a one-eyed monster (as Odysseus does), slaying a monster (as Beowulf does in the Old English epic), leading the enslaved Israelites safely out of Egypt and across the Red Sea, as Moses does in Exodus, and daring to pass through the gates of hell, from which no living human returns, as Dante does in *The Divine Comedy*. The epic hero brings enormous, godlike mental, physical, and spiritual power to the task of overcoming supernatural enemies. In each instance, the epic hero reenacts defining moments in the early development of a national culture.

Epics were sometimes literary constructs of a single, identifiable author and sometimes part of folk traditions, told and retold, read and reread, not only for entertainment but also to fortify a society, to encourage cohesiveness and identity.

The impact and influence of *The Odyssey* are scarcely matters of debate, but many issues surrounding the epic remain mysterious:

- Was *The Odyssey* composed by one person?
- Did a poet whom we call Homer actually exist?
- If so, when and where did he live?
- Was he blind, as tradition has it?
- Did the person who composed *The Odyssey* also compose *The Iliad*?

Introduction

- Was the poet called Homer literate, that is, did he actually write the epic? Or did he transmit it orally, by singing or reciting it, as was the tradition?
- Was his an original story, or one he constructed of older legends and myths?

Despite the continual scholarly argument over these issues and many recent archaeological findings, the likelihood of ever reaching certainty on what is labeled "the Homeric Question" is remote. One credible assumption is that a single poet, referred to by the classical Greeks as Homer, was the single creator, from many ancient oral stories, of two unified epics, *The Iliad* and *The Odyssey*. In part because the epics were first transmitted in Greek dialects used in Asia Minor, it is assumed that he came from the island of Chios, located near Asia Minor. The time of Homer's life has been a matter of wide disagreement, different scholars placing him in the seventh, eighth, or ninth century, but the evidence at hand seems to point to his having lived somewhere around the eighth century B.C. Current historians have found little evidence for the traditional notion that Homer was blind, a view that developed as long ago as classical Greece, perhaps because of interpretations of his name in Greek and perhaps because he has been identified with the blind singer Demodocos in *The Odyssey*.

The stories in *The Odyssey* are considered by most scholars to have originated and been conveyed orally by professional singers over hundreds of years. Several traditions of these orally transmitted tales are apparent in *The Odyssey*: the repetition of short epithets like "wily Odysseus" or "Odysseus, Sacker of Cities," and longer stock descriptions of such things as the entertaining of guests and of bathing. This has led some scholars to argue that the composition of the two epics was a group effort and, because of the difference in interests in the two epics, not the work of a single person. Others insist that though the stories had been transmitted orally for many years, they culminated or evolved into the two unified tales through the efforts of a single person, probably the man called Homer.

One part of the "Homer Question" is whether or not Homer actually wrote down the epics or only recited them. Some scholars argue that Homer was part and parcel of the Dark Ages (see chapter 5) in Greece, when there was no written language, and that *The Odyssey* was not actually written down until the sixth century B.C., some two to three centuries after Homer lived.

But those closest in time to Homer—the classical Greeks—assumed that he had written down the epics. And some current scholars (see Bernard Knox's "Introduction" to Robert Fagles' translation of *The Odyssey*, New York: Penguin, 1990) contend that Homer wrote *The Odyssey* after the Dark Ages, when a Greek alphabet had already appeared. Homer may well have either written the epics down himself or dictated them to someone else. If this were the case, it is assumed that Homer honed the stories in oral performance and then gradually wrote down one episode at a time, all along unifying the whole, refining, and enlarging on them. Knox writes:

> It is not surprising that many recent scholars in the field have come to the conclusion that writing did indeed play a role in the creation of these extraordinary poems.... They envisage a highly creative oral poet, master of the repertoire of inherited material and technique, who used the new instrument of writing to build, probably over the course of a lifetime, an epic poem on a scale beyond the imagination of his predecessors. (p. 20)

Despite the controversies surrounding the author, *The Odyssey* continues to be one of the most frequently studied works of the ancient world. *Understanding The Odyssey* is intended to provide those coming to this extraordinary epic with a historical context as well as an investigation of the enduring issues in the epic that have relevance to contemporary society. To approach the matters of context and issues, the first chapter is a literary analysis of major themes in the epic, as a self-contained, self-evident work of literature. Chapters 2 through 6 are explorations of the context of the epic: the mythology and geography needed for an understanding of the work; the archaeological excavations that have thrown light on the time of Odysseus; the history of the period; the Trojan War, which lies behind Odysseus' return home and to which *The Odyssey* repeatedly refers; and the underlying class structure of slaves and servants so critical to the society in which Odysseus and his son Telemachos move.

The final three chapters are examinations of the contemporary relevance of themes in *The Odyssey*. The first of the three is about Homeric vengeance or retribution in contemporary life, with particular reference to ongoing conflicts between Catholics and Protestants in Northern Ireland, the war between Israel and the Palestinians in the Near East, and the war that ensued in Afghanistan after the attacks by fanatical Muslims on America in 2001. The second current issue is athletics—a study of the importance and meaning of the athlete and athletics in Homer's day and in our own. The final chapter is on the evolution of the heroic ideal, from the time of Odysseus and Achilles to the heroes of World War I and World War II, the Vietnam War, and September 11, 2001.

Each chapter on the context and issues includes a comprehensive general introduction that provides a pertinent history of the idea under discussion and traces it through the text of the epic. Following the general introduction are documents relevant to the context: excerpts from ancient Greek history, drama, geography, poetry, and nineteenth- and early twentieth-century archaeology and mythology. The last chapters on contemporary relevance contain excerpts from diaries, citations, governmental hearings, and newspaper reportage. Each document is introduced with an essay identifying the excerpt and its author, explaining how the document is useful in the study of *The Odyssey*, and directing the reader's attention to pertinent ideas within the document.

Each chapter concludes with projects for oral and written exploration and lists of books for further reading.

The book is designed to be accessible to students and teachers alike.

In the following chapters, we have made use of a number of different prose and verse translations of *The Odyssey* that are available, identifying each by book and translator. Although any one of a number of translations is appropriate for study, we suggest that all members of the class read the same edition.

1

A Literary Analysis of Homer's *The Odyssey*: Transformation and Return

The twenty-four books of dactylic hexameter that comprise the story of Odysseus' ten-year journey home after the end of the Trojan War encompass myriad themes that have resonated in thousands of works of literature, in every nation, for roughly twenty-seven centuries. In the nineteenth century, for the Victorian poet Alfred Tennyson, Odysseus represented active, adventuresome, aspiring humanity: "strong in will to strive, to seek, to find, and not to yield." For the Dubliner James Joyce, *The Odyssey* provided the framework for a mythic journey, within one city in the period of a single day, of a twentieth-century Ulysses, that is to say, a middle-class, somewhat bumbling salesman who, as a Jew, is something of an alien in his own land.

In Western civilization, *The Odyssey* is the original, universal myth of the eternal journey; the longed-for, arduous return; the initiation into manhood; and the search for the father. It contains the elements of transformation, disguise, pretense, and trial on which such religious and psychological passages are constructed. Deception and storytelling contribute to two fundamental themes in *The Odyssey*: first, initiation, and second, return and resolution.

Before examining these particular elements in the work, however, it is important to have a clear grasp of the time frame of the epic; its major characters; the chronology of the events as they occur in the story of Odysseus and his son Telemachos; an understanding of the structure of *The Odyssey*, in which events are not presented in the order in which they actually occurred; and, finally, the technique of storytelling.

A representation of a scene of Odysseus' encounter with Circe (KIRKA), from a fifth-century B.C. Greek vase in the British Museum. Circe is presenting him with the magic drink. In the middle is her loom, and on the far right one of Odysseus' men is in the process of being turned into a swine. Source: *Illustrations of School Classics*. G. F. Hill, London: Macmillan, 1903, p. 115.

TIME FRAME

At the beginning of the poem, it has been twenty years since Odysseus left his home in Ithaca to fight in the war against Troy. That war lasted for ten years, and for the next ten years Odysseus has been trying to get home. The action of the story takes place in the last year of his journey. His adventures during the previous ten years are told by him in flashback. Telemachos, his son, had been an infant when Odysseus left for the Trojan War. As the narrative opens, he is in his early twenties.

MAJOR CHARACTERS

The major characters in *The Odyssey* fall into several categories: there are, for example, mortals, gods, and those characters, like giants, who have superhuman strength but are not easily classified as either humans or gods. There are characters who share in the action of Odysseus' journey back to Ithaca and those who are equally important but who live only in memory and do not participate in the action at hand.

Although Homer makes reference to many gods in the Greek pantheon, three of them have major roles to play in *The Odyssey*: Zeus, the chief of all the gods and the one to whom Athena makes continual appeals on Odysseus' behalf; Athena, Odysseus' protector and the goddess of wisdom, who is also associated with warfare; and Poseidon, god of the sea, who causes most of the impediments to Odysseus' return home. There are also the minor goddess Calypso, who imprisons Odysseus on her island for seven years, and Circe, an enchantress who keeps Odysseus with her after initially turning his men into swine.

The epic centers on the human character of Odysseus, and secondarily on his son Telemachos. The other major mortals whom Telemachos and Odysseus encounter on their journeys include the following:

Penelope: Odysseus' wife

Laertes: Odysseus' father

Antinoos, Eurymachos, and Amphinomos: leaders of Penelope's suitors

Eurycleia: a faithful servant of Odysseus'

Nestor: an old warrior whom Telemachos visits

Peisistratos: Nestor's son, who accompanies him

Menelaos: Greek warrior whom Telemachos visits

Helen: Menelaos' wife, whose kidnapping by Paris twenty years earlier had provoked the Trojan War

Nausicaa: king of Scheria's young daughter, who finds Odysseus washed up on the beach

Alcinoos: king of the Phaeacians of Scheria, who entertains Odysseus and helps him return to Ithaca

Demodocos: a blind singer of tales in the court of Alcinoos

Polyphemos: a Cyclops, son of Poseiden, whom Odysseus blinds in an attempt to escape

Telepylos: king of the giant Lestrygonians, who wreck all of the ships in Odysseus' party save one

Eumaeos: a swineherd in Ithaca, loyal to Odysseus

Some of the dead whom Odysseus encounters in Hades include the following:

Anticleia: Odysseus' mother

Tiresias: a blind seer, who warns him about dangers in returning home

Agamemnon: leader of the Greek or Achaean forces, who had fought beside Odysseus in Troy and returned home, where he was murdered by his wife's lover

Achilles: greatest of the Greek warriors who died in battle

CHRONOLOGY OF EVENTS

- The Trojan War ends
- Odysseus leaves, and is swept to the Cicones, where he and his men sack one city, kill the men, and take the women as slaves. Some of his men are killed in the process.
- Tempestuous winds carry them to the Land of the Lotus-Eaters. He has to drag his men back to the ship.

- They are imprisoned by the Cyclops, then blind him in their escape, taunting him as they speed away. This enrages the Cyclops' father, Poseiden, god of the sea.
- Aelios gives Odysseus a bag of wind to help him navigate well, but his men open the bag and release the wind while he is asleep, thus blowing them off course.
- They are swept to the land of the giant cannibal Lestrygonians, who eat many of the men.
- From there they are swept to the island ruled by Circe, a witch who initially turns the crew to pigs, and then takes Odysseus as a lover. He stays with her for a year.
- Circe sends Odysseus on a trip to Hades, where he learns of his wife's suitors and his own fate; he also meets and talks with many of the dead, including Achilles.
- Odysseus, now again headed home, successfully sails past the Sirens.
- He sails past Scylla and Charybdis, but not without losses.
- In Thrinacia, where the crew stops, the men disobey Odysseus' directions and eat the cattle of Helios. The ship is destroyed in revenge.
- Odysseus drifts alone to the island of Ogygia, where Calypso holds him as her lover for seven years.
- When Calypso lets him go, at the urging of the gods, he drifts and swims to the land of the Phaeacians, where he is found by Nausicaa, is entertained by King Alcinoos, and outfitted for a return to Ithaca.
- Back in Ithaca in disguise, Odysseus reveals himself to his son Telemachos, who has escaped ambush by the suitors; slays them with Telemachos; and is reunited with Penelope.

NARRATIVE SEQUENCE

While the above chronology indicates the sequence in which Odysseus' adventures occur, *The Odyssey* actually begins *in medias res,* that is, in the middle of things, with Telemachos' journey as an adult to find news of his father and with Odyssey's entrapment by Calypso. Only when Odysseus has been allowed to leave Calypso and finds himself in the land of King Alcinoos, does the reader discover Odysseus' earlier adventures after the Trojan War, as he relates his story to Alcinoos' courtiers.

LITERARY TECHNIQUE OF STORYTELLING

Storytelling shapes *The Odyssey*, and Odysseus himself tells stories to survive and make possible his return home. The epic opens as an unidentified "I" begins telling the story of Odysseus, starting with an assembly of the Olympian gods, called to order while Poseidon, god of the Sea, who is furious with Odysseus, is in Ethiopia. This, we can assume, is the voice of the poet Homer, who was supposedly a court storyteller like those mentioned in his tale. Most prominent in the epic are the singer at the court of Menelaos; the blind poet Demodocos, at the court of King Alcinoos; and Phemios, the bard in Odysseus' house, who sings for the suitors.

Homer begins telling a story that is composed of many true and false tales told by a variety of characters, not just the professional storytellers. Telemachos tells Athena (in disguise) the story of the disarray in his father's house, and repeats it in the Ithacan assembly in a futile effort to convince the elders to stop supporting the suitors. Nestor and Menelaos tell Telemachos stories of the defeat of Troy, their difficulty in getting home, and the scandalous murder of their leader Agamemnon. Helen of Troy, now back home with her husband Menelaos, also tells Telemachos stories about his father and the Trojan Horse.

The chief story within Homer's tale is told by Odysseus, who relates his own adventures to the court of King Alcinoos. He has earlier assumed a fake identity and told the king a false story about himself; but after he has been in the court long enough to get a sense of their loyalties, he reveals his true identity and tells them what has happened to him. The story he tells begins with the defeat of Troy and ends with his imprisonment on the island of Ogygia by Calypso and his washing up on Phaiacia. There are stories within stories within stories: within Homer's story is Odysseus' story, and within Odysseus' story are the stories he hears in the Land of the Dead, especially those of his mother, Agamemnon, and Achilles.

When Odysseus arrives back in Ithaca, he again assumes false identities and makes up stories about himself—to tell his friend the swineherd, his son, and his wife. He soon reveals his true self only to his son. As Odysseus is inventing wild tales to cover his deception, he is also hearing stories told by Telemachos, Helen, the swineherd, and a friendly visitor to Ithaca.

We see that these stories, many of them repeated several times, are not just forms of entertainment. They are also often ways of seeking assistance and ways of deceiving others and protecting one's self. Sometimes in stories of the past there are warnings of future danger. Most important, however, storytelling is a way of seeking truth and value in personal and tribal remembrance.

INITIATION AND RESOLUTION: TELEMACHOS

One of the major themes running throughout *The Odyssey* is the transformation of Telemachos from a boy into a man, the story that begins and ends the epic. The reader learns that Telemachos was only an infant when his father went to aid Menelaos and Agamemnon in their war against Troy in order to retrieve Menelaos' wife, Helen. As *The Odyssey* opens, however, Telemachos is twenty years old. Although he is physically an adult and the only male in his father's household, he is still a boy in the house because he is at the mercy of over one hundred of his mother's unwanted suitors. They have invaded his house uninvited. There they play loud and disruptive games, take the household's serving maids to bed, and are rapidly depleting Odysseus' estate as every day they consume enormous quantities of wine, bread, and meat, a situation that has prevailed since Telemachus was about eleven years old. The beginning of his initiation into manhood at the age of twenty is marked by the appearance of a goddess, Athena, in the guise of a human, to whom he complains that the suitors are wasting his home away and there seems to be nothing he can do about it. Athena notes his immaturity by telling him that he is too old to cry and whine about the situation; such behavior is mere childishness. He needs to grow up and take action, she says.

In this case, as in others, the appearance of a god often signals a change in a character's situation or mentality. Shortly after Athena disappears, Telemachos assumes a degree of authority and manhood, amazing his mother by his bold speech as he tells her to come into the house and resume her normal activities so that the household will be reassured, himself included. He asserts, "The power in the house is mine." He also stuns the suitors by ordering them out of his house and vowing that if they don't leave (and they don't at this time), he will call on the gods for assistance in seeking retribution against them.

Telemachos' growing maturity is further seen in his decision to call into session the assembly of Achaians, the first time the body has met since the departure of Odysseus. Telemachos presents his case to these older men, pleading with them not to encourage the suitors, many of whom are their sons. But at the end of this session, his command and composure break as he hurls to the ground the scepter (given to the person who is addressing the assembly) and, like a child, bursts into tears.

Two symbolic details mark Telemachos' struggle toward manhood as archetypal, that is, part of the universal tradition of transformation: the guidance of a wise teacher and the journey over water, itself a symbol of rebirth and renewal. Telemachos has guidance in the form of the wise mortal, Mentor, and in the goddess Athena, who takes on the form of Mentor to arrange a ship, a crew, and provisions for him to sail to Pylos and Sparta to seek news of his father. This journey is seemingly the first that Telemachos has undertaken. Once in Pylos, he tells Athena, still in the guise of his teacher Mentor, that he has no experience, and desperately needs advice about how to conduct himself in approaching the renowned warrior Nestor.

In the aging Nestor's account of what happened to the Greek warriors after the fall of Troy, Telemachos hears a parallel account of a son wanting vengeance against his father's enemies, who have taken advantage of the warrior/father's long absence. Nestor tells him of Aegisthus, who took over the household and wife of the great warrior Agamemnon during the Trojan War. Aegisthus and Agamemnon's wife, Clytemnestra, murdered Agamemnon and his Trojan slave Cassandra when he returned, and it is incumbent upon Agamemnon's son Orestes to avenge his father's death by murdering Aegisthus and his own mother. Telemachos responds to Nestor's story by praising Orestes and hoping that he, too, can seek revenge against the suitors who harm his father's household.

At the end of Odysseus' story, Telemachos continues his transformation into manhood as he overcomes his first trial; he returns to his homeland without being ambushed by the suitors, a feat he is able to accomplish with the help of Athena. On the heels of this escape, he finds the father he has been seeking and embraces him at the home of the swineherd, an act that symbolizes a wholeness and self-definition of the boy-turned-man. But in this case, action, vengeance, and victory over wrong are needed to validate his manhood. The transformation and resolution are complete when he joins his father in slaying the suitors.

Telemachos, then, goes through the archetypal journey to manhood in that he leaves his mother and homeland on a dangerous voyage, which becomes a rite of passage, to new worlds. In a classic study of mythology, *The Hero with a Thousand Faces*, Joseph Campbell, a world-renowned mythologist best known for his linking of myths in different cultures, writes of the similar traits shared by heroes in multiple societies. Telemachos is typical of the youthful hero who goes through a pattern of separation, initiation, and return.

RESOLUTION AND RETURN

The resolution that Telemachos finds in his emergence into manhood parallels the resolution that can come to Odysseus only when he returns home and restores the integrity of his household. Odysseus also follows the pattern of the archtypal hero in his prime in that he heeds the call to adventure; continually undergoes tests and trials, making many passages; encounters the supernatural and the gods who both sponsor and impede him; must contend with temptresses; in a turning point, a trip to the underworld, acquires new knowledge; and, finally, must actually return. As Campbell writes, "*The return and reintegration with society*, which is indispensable to the continuous circulation of spiritual energy into the world, and which, from the standpoint of the community, is the justification of the long retreat, the hero himself may find the most difficult requirement of all" (p. 36). Home is permanence, family, domesticity, peace, certitude, connection to the past, society, commitment, responsibility. On the other hand, the ocean, on which he wanders, is adventure, turbulence, changefulness, solitude, uncertainty. Although he professes a desire to reach home, Odysseus is undoubtedly torn between the two extremes, and much of the ten-year delay in his reaching Ithaca is ultimately attributable to his own arrogant, foolhardy character, his immense intellectual curiosity, and his reckless actions.

The irony, to which the stories of return embedded in *The Odyssey* attest, is that the battle a soldier faces after he returns home may be of greater magnitude than the ones he fought in a declared war with an enemy. For through time, the world at home has changed, and he himself has been profoundly altered by what he has seen and experienced. Having heard about his buddies getting "Dear John" letters, he has to wonder if his own lover or wife has waited for him, or will continue to be faithful to a man who comes back so different from the man she once loved. For that matter, will he, who has changed so drastically, be able to love the woman his former self cherished? Back home, he realizes that his life has been interrupted. Typically, the twenty-three-year-old returns to take up where life stopped at eighteen.

The story of Telemachos, which opens the epic, is joined to his father's story of return because the son cannot make a show of his manhood among the suitors without his father's assistance. In his search for his father, Nestor and then Menelaos tell Telemachos tales that focus more on the warriors' return home than they do on the battles they fought.

The initial difficulty that Odysseus (and other Greek warriors) encounter in making their way home is caused by their brutal sacking of Troy, their desecration of temples, and their taking of women prisoners, actions that so enraged Zeus and Athena that Zeus scattered the fleet as the Greeks prepared to sail for home with their war booty. Though he goes back to Troy to offer sacrifices to the gods, Odysseus continues to enrage them by taking the opportunity to pillage the city of Ismaros, sympathetic to the Trojans. There, as Odysseus reports to King Alcinoos, "I destroyed the city and killed the men. We spared the women and plenty of cattle and goods, which we divided to give each man a fair share" (*The Odyssey*; trans. W.H.D. Rouse. New York: Signet Library, 1999 p. 101). Furthermore, when his men insist on staying behind to eat and drink, they are attacked by natives from other parts of the island who kill scores of them, and when the survivors finally put to sea again, Zeus in his anger again punishes them with tempestuous storms.

After nine days at sea, they land on the island of the Lotus Eaters. Odysseus' curiosity leads him to send men to seek out the Lotus Eaters instead of promptly continuing on the way. The men, who have become contented to join the Lotus Eaters in savoring their narcotic, fail to return to ship, and

Odysseus must spend more time hauling them back by force and tying them down before they can continue on their way.

One of the most disastrous detours is clearly a path that Odysseus chooses—not from necessity but from curiosity and a desire for more riches. When they near the land of the Cyclopes, who are known to be dangerous giants, they gather all the provisions they can possible carry on a nearby island of goats to which the Cyclopes never sail. But Odysseus announces his plan to take a crew and "see who these people are" (Rouse translation; p. 103). Having arrived in Polyphemos' cave, Odysseus' men want to just steal his cheese and lambs and leave, but Odysseus admits that he "would not listen" because he wanted to observe the giant and hoped that he (Odysseus) would be provided with gifts. The results of this calamitous decision, of course, are that they are imprisoned, several of the men are eaten alive, and, to escape, Odysseus has to blind the giant and hide his men beneath the sheep going out to pasture. His blinding of the giant brings on perpetual disaster and obstacles to reaching home because it infuriates the giant's father, who is no less than Poseiden, god of the sea.

Moreover, after the ship has set sail for the goat island where the rest of the men are waiting, Odysseus insists, against the urgent pleading of his men, on satisfying his vanity by taunting the Cyclops, who hurls a stone that forces the ship back to shore. They escape a second time, but even though his men again plead with him to be silent, he again taunts the Cyclops, and even shouts out his true identity. Now Poseiden has no doubt about whom to punish for harming his son.

Odysseus does not reveal himself eager to reach home when they come to their next stop, the Island of the Winds. They choose to stay here for a month, living off the fat of the land as King Aeolios' guests. When they finally leave, the king puts all hostile winds into a bag and gives the bag to Odysseus. This will enable him to get home. Odysseus guards the bag with his life until their ship is within sight of home. Then a strange urge leads him to fall asleep (did he really want to go home at this point?), after which his men open the bag and are blown back to the Island of the Winds. King Aeolios recognizes, and is enraged at, Odysseus' irresponsibility in having ruined his chances of landing at home. He calls him a sinner and an enemy of the gods, and tells him to get off his island at once.

At Aiaia, the next island they encounter, Odysseus is apprehensive enough about the inhabitants to leave his ship anchored at the outer edge of an inlet; he sends some of his men to investigate the people who live there. This intrusion causes the native giants to gobble up some of the men and destroy all the ships in the inner harbor. Only one ship, Odysseus', and its crew escape.

Nor does Odysseus' next venture show a man determined to find his way home. He and his shipmates remain for *a year* in the house of Circe, the enchantress who initially turned his men into swine, then restored them to their natural form, and took Odysseus as her lover. The epic leaves the impression that Odysseus would have remained there indefinitely had not the members of his crew chided him that it was time to go home: "But when the year was past and the seasons came round again, my companions called me aside, and said, 'Good heavens, have you forgotten home altogether?'" (Rouse translation, p. 121).

The next stage on Odysseus' voyage, one that changes his approach to a return home, is a classic turning point of universal mythic importance in the life of the typical hero. That is his trip to the Kingdom of the Dead. Here, especially in his interviews with his mother, Agamemnon, and Achilles, his eyes are opened. His mother and Agamemnon throw light on the return home in different ways. His mother informs him that his wife has been faithfully awaiting his return, but that his father's health has been destroyed grieving for Odysseus. Agamemnon paints a gruesome picture of return, telling Odysseus of his own faithless wife, the assumption of power by Aegisthus in his absence, and finally Agamemnon's own return home, where he was slaughtered. In short, while returning home is an act of assuming responsibility, it can also be perilous.

Achilles throws light on the character of ambition and honor—the very attributes that Odysseus has been seeking—as compared to the simple values of nature and family. This can be seen in the conversation between Odysseus and the shade of Achilles in Hades. Achilles opens the conversation by calling Odysseus rash, foolhardy, and always looking for some unusual adventure, the most astonishing of which is his living presence in the Kingdom of the Dead. Odysseus answers by telling Achilles that he is fortunate in having died a hero, honored like a god throughout the world, and in now being the most important person in Hades. Achilles, once as insistent on fame and honor as Odysseus has been, says, "Don't bepraise death to me, Odysseus. I would rather be plowman to a yeoman farmer on a small holding than lord paramount in the kingdom of the dead" (Rouse translation, p. 134).

Scholars have long debated whether or not Odysseus fundamentally changes in the course of his journey. He continues to the last to be wily, arrogant, violent, and manipulative. He is still prone to take dangerous risks. He is still an adventurer who belongs on the sea rather than on land. For example, though he has the option of merely stopping up his own ears with wax, as he is instructed to do with his men, so as not to be lured by the Sirens, he decides to have his men chain him to the mast so that he can hear the Sirens' song without being able to approach them. And as Circe is telling him how to escape the perils he will encounter, he interrupts to asks if it would be possible for him to fight Scylla, to keep her from grabbing six of his men. Her reply is telling: "You hothead! fighting and asking for trouble is all you care about!

Will you stand up even to the immortal gods?" (Rouse translation, p. 140.). When they actually reach Scylla, he does at least have the men row past fast, though even here he forgets, and puts on his armor, which Circe had instructed him not to do. So in many ways, he is the same Odysseus.

After his trip to the underworld, or Land of the Dead, however, Odysseus's attitude seems to change in one important particular—he is now a man single-mindedly bound for home. This change is seen in his insistence that the men avoid landing on the island of Helios. This time, the men overrule him and land on the island despite his warnings. Tempests trap them there for a month. Finally, the men again disobey him and kill the cattle of the sun, as a result of which Zeus smashes the ship, leaving only Odysseus alive, clinging to the floating spars.

For the next seven years he has no thought except a futile hope to return home. Although he seems at one time to have cared for Calypso, who entraps him on her island, for seven years he resists her plea to become her husband and an immortal. He has no choice but to remain because he has no ship and no crew, and has no idea where he is. After Hermes' visit to Calypso to tell the goddess to release him, Calypso finds him weeping and pining on the beach, as usual: "he spent the days sitting upon the rocks or the sands staring at the barren sea and sorrowing" (65).

There is little doubt, as well, that Odysseus could have remained in Phaeacia for as long as he liked, highly honored as a warrior and adored by the princess Nausicaa, who had saved his life and who looks "as lovely as if she had stepped down from heaven." But he has, since his visit to the underworld, been fixed on the return home.

The other prominent theme of the returning warrior, which reverberates throughout the epic as a counterpoint of forewarning and emphasis to Odysseus' journey, is the story, repeatedly told, of a disastrous return home—the slaughter of Agamemnon by his wife and her lover. References to Agamemnon open the epic as Zeus tells of this warrior's cataclysmic return. Then the story is enlarged upon by Nestor and Menelaos, Agamemnon's brother. It is repeated by Agamemnon himself when Odysseus encounters him in the underworld. Agamemnon and Odysseus are both returning soldiers. Both have left wives and a son behind. Both of their houses are invaded by usurpers in their absence. The usurpers in both cases plan ambushes, and the return of both men is marked by unspeakable carnage. The difference is that Penelope, Odysseus' wife remains faithful to her husband, whereas Agamemnon's wife, Clytemnestra, yielded to the seductions of Aegisthus. The other difference is that Odysseus is forewarned of the presence of the suitors, just as his son Telemachos is warned of their planned ambush against him. The story of the slaughter of Agamemnon and Cassandra, the Trojan princess he has brought home as his slave, is a perpetual reminder to Odysseus that he must be wily enough to wipe out those who have desecrated his household before they kill him.

The epic contains numerous other embellishments on the theme of the return home. A twist on the theme, referred to in *The Odyssey*, is that the whole Trojan War was fought, at the insistence of Menelaos and his brother Agamemnon, to bring Helen home. As a result, numerous men leave home never to return. Odysseus meets some of them in the Land of the Dead, where Achilles states the feelings of many: that he would trade all his glory and all his social importance just to be home again. Nor should one overlook the fact that none of the men under Odysseus's command have the luxury of returning home again. Many of them have fallen victim to Odysseus' lust for adventure. The stories of Nestor and Menelaos are reminders early in the epic that, for those who do live through the war, the soldier's return home is arduous and fraught with danger, and may take months, even years.

Another slant on the theme of the return home in *The Odyssey* is that the many slaves sold or taken in battle can never return home again. One of those mentioned by name is Cassandra, daughter of King Priam of Troy, who is taken from Troy by Agamemnon as part of the spoils of war. Many other Trojan women, who go unnamed in *The Odyssey*, are taken as slaves after their husbands and fathers have been killed. Those who are taken by Odysseus' men are never mentioned again, but undoubtedly die in the ships along with the crews. Others who never see home again serve as slaves in the households of Nestor and Menelaos and other warriors. Odysseus' swineherd has suffered such a fate. He was actually the son of a king who was kidnapped from home and sold to Odysseus' father, Laertes. Although he loves Odysseus, he confesses that he is deeply grieved that he will never return to his homeland to see his own mother and father.

Even after Odysseus has planted his feet on Ithacan soil, he still cannot say that he has returned home, because his home has been stolen and occupied by approximately 126 men. It is not until he slaughters these parasites, hanged their women, and negotiated a truce with their families that he can be satisfied that he has returned home.

Even so, he knows from Tiresias, whom he encountered in the Land of the Dead, that he is fated to leave home again, and that he will not die in bed at home. Death will come to him from the sea.

QUESTIONS AND PROJECTS FOR FURTHER EXPLORATION

1. Write an extensive essay, comparing and contrasting the fates of Agamemnon and Odysseus.
2. Write a description of Odysseus' visit to the land of the Cyclops from Polyphemos' point of view.
3. Write your own journal entry of a woman taken as a slave by one of Odysseus' crew after the fall of Troy.
4. Stage a debate on the following topic: Odysseus changes in the course of his journey home.
5. Using the dialogues and stories told in Homer's epic, indicate what Homer and his age regarded as heroic values.
6. Illustrate the heroic values of your own age, referring to specific heroes, and compare and contrast them with those of Homer.
7. Construct your own definition of a hero. You may want to refer to another novel or to a movie you have enjoyed.
8. Write an essay on the importance of hospitality in *The Odyssey*.
9. As a class project, write a one-act play, based on your interpretation of one of Odysseus' adventures, and stage it.

SUGGESTIONS FOR FURTHER READING

Alvis, John. *Divine Purpose and Heroic Response in Homer and Virgil.* Lanham, MD: Rowman and Littlefield, 1995.
Anton, John Peter. *Art and Society.* Salt Lake City: Utah Humanities Research, 1960.
Atchity, Kenneth, ed. *Critical Essays on Homer.* Boston: G.K. Hall, 1987.
Baldick, Julian. *Homer and the Indo-Europeans.* London: I.B. Tauris, 1994.
Bowra, C.M. *Homer.* London: Duckworth, 1972.
Campbell, Joseph. *The Hero with a Thousand Faces.* Princeton: Princeton University Press, 1949.
de Jong, Irene J.F., ed. *Homer: Critical Assessments.* London: Routledge, 1999.
Finkleberg, Margalit. *The Birth of Literary Fiction in Ancient Greece.* New York: Oxford University Press, 1998.
Griffin, Jasper. *Homer on Life and Death.* Oxford: Clarendon Press, 1980.
McAuslan, Ian, and Peter Walcot, eds. *Homer.* New York: Oxford University Press, 1998.
Michalopoulos, Andre. *Homer.* New York: Twayne, 1966.
Rubino, Carl A., and Cynthia W. Shelmerdine, eds. *Approaches to Homer.* Austin: University of Texas Press, 1983.
Rutherford, R.B. *Homer.* Oxford: Oxford University Press, 1996.

Shannon, Richard Stoll. *The Arms of Achilles and Homeric Composition.* Leiden: Brill, 1975.
Steiner, George, and Robert Fagles, eds. *Homer: A Collection of Critical Essays.* Englewood Cliffs, NJ: Prentice-Hall, 1962.
Thalmann, William G. *The Odyssey: An Epic of Return.* New York: Twayne, 1992.
Webster, T.B.L. *From Mycenae to Homer.* London: Methuen, 1958.

2

Greek Mythology and Homer

DEFINITION OF MYTH

In ancient Greece, as in every culture, mythology was at the heart of everyday life, as well as of its literature, including Homer's *The Odyssey*. Mythology was a complex structure of traditional narratives in which a hierarchy of gods and goddesses and other supernatural beings played the central roles. Often, mythology is commonly referred to as a widely accepted idea that is simply untrue. But in the context of the study of literature especially, it has the opposite meaning. That is, a myth is a set of commonly held beliefs that expresses a higher, sometimes spiritual or psychological truth that cannot, in the culture in which it exists, be explained in literal, scientific terms.

Cultures turn to myth, for example, to explain the creation of the world, the existence of evil, and natural phenomena for which they have no scientific explanation. In Greece a particular god was identified with every aspect of nature. The Greeks, for example, explained the seasons with the myth of Demeter and her daughter Persephone. When Persephone, who had been kidnapped by the god of the underworld, is allowed back on earth in spring and summer to visit her mother, Demeter, the goddess of the harvest, plants grow, blossom, and produce food. But when Persephone has to return to the underworld in winter, the distraught mother causes plants to turn brown and die. In this way, myth explained the seasons, as nothing else then did. In *The Odyssey*, the winds are explained by the gods. Odysseus is able to sail close to home because the god of the winds, Aeolios, has closed up unfavorable winds in a bag and given

This is a statue by the Greek sculptor Lysippus of the god of the sea, Poseidon (Lateran Museum, Rome), who throws barriers in the way of Odysseus' return home. A dolphin is to his left; the prow of a ship is under his feet; an ornament from the stern of a ship is in his right hand; and a trident is in his left hand. Source: Hill, G.F. *Illustrations of School Classics*. London: Macmillan, 1903, p. 23.

them to Odysseus, telling him not to open the bag and let them out. When Odysseus falls asleep and his men, out of curiosity, open the bag, they release the ill winds, which blow them back out to sea. When a deadly lull in the winds keeps the Greek army from sailing for Troy, they explain it by determining that the gods are punishing their leader, Agamemnon, for killing a deer sacred to the goddess Diana.

Mythic stories also explained the course of history. Thus, the fall of the city-kingdom of Troy is traced ultimately not to tribal greed and imperialism but, as chapters 5 and 6 explain in more detail, to vanity, jealousy, and vengeance as they are embodied by the immortals.

Mythic stories also explained human psychology, those mysterious, unseen forces within human beings. Gods were the embodiments of human characteristics. Every human urge, every human characteristic was controlled to some extent by a particular god, and the often senselessness of human actions was explained by the actions of a god. For example, when the young Greek warrior Achilles is about to kill Agamemnon, the leader of the Greeks who has

The death of Aegisthus at the hand of Orestes, from an early fifth-century B.C. vase. Orestes has stabbed Aegisthus once and is stabbing him again, as he holds him by the hair. His sister Chrysothemis, who had accommodated herself to Aegisthus and Clytemnestra, the killers of her father, turns away from the scene. Source: Hill, G.F. *Illustrations of School Classics*. London: Macmillan, 1903, p. 117.

humiliated him, Athena, the goddess of wisdom, is said to have stayed his hand. In short, when at the last moment Achilles comes to possess some common sense, realizing that killing Agamemnon would destroy not only the Greek army but also his own reputation, his actions are attributed to a god. Likewise, in *The Odyssey*, when Helen leaves her husband to go to Troy with Paris, she explains to Telemachos that she was overcome by Aphrodite, the goddess of physical love.

DEVELOPMENT OF THE GODS IN GREECE

The so-called pre-Hellenic period began to erode in the years around 2000 B.C. with the invasion of the Balkan Peninsula by Indo-European tribes from the north. These earlier inhabitants were an agricultural people who assigned an evil spirit, which issued from an underworld, to every aspect of nature that hindered their farming and made existence difficult, and that had to be assuaged by rituals and sacrifices. Eventually, these vague spirits assumed human shape and entered the local mythology as gods and goddesses. Predominant among them were female deities associated with farming, harvest, and fertility. Demeter, the goddess of earth and harvest; Hera, also identified with Mother Earth; and Dionysus, the god of wine and vegetation, were prominent among them. They were goddesses and gods associated with earth and the life force, but they were not necessarily kindly, maternal deities: the sacrificial rituals demanded by them often incorporated the bloodthirstiness and cruelty of Nature herself in the raw. When tribes from the north of the Greek peninsula invaded, they brought with them a new pantheon of gods, based on conquest, force, prowess in battle, and violent heroism—death not from nature but from man. Zeus, the great sky god of the invading Indo-Europeans, superseded Hera as the chief god in Greece. And Athena, once an agricultural deity, adopted the war helmet and the spear of a warrior goddess of wisdom. Other older female deities of the agricultural world fused with those of the more powerful invaders or else faded into insignificance.

A powerful Zeus reigned over the earth from Mount Olympus, the cloud-covered highest peak in Greece, where most of the other gods and goddesses lived with him. The two other homes of gods included the underworld, where Hades, one of Zeus' two brothers, held sway, and the sea, the domain of the third brother, Poseidon.

HOMER'S USE OF THE GODS

It has been observed, as with the case of Helen, who attributes her own passion to Aphrodite, that in Homer's epics the gods are often conveniences to explain what characters would have done anyway, without the interference of the gods. Still, *The Odyssey* is, in itself, a mythic narrative in which the gods play major roles—especially Athena, who constantly comes to Telemachos' and Odysseus' aid and argues Odysseus' case before the other gods on Mount Olympus. Poseidon also plays a major role, doing everything he can to hinder Odysseus' return home. And there are other gods, supernatural beings, and children of the gods who are important characters in the epic, including King Aeolios, the Sirens, Calypso, Circe, and Polyphemos.

A FAMILY TREE OF THE GODS

As with any mythological system, there is a definite hierarchy among the Olympian gods, defined by their relationships and their roles. The ancestry of the Olympian gods had its beginning when out of Chaos came Light, and out of Light came Earth (or Gaea). The son and husband of Earth/Gaea was Uranus, god of the heavens or sky. With the help of Gaea, their son Cronus, a Titan, murdered his father by castration, and assumed the preeminent position among the gods, marrying his sister Ops. The period of Cronus' reign as chief god was known as the Golden Age, somewhat equivalent to the Garden of Eden, when humankind flourished in an idylic world free of war, strife, and the necessity to work. From these Titans, Zeus was born, becoming the chief of the Olympian gods when he overthrew his father, Cronus. There were some variations on the story of the gods, but the following chart indicates the Olympian relationships as Homer used them and as his audience knew them.

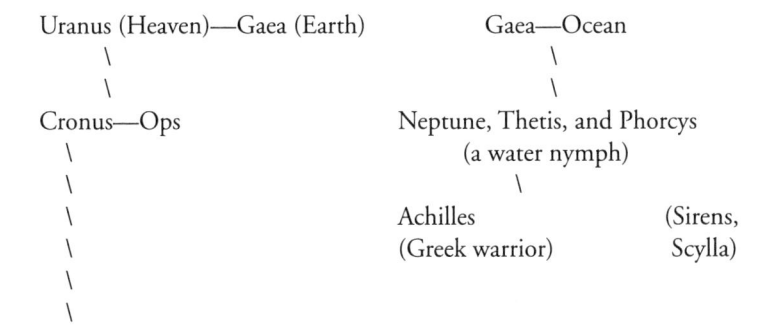

```
Uranus (Heaven)—Gaea (Earth)        Gaea—Ocean
     \                                  \
      \                                  \
   Cronus—Ops                  Neptune, Thetis, and Phorcys
      \                              (a water nymph)
       \                                  \
        \                              Achilles            (Sirens,
         \                           (Greek warrior)        Scylla)
          \
           \
```

Pluto (or Hades): god of the underworld, which Odysseus is allowed to visit by Circe.

Poseidon: god of the sea, father of Polyphemos, the one-eyed Cyclops. Supporter of the Greeks in the Trojan War, but angered by Odysseus after the blinding of Polyphemos.

Demeter: goddess of agriculture and harvest

Hera: Zeus' consort

Zeus: chief of the Olympian gods

The gods who were the children of Zeus include the following:

Athena: goddess of wisdom, associated with war; on the Greek side in the Trojan War; a champion of Odysseus, a helper of his son.

Aphrodite: goddess of physical love; winner of the apple of discord; on the side of Troy in the Trojan War; oversaw Helen and Paris.

Hermes: the messenger god who assists Odysseus at Athena's request, provides him with an herb to resist Circe.

Artemis: virgin goddess of the chase

Apollo: god of light and prophecy; helped build the walls of Troy.

Dionysus: god of the vine

Ares: god of war, prominent in Homer's *The Iliad*.

Hephaestus: god of the forge, story told in *The Odyssey* of his being cuckolded by wife, Aphrodite

Persephone: queen of the underworld.

Zeus also is the father of the Fates, the three Graces, and the nine Muses. Other immortals who appear in *The Odyssey* are the following:

Aeolios: god of the winds
Atlas: supports the heavens; Calypso's father
Calypso: imprisons Odysseus for seven years
Circe: a witch who imprisons Odysseus
Polyphemos: a giant Cyclops

Zeus and other gods also coupled with mortal women. Three half-god, half-mortal characters are especially relevant to the study of Homer:

Helen: the daughter of Zeus and Leda, wife of the Greek Menelaos; kidnapped by Paris, causing the Trojan War; speaks with Telemachos in *The Odyssey*

Achilles: son of Peleus and the water nymph Thetis; a Greek warrior; speaks with Odysseus in the Land of the Dead.

Alcinoos: grandson of Poseidon, who punishes him for helping Odysseus reach Ithaca.

MYTHICAL NARRATIVES RELEVANT TO *THE ODYSSEY*

Natural phenomena and causes and effects in history, whether an earthquake, a plague, a cataclysmic war, the fall of a city, or the demise of a once powerful leader, were often explained or magnified by mythical narratives involving the immortals. These would have been familiar to Homer's readers. Odysseus' return home is, itself, one of the formative mythic narratives of Greece, as is the tale of the Trojan War (which will be treated in more detail in chapter 6). In addition, mythic narratives are interwoven into *The Odyssey*, to clarify happenings, to explain disasters, and to serve as warnings. The following are the most important mythical narratives pertinent to *The Odyssey*, discussed in chronological order.

The Birth of Helen

According to some legends, when Aphrodite, the sensual goddess of love, first appeared on Olympus, she was pursued by several gods, Zeus among them. When she rejected his advances, Zeus forced her into marriage with Hephaestus, the lame god of the forge. Aphrodite became his loving but not faithful wife. In book VII of *The Odyssey*, Homer relates a story of her "secret" affair with Ares, the handsome god of war, and of Hephaestus' ingenious revenge for his wife's infidelity. Aphrodite exacts her own kind of revenge upon Zeus by forcing him to fall in love with mortal women. This is intended as a humiliation for a god, but Zeus does not seem to mind.

One of the women for whom Zeus conceives a mad passion is Leda, daughter of the king of Aetolia and wife of Tyndareus, king of Sparta. Zeus appears to Leda in the form of a swan and ravishes her. As a result, Leda lays an egg from which Helen and Castor and Polydeuces (Pollux) are hatched.

With Tyndareus as the mortal father, Leda also gave birth to Clytemnestra. Tyndareus had once failed to sacrifice to Aphrodite; and as a result she decreed that his daughters, Helen, to whom he was a mortal father, and her sister Clytemnestra, would be unfaithful to their husbands. The poet Hesiod, coming a few years after Homer, called Clytemnestra and Helen "*lipesanores*," or "husband-deserters." They were much more than that, however—they were two of the most famous women in classical literature, the one noted for a fierce, ironlike, and unflinching character; the other, for unsurpassed sensual beauty and for, in effect, starting the Trojan War. One was one of the strongest women in classical legends; the other, one of the weakest.

Birth of Paris Alexander

When King Priam of Troy and his queen, Hecuba, discovered that they were soon to have a child, she (or, as some stories have it, her daughter Cassandra) had a dream that the child would be a "firebrand" who would destroy Troy. This was Paris, the man who eventually caused the Trojan War and the fall of Troy. After his birth, King Priam took measures to see that the prophecy did not come true. When the child was born, a shepherd in the employ of the king was told to take the child and kill it, but being unable to take the child's life himself, he left it on a hillside to die. The baby was found by a bear, who fed and cared for him. When the shepherd found that the child was still alive, he took it and raised it as his own. From boyhood, Paris had a local reputation for his handsome looks and athletic prowess.

Thus it was only a matter of time before he went to the city of Troy to participate in athletic games that were, ironically, being held in honor of the child Priam thought he had had killed. In Troy, Paris excelled at every event, but he was again in danger of being killed. One story has it that other young men, jealous of his achievements, plotted his death. Another has it that when Paris refused to allow his brother Hector to slaughter one of his favorite animals, Hector determined to kill him. It was Cassandra, his sister, who recognized who he was and saved his life. He was welcomed with open arms by his family, and entertained like the royalty he was. Soon, however, he returned to the mountains of his youth to resume his life as a shepherd and marry (or become the lover of) a young nymph named Oenone.

Courtship and Wedding of Helen

Helen was reputedly the most beautiful of mortal women. Her beauty and her status growing up as a princess in the house of Tyndareus, king of Sparta, caused her to collect many ardent suitors for her hand in marriage. Before she could choose a husband, she was kidnapped by Theseus, a prince of Athens, but her brothers managed to rescue her. Her subsequent suitors included Odysseus himself as well as other prominent figures. Tyndareus, Helen's mortal father, became apprehensive that when Helen made her choice, the rejected suitors might cause trouble. Odysseus, one of those doomed to be rejected, supposedly told Tyndareus that if he would help Odysseus marry Icarius' daughter Penelope, Odysseus would tell him how to avoid the feared quarrels. Tyndareus agreed, whereupon Odysseus told him to exact an oath from each suitor that he would defend Helen and her husband against whoever should cause trouble in the future. Odysseus was then able to win Penelope, while Helen chose Menelaos. Thus the most beautiful woman in the world married the rich and handsome prince, who was shortly (upon the death of Tyndareus) to become king of Sparta and one of the most powerful men in the world.

Apple of Discord

Thetis, a beautiful sea nymph, attracted the attention of Zeus and Poseidon, both of whom fell in love with her. But they were told that any son of Thetis would be greater than his father. This cooled the interest of both gods, who decided that Thetis should marry a mortal. Peleus was the man they encouraged. The marriage of Peleus and Thetis was a splendid social occasion that all the Olympic gods looked forward to attending. And all were invited except for Eris, the goddess of discord. Eris was so enraged at not being invited that she came anyway and threw a golden apple into the midst of the festivities—an apple on which was written, "for the fairest." The act was doomed to cause discord because each of the female guests believed that she was the rightful owner of what came to be called "the apple of discord." Finally there was an agreement that the claimants for the apple would be narrowed down to three—the three most powerful goddesses on Olympus: Hera, Aphrodite, and Athena. The gods were too politically astute to try to make the judgment themselves, so an exceptionally handsome young shepherd who was tending his sheep nearby was called upon to decide. This, of course, was Paris Alexander. Paris took his task seriously, insisting that he be allowed to meet with each goddess in private and to view her in her natural state.

Since much standing and feminine honor rested on the choice, none of the three goddesses was above offering Paris a bribe. Hera, the chief goddess of Olympus, offered him power. Athena, the goddess of wisdom, offered him the cunning to be a successful warrior. But Aphrodite, the goddess of physical love, offered him the most beautiful woman in the world. The young Paris awarded the apple of discord to Aphrodite.

Abduction of Helen

The most beautiful woman in the world, promised to Paris Alexander, was, however, married to someone else—Menelaos the king of Sparta. This was scarcely a discouragement for Paris, who was determined to secure his promised bribe. Using his status as a prince of Troy and with his intention well hidden, he sailed to Sparta. There Menelaos and his court welcomed him with open arms, as they would any handsome prince. He remained in Sparta for many months, biding his time. When Menelaos was called away on business, Paris seized the opportunity to take the king of Sparta's wife, and as much of his treasure as he could load, onto his ships, and sail for Troy. Helen was either abducted against her will (as she would claim at the end of the Trojan War, according to some legends) or she went willingly, bewitched by the goddess Aphrodite, who had promised her to Paris (as she told Telemachos). The Trojans made matters worse for themselves by welcoming Paris, with his stolen woman and stolen treasure, and refusing to negotiate when a delegation of Greeks came to ask for the return of Helen and the stolen goods.

At this point, Menelaos called upon his powerful brother, Agamemnon, and Helen's former suitors, who had signed an oath to come to her husband's aid should anything happen to her. These, the most powerful men across Greece, marshaled forces to go to war with Troy.

The Trojan War

The Trojan War, the myth of the Greek war with the Trojans and the sacking of the city of Troy, is constantly in the foreground of *The Odyssey*, the story of a soldier returning from that war. For this reason, the Trojan War will be considered in greater detail in chapter 6.

Agamemnon and the House of Atreus

In the *Odyssey*, Homer uses the story of Agamemnon's homecoming and his murder by Clytemnestra (and Aegisthus) as a contrast with the homecoming of Odysseus, and as a warning to him. To inject the curse of the house of Atreus would have vitiated the point of the contrast. Nevertheless, it was a mythic story that most of his audience would have understood as the context for repeated references to Agamemnon's murder. The grandfather of Agamemnon, King Pelops of Mycenae, had two sons, Atreus and Thyestes. Being proud, hostile, and ambitious, they ruthlessly vied with one another for the throne upon his death. The curse on the house of Atreus begins with the competing brothers.

The god Pan, acting at the behest of Hermes, put among the flock of ordinary sheep that Pelops had left to the two brothers a special horned lamb with a golden fleece. Atreus sacrificed the flesh of the lamb to Artemis, but secretly kept the magnificent golden fleece hidden in a chest. Being a proud man, however, he could not resist boasting about his possession to loungers and friends in the town square (the ancient equivalent of the friendly pub or the general store); as a result, Thyestes learned of it. At the same time, Aerope, the wife of Atreus, developed a passion for Thyestes, who agreed to become her lover if she would secure the fleece for him.

Atreus claimed the throne because he was the older of the two and possessed the magic fleece, which, as the people agreed at his urging, was a true indicator of the right to kingship. After the coronation celebrations began, however, Thyestes led the deciding judges to his home and there revealed that he, not his brother, was in possession of the empowering fleece. So Thyestes, rather than Atreus, became king.

Zeus favored Atreus, and to show his displeasure with Thyestes, he caused the sun to go backward and set in the east, and all the stars to go backward. The people, seeing this as a directive from god, deposed Thyestes, and Atreus became king. Atreus, belatedly learning that Thyestes and his wife had betrayed him, plotted revenge. He invited Thyestes to return, feigning reconciliation and planning a grand feast to which his brother and his brother's children were invited. Thyestes accepted, and Atreus secretly slaughtered all but one of the children and served them in a stew to Thyestes. After it was too late for anyone to call back the horror, Atreus, holding up parts of the dead bodies, revealed the terrible secret: Thyestes had eaten the flesh of his own children. As Thyestes fled with his remaining son, Aegisthus, he thundered a curse on the entire house of Atreus.

Agamemnon, the son of Atreus, succeeded his father as king of Mycenae. In order to secure Clytemnestra, the sister of Helen, for his wife, he murdered her husband Tantalus, the son of his uncle Thyestes, and their infant. Years passed, and Agamemnon left for the Trojan War. Waiting with his troops to set sail for Troy from Aulis, Agamemnon killed a deer sacred to the goddess Artemis. She punished him by seeing that the winds were stilled so that they could not leave, and told him that he could sail only if he sacrificed his and Clytemnestra's daughter Iphigenia. Agamemnon sent for Iphigenia, telling his wife that their daughter was being summoned as a bride for the illustrious Achilles. But when Iphigenia arrived, she was killed so that the fleet could sail for Troy.

Meanwhile, with Agamemnon gone, Aegisthus, the son of Thyestes, returned, ultimately winning the trust and the love of Clytemnestra and, with her, ruling the country.

After the war, when Agamemnon returned home, bringing with him his concubine Cassandra, the daughter of Priam, Aegisthus and Clytemnestra killed them both.

Myth of Achilles

Achilles, a major figure in the Trojan War and a friend and fellow warrior fighting beside Odysseus, makes a crucial appearance in *The Odyssey* from the Land of the Dead. His words may create the turning point of the epic in that he tells Odysseus he would relinquish all his military glory and reputation to be alive and perform the humblest tasks on earth. At that moment Odysseus seems to see the light about himself, and makes a more determined effort to reach his home. The myth of Achilles lies behind the awe with which storytellers in *The Odyssey* regard him.

Ironically, it was at the wedding of his mother, Thetis, a mermaid, and his father, Peleus, that the apple of discord was thrown among the beautiful guests, ultimately resulting in the Trojan War, in which Achilles found fame and death. To repeat, Thetis was married to Peleus, a mortal, because the gods who coveted her had been told that her son would be greater than his father. Being an immortal herself, she wanted immortality for her son, Achilles, so according to the more famous version of the story, she dipped him in the River Styx, holding him by his heel and, therefore, leaving his heel vulnerable. When her husband caught her at her magic, she fled back to the sea, leaving Achilles' upbringing to his father. For a time, he was raised by the half-man, half-horse Chiron, who taught him the ways of survival. While still a boy, he was brought back to his father's house to be educated. One version of the Achilles story says that Thetis, realizing the danger her son would be in later in life, had him hidden as a girl among the daughters of Lycomedes, where Odysseus later found him. In *The Iliad*, Achilles, who has withdrawn from battle because of his anger at being dishonored by Agamemnon, lends his armor to his friend, Patroclus, who *is* going into battle. Hector, however, slays Patroclus and takes Achilles' armor.

At the request of Thetis, Hephaestus constructed a new suit of armor for Achilles: this is one of the crucial events in *The Iliad*, for the shield contains fine thematic images of war and peace, including Homer's only consistent images of the life of the common man, a series of rural and pacific scenes that stand in striking contrast to the entire tone of the epic. It is also in contrast to the values inherent in the work and in the Heroic Age.

After killing Hector, King Priam's son, Achilles was himself killed by Paris, who shot an arrow into his heel.

CONCLUSION

To achieve the proper order, pace, focus, and tone, Homer omitted many details of the mythic narratives in his epics. In neither epic is there a discussion, for example, of the grisly beginnings of the curse of Atreus, or the sacrifice of Iphigenia by Agamemnon, or the story of Achilles' vulnerable heel. But these were details well known to his audience from older, now extinct accounts that form the context of Homer's stories.

For a thousand years the Greeks retained their beliefs in the Olympian gods very much as that mythology had been conveyed to them by Homer in the late ninth or early eighth centuries B.C. Even as late as the second century A.D. one could still find evidence that many Greeks clung to a belief in the ancient Homeric mythology. That most magnificent of Greek structures, the Parthenon, designed by the artist/architect Phidias and constructed around 438 B.C. atop the highest hill near Athens, was intended not only as a storehouse but also as an extravagant homage to the gods, particularly Athena, to whom a forty-foot, gold-covered statue was erected. The perceived erosion of social cohesion, discipline, and order that ensued from the time of Homer was often attributed to the decline of respect for the gods; hence, the people were often encouraged to continue to honor them to restore positive virtues. Although the Greeks were usually not dogmatic about their mythology, some measure of the extent to which those in power clung to the old gods is suggested in their execution of Socrates in 399 B.C., partially on the grounds that he refused to recognize the old gods. While many writers urged the honoring of the old gods, many philosophers, from the sixth century B.C. on, altered the old mythology by making the behavior of the gods less offensive, by interpreting them poetically rather than literally, or by flatly denying that the myths had any validity at all.

The final overpowering of the old Greek Olympian religion by the more powerful doctrine of Christianity is seen as the Parthenon, dedicated to Athena, became a Christian church in the fifth century A.D.

Nor was the power of Greek mythology restricted to the Greek peninsula, for the Greeks, who were colonizers—sending soldiers, settlers, and businessmen to every part of the Mediterranean—exported their religion throughout the area. Alexander the Great took Greek culture, which included Greek mythology, all the way to India.

As the Greek influence moved into Italy (according to legend) when the Trojan warrior Aeneas founded the city of Rome, the Greek gods were transplanted to Italian soil. The old Greek names were replaced there with Latin names, more familiar to contemporary society than the older names. Thus, Zeus became known as Jupiter; Cronos became known as Saturn; Hera became Juno; Poseidon became Neptune; Athena became Minerva; Dionysus became Bacchus; Aphrodite became Venus; Artemis became Diana; Hermes became Mercury.

Judaism and Christianity were considered heresies throughout the Roman Empire until the supposed conversion of the Emperor Constantine to Christianity in the fourth century A.D. Even then one finds the older rites of the Greek and Roman gods mixed in with Christian rites.

Although the Greek and Roman mythologies were no longer part of a state religion, the power of Greek mythology continues to the present in Western culture, especially in its poetry, drama, fiction, art, and music. The stories continue to be emblematic of human interactions, passions, foibles, and greatness, explaining them as nothing else does.

The documents included here enlarge on the Greek mythology from which Homer drew, and place *The Odyssey* in the context of early Greek religion. The first, from Thomas Bulfinch's 1855 classic, provides an idea of how the Greeks conceived of the physical world that their gods inhabited. The second, by the fifth-century B.C. Greek prose writer and historian Herodotus, tells how the ancient world traced the introduction of the particular Olympian gods into Greece. The third document comes from Hesiod, the eighth-century B.C. poet who also provided Greece with written accounts of gods and mythology. The excerpts from his *Theogony* give details about the rise of Zeus and a catalog of goddesses, some of whom are mentioned in *The Odyssey* without showing their relationships to one another. The excerpts from the classicist Alexander S. Murray (1888) provide details about Pallas Athena and Poseidon, who have major roles in *The Odyssey*, again details with which Homer's hearers would have been familiar. Another selection, this one by Pausanias, from the second century A.D. in Greece, shows the extent to which later Greeks believed or were skeptical of the mythology like that which pervades *The Odyssey*. Finally, from Plato's *Republic*, we find the reasons why this fourth-century B.C. philosopher found Homer's treatment of Greek mythology to be dangerous for young children.

A MYTHOLOGICAL ATLAS

Thomas Bulfinch's study of mythology, which first appeared in 1855, is still the most popular and useful book on classical Greek mythology in English. In a field—the classics—usually dominated by Englishmen, Bulfinch was an American, a Harvard College graduate, and a friend of the American poet and philosopher Ralph Waldo Emerson and of the poet Henry Wadsworth Longfellow. Using classical sources, Bulfinch wrote his mythology before excavations revolutionized our understanding of Greek history.

The excerpt included here is Bulfinch's explanation of the mythological atlas of the universe where Homer's gods held sway and where, on the periphery, giants and monsters and other supernatural beings roamed. Bulfinch also includes a description of the daily life of the gods. He uses Roman rather than Greek names. Jupiter is the Roman name of Zeus, and Hebe, whom he also mentions, is the daughter of Zeus and Hera, wife of Heracles, and the handmaiden of the gods.

FROM THOMAS BULFINCH, *THE AGE OF FABLE*

(Philadelphia: David MacKaye, 1898)

In order to understand these stories, it will be necessary to acquaint ourselves with the ideas of the structure of the universe which prevailed among the Greeks—the people from whom the Romans, and other nations through them, received their science and religion.

The Greeks believed the earth to be flat and circular, their own country occupying the middle of it, the central point being either Mount Olympus, the abode of the gods, or Delphi, so famous for its oracle.

The circular disk of the earth was crossed from west to east, and divided into two equal parts by the *Sea*, as they called the Mediterranean, and its continuation the Euxine, the only seas with which they were acquainted.

Around the earth flowed the *River Ocean*, its course being from south to north on the western side of the earth, and in a contrary direction on the eastern side. It flowed in a steady, equable current, unvexed by storm or tempest. The sea, and all the rivers on earth, received their waters from it.

The northern portion of the earth was supposed to be inhabited by a happy race named the Hyperboreans, dwelling in everlasting bliss and spring beyond the lofty mountains whose caverns were supposed to send forth the piercing blasts of the north wind, which chilled the people of Hellas (Greece). Their country was inaccessible by land or sea. They lived exempt from disease or old age, from toils and warfare.

...

On the south side of the earth, close to the stream of Ocean, dwelt a people happy and virtuous as the Hyperboreans. They were named the Ethiopians. The gods favored them so highly that they were wont to leave at times their Olympian abodes and go to share their sacrifices and banquets.

On the western margin of the earth, by the stream of Ocean, lay a happy place named the Elysian Plain, whither mortals favored by the gods were transported, without tasting of death, to enjoy an immortality of bliss. This happy region was also called the "Fortunate Fields" and the "Isles of the Blessed."

We thus see that the Greeks of the early ages knew little of any real people except those to the east and south of their own country, or near the coast of the Mediterranean. Their imagination meantime peopled the western portion of this sea with giants, monsters, and enchantresses, while they placed around the disk of the earth, which they probably regarded as of no great width, nations enjoying the peculiar favor of the gods and blessed with happiness and longevity.

The Dawn, the Sun, and the Moon were supposed to rise out of the Ocean, on the eastern side, and to drive through the air, giving light to gods and men. The stars also, except those forming the Wain or Bear, and others near them, rose out of and sank into the stream of Ocean. There the sun-god embarked in a winged boat, which conveyed him round by the northern part of the earth back to his place of rising in the east.

...

The abode of the gods was on the summit of Mount Olympus, in Thessaly. A gate of clouds, kept by the goddesses named the Seasons, opened to permit the passage of the celestials to earth and to receive them on their return. The gods had their separate dwellings; but all, when summoned, repaired to the palace of Jupiter, as did also those deities whose usual abode was the earth, the waters, or the underworld. It was also in the great hall of the palace of the Olympian king that the gods feasted each day on ambrosia and nectar, their food and drink, the latter being handed round by the lovely goddess Hebe. Here they conversed of the affairs of heaven and earth; and as they quaffed their nectar, Apollo, the god of music, delighted them with the tones of his lyre, to which the Muses sang in responsive strains. When the sun was set, the gods retired to sleep in their respective dwellings. (1, 2, 3, 4)

THE GODS

Herodotus, the first Greek historian and the first writer of prose in Greek, was born between 490 and 480 B.C. His sources were primarily individuals whom he interviewed about the wisdom that had been handed down orally through generations. Few documents were available to him. While he is not as skeptical of the gods and mythology as later historians were, he does not accept the stories entirely without question. The excerpt included here is useful in conveying something of the beliefs at the time about the introduction to Greece of what came to be known as the Olympian gods, as they appeared in Homer. The word *Pelasgians*, used in the excerpt, was the name invaders of Greece gave to the people they conquered. *Dodona* is the Greek site of what Herodotus calls the first Olympic oracle. *Oracles* were temples to particular gods. The priests and priestesses in such temples issued messages and prophecies from the gods to humans. In writing of the first appearances of the Olympians in Greece, Herodotus follows legends concerning the origins of their oracles on Greek soil. Note his own rational explanation of some of the supernatural details in the legend related to him by those who seem to take the story without question.

FROM HERODOTUS, *THE HISTORIES*, BOOK II, TRANS. HENRY CARY

(London: Henry G. Bohn, 1854)

The names of nearly all the gods came to Greece from Egypt. I know from the inquiries I have made that they came from abroad, and it seems most likely that it was from Egypt, for the names of all the gods have been known in Egypt from the beginning of time, with the exception (as I have already said) of Poseidon and the Dioscuri—and also of Hera, Hestia, Themis, the Graces, and the Nereids. I have the authority of the Egyptians themselves for this. I think that the gods of whom they profess no knowledge were named by the Pelasgians—with the exception of Poseidon, of whom they learned from the Libyans; for the Libyans are the only people who have always known Poseidon's name, and always worshipped him.

...

In ancient times, as I know from what I was told at Dodona, the Pelasgians offered sacrifices of all kinds, and prayed to the gods, but without any distinction of name or title—for they had not yet heard of any such thing. They called the gods by the Greek word *theoi*—"disposers"—because they had "disposed" and arranged everything in due order, and assigned each thing to its proper division. Long afterwards the names of the gods were brought into Greece from Egypt and the Pelasgians learnt them—with the exception of Dionysus, about whom they knew nothing till much later; then, as time went on, they sent to the oracle at Dodona (the most ancient and, at that period, the only oracle in Greece) to ask advice about the propriety of adopting names which had come into the country from abroad. The oracle replied that they would be right to use them. From that time onward, therefore, the Pelasgians used the names of the gods in their sacrifices, and from the Pelasgians the names passed to Greece.

But it was only—if I may so put it—the day before yesterday that the Greeks came to know the origin and form of the various gods, and whether or not all of them had always existed; for Homer and Hesiod, the poets who composed our theogonies and described the gods for us, giving them all their appropriate titles, offices, and powers, lived, as I believe, not more than four hundred years ago. (122, 123, 124)

A FAMILY TREE OF THE GODS

Along with Homer, the poet Hesiod provided Greece with written accounts of the Olympian gods and Greek mythology. Hesiod, who lived a generation after Homer (probably in the eighth century), is best known as the author of *Theogony*, a history of the gods, and *Works and Days*, a treatise on work and justice. The account we have in *Theogony* is that of a religious man who, while he may question some of the details in the mythology he relates, is basically a true believer in the immortality of Zeus.

The first excerpt is his poem on the rise of Zeus. The myth is pertinent to a study of *The Odyssey* in its theme of father-son relationships that are opposite in character from those in Homer's epic. Here, at the dawn of the gods, we find the divine father's well-justified fear of his son and the son's vengeance against the cruel father. In *The Odyssey*, human father and son honor one another and vengeance is directed at those who harm the immediate family.

The second excerpt consists of two catalogs of gods and goddesses. The first is about the births of Hermes, Dionysus, and Herakles, all children of Zeus. The second is a catalog of goddesses that includes reference to Odysseus.

FROM HESIOD, *THEOGONY*, IN *HESIOD: THE HOMERIC HYMNS AND HOMERICA*, TRANS. HUGH G. EVELYN-WHITE

(London: William Heinemann, 1914)

THE RISE OF ZEUS

The Birth of Zeus and the Other Olympians, the Children of Kronos and Rhea

And Rhea, mating with Kronos, bore him glorious children:
Hestia, Demeter, and Hera, who walks on sandals of gold;
powerful Hades, who dwells in a mansion under the earth
and has a pitiless heart; the roaring Shaker of Earth; and
Zeus of the Counsels, who is the Father of Gods and of Men
and at the sound of whose thundering a trembling seizes the broad earth.
Great Kronos swallowed each of these children as each of them came
out of the holy womb of their mother and fell at her knees,
this his set purpose, that no other lordly descendant of Ouranos
should possess the honor of kingship among the immortals.
For he had learned of the future from Gaia and star-studded Ouranos,
how he was destined to meet with defeat at the hands of his son;
this was to be in spite of his strength, for great Zeus would plan it.
Therefore no blind man's lookout was his, but he being watchful
swallowed his children, and Rhea was seized with a grief unforgettable.

But when she was finally about to give birth to Zeus,
the Father of Gods and of Men, then she begged her dear parents,
Gaia and star-studded Ouranos, who were her mother and father,
that they should tell her how she might secretly bear her dear baby,
and how her father's Erinys might be an avenger against
great Kronos, the clever deviser, in payment for swallowing her children.
They then heeded their daughter's request and did as she asked them,
telling her all that was destined to be, revealing the future,
what was to happen to Kronos the king and her stout-hearted son.
And they sent her to Lyktos, off in fertile-soiled Krete,
when she was going to bear him, her youngest, the last of her children,
Zeus, great Zeus. There in the broad isle of Krete huge Gaia
received him from her in order to nurse him and rear him to manhood.
Bringing him there she came in the covering darkness of swift night
first to Lyktos, and taking him into her hands she put him
into a cave under the holy earth high up
on Mount Aigaion, where is abundant thickly grown forest.
And she swaddled a great stone and put it into the hands of
Ouranos's son, the great lord, king of the earlier gods,
who, having taken it from her, sent it down into his stomach,
hardhearted wretch, nor did he foresee what was going to happen,
that his son, replaced by the stone, unconquered and carefree,
still surviving, would prove himself victor by force of his hands and
drive him out of his honor and rule as king of the gods.
Then the strength and the glorious power of the limbs of this king
rapidly grew and, the circling year having come to completion,
great Kronos, the clever deviser, being the dupe of Gaia's
very superior advice, sent up his children again,
for he was brought to defeat by the trickery and force of his son.
First he was forced to spew up the stone—he had swallowed it last—and
this was established and fixed by Zeus in the wide-wayed earth at
holy Pytho down in the hollow beneath Mount Parnassos,
there to remain as a sign, a marvel for mortal men. (113–117)

...

THE KINGSHIP OF ZEUS AND HIS MARRIAGES

But when the blessed gods had finished the struggle of fighting,
when they had won in the war with the Titans the contest for honors,
then they, following the advice of Gaia, urged the Olympian
far-seeing Zeus to rule as their lord and take up the kingship
over immortals; and so he fairly apportioned their honors.
Zeus the King of the Gods took as his first wife Metis,
who among gods and mortal men was the wisest of all.
But when her time came to bear him the gray-eyed goddess Athena,
then he, deceiving her mind by means of a trick and using

flattering words to beguile her, put her into his stomach,
following the advice of Gaia and of star-studded Ouranos.
So they advised him in order that no one besides Zeus, no other
one of the ever-living gods, might possess the honor of kingship.
Metis, they said, was going to bear him two powerful children:
first a daughter, the gray-eyed goddess Tritogeneia,
who would equal her father in strength and excellent counsel;
then a son who would be the King of Gods and of Men;
she was going to bear him a son of invincible might.
But before this could happen Zeus put her into his stomach
so that this goddess might help him to plan both good things and bad.
Then he took as his wife shining Themis, who bore him the Horai:
Orderly Government, Justice, and Peace, a bountiful goddess;
and the Moirai, whom Zeus of the Counsels gave greatest honor:
Klotho, Lachesis, Atropos, powers that determine the fates and
grant to mortal men to have both good things and bad.
Then Eurynome, the daughter of Okeanos, a beautiful girl,
bore of her union with him the three lovely-cheeked Graces:
bright Aglaia, joyful Euphrosyne, charming Thalia.
Love which drops from their eyes strikes whomever they look on,
loosening his limbs; under their brows their eyes glance with loveliness.
Next he came to the bed of Demeter, the feeder of many,
and she bore him white-armed Persephone, who was by Hades
seized from her dear mother's side, as Zeus of the Counsels permitted.
Then he mingled in love with the lovely-haired Mnemosyne,
and she bore him the Muses crowned with headbands of gold,
nine of them, who are delighters in feasts and the joy of the song.
Then Leto bore him Apollo and Artemis, expert in archery, children surpass-
    ing in beauty all other descendants of Ouranos;
these she conceived by mingling in love with Zeus of the Aigis.
Last of all it was Hera he took as his blossoming bride,
and she bore him Hebe and Ares and Eileithyia
when she had mingled in love with the King of Gods and of Men.
Then he produced of himself from his head the gray-eyed Athena,
frightening rouser and leader of armies, the weariless one,
who is the mistress delighting in war and the tumult of battle.
And Hera, angered with him and trying to rival her husband,
bore of herself without mingling in love glorious Hephaistos,
who surpasses in skill of his hands all descendants of Ouranos.

MORE UNIONS OF ZEUS AND OTHER GODS AND GODDESSES

And Amphitrite bore to the roaring Shaker of Earth
Triton, a mighty, wide-ruling power, who with his mother
and with his lordly father holds the depths of the sea and
dwells in a gold house, a frightening god. And Aphrodite,

queen of Kythera, to shield-piercing Ares bore Phobos and Deimos,
frightening powers who accompany Ares the Sacker of Cities
as they scatter the thick ranks of men in the onslaught of chill war;
and she bore Harmonia, the wife of high-spirited Kadmos.
And Maia, the daughter of Atlas, bore the herald of the gods,
glorious Hermes, to Zeus, after mounting his sacred bed.
And Semele, the daughter of Kadmos, having mingled in love with Zeus,
bore him a shining son, Dionysos the Bringer of Joy,
she a mortal producing a god; now both are immortals.
And Alkmene gave birth to the wonderful strength of Herakles,
when she and Zeus of the Storm Cloud had mingled together in love.
And Hephaistos, the far-famed god who is lame in both legs,
took Aglaia, the youngest Grace, as his blossoming bride,
And golden-haired Dionysos took the blond Ariadne,
who was the daughter of Minos, as his blossoming bride;
and she was made an unaging immortal by Zeus, son of Kronos.
And powerful Herakles, the valiant son of fair-ankled Alkmene,
when he had finished his strenuous labors, married Hebe,
who was the daughter of almighty Zeus and golden-shod Hera;
she became his praiseworthy wife on snowy Olympos,
where, his great work complete, among the immortals he blessedly
dwells, living the life of a painless, unaging divinity.
And Perseis, one of Okeanos's glorious daughters,
to weariless Helios bore Kirke and King Aietes.
And Aietes, the son of Helios the Bringer of Light,
married by will of the gods Idyia, a lovely-cheeked girl,
a daughter of Okeanos, the river that flows in unending completion;
and she bore him fair-ankled Medeia, when she had come and
yielded to him in love through Aphrodite the Golden.
Farewell now, you gods who have your homes on Olympos,
and you islands and mainlands and salty sea lying within.
Now, O sweet-sounding voices, Muses who dwell on Olympos,
daughters of Zeus of the Aigis, sing of the race of goddesses,
of all those who lay in love with mortal men and
bore, they being immortal, children resembling the gods.
Demeter gave birth to Ploutos, she a goddess divine
having mingled in passionate love with the hero Iasion,
lying with him in a thrice-plowed field of Krete's fertile island;
goodly Ploutos goes over earth and the sea's broad back
everywhere, granting the good luck of wealth and a blessed existence
to all whomever he meets and into whose hands he comes.
And Harmonia, the daughter of golden Aphrodite,
bore to Kadmos in the well-crowned city of Thebes
Ino, Semele, lovely-cheeked Agaue, Autonoe,
who was the wife of the long-haired Aristaios, and Polydoros.

And Kallirhoe, who was one of Okeanos's daughters,
when she had mingled in love with mighty-hearted Chrysaor
through Aphrodite the Golden, bore him the strongest of all men,
Geryon, whom the wonderful power of Herakles slew
as he defended his shambling herd in the isle Erytheia.
And Eos bore to Tithonos bronze-helmeted Memnon,
the Ethiopians' king, and the lordly Emathion.
And she bore of Kephalos's love a glorious son,
powerful Phaethon, who was a man resembling the gods.
On his coming of age, in the tender flower of young manhood,
while still boyish in thought, smile-loving Aphrodite,
seizing and carrying him off, made him a spirit divine
dwelling within her holy temple's innermost shrine.
And Medeia, the daughter of Zeus-nurtured King Aietes,
Aison's son, Iason, by will of the immortal gods
took as his wife, when he had finished his strenuous labors,
those many tasks which Pelias, that great, overbearing king,
that hybristic, wicked worker of outrage, had ordered.
When with a great deal of trouble he had completed these labors,
Aison's son in his swift ship sailed back home to Iolkos
with that girl of the bright eyes and made her his blossoming bride.
And Medeia in love with Iason, a shepherd of people,
bore him a son, Medeios, whom Philyra's offspring Cheiron
reared in the mountains; so great Zeus's purpose was brought to fulfillment.
And one of the daughters of Nereus, the Old Man of the Sea,
the divine goddess Psamathe, gave birth to Phokos,
when she had mingled with Aiakos through Aphrodite the Golden;
and another, the goddess silver-foot Thetis,
having yielded to Peleus's love, bore man-slaying, lion-hearted Achilleus.
And Aphrodite, the lovely-crowned goddess of Kythera,
bore Aineias, when she had lain in passionate love with the
hero Anchises in the heights of the many-valed, windy Mount Ida.
And Kirke, the daughter of Helios, the son of Hyperion,
bore, after mingling in love with much-enduring Odysseus,
blameless Agrios and the mighty hero Latinos.
These in a region remote, in islands secluded and holy,
rule over all the Tyrsenians, a people of great renown.
And the divine goddess Kalypso bore to Odysseus,
when they had mingled in love, Nausithoos and Nausinoos.
These, then, are those goddesses who lay in love with mortal men and
bore, they being immortal, children resembling the gods.
Now, O sweet-sounding voices, Muses who dwell on Olympos,
daughters of Zeus of the Aigis, sing of the race of women. (143–155)

ATHENA AND POSEIDON

Alexander S. Murray, a nineteenth-century classicist and director of Greek antiquities in the British Museum, wrote his *Manual of Mythology* to bring together different stories in the histories of the gods, gleaned from a wide variety of ancient sources that had not been translated into English. His accounts of Pallas Athena and Poseidon, the two most active divine antagonists in the story of Odysseus, provide many details that Homer likely assumed his audience already knew.

FROM ALEXANDER S. MURRAY, *MANUAL OF MYTHOLOGY*

(New York: Charles Scribner's Sons, 1888)

PALLAS-ATHENE, OR MINERVA,

Called also Tritogeneia or Tritonia and Athenæa, is usually described, in the myths concerning her birth, as having sprung into life, fully armed, from the head of Zeus, with its thick black locks, all heaven and earth shaking meanwhile, the sea tossing in great billows, and the light of day being; extinguished. Zeus, it was said, had previously swallowed his wife Metis (Intelligence), to prevent her giving birth to a son. The operation of laying his head open, that Pallas might come forth, was performed by Hephæstos (Vulcan), or, according to other versions of the story, Prometheus. There is, however, another myth, which ascribes her origin to a connection of Poseidon (Neptune) with the nymph Tritonis, adding that Zeus merely adopted her as his daughter. But this seems to have had no foundation in the general belief of the people, and to have been only an invention of later times, when her name, Tritogeneia, or Tritonia, had become unintelligible.

No being connected with the earth, whether deity or mortal, had a part in her birth. She was altogether the issue only of her father, the god of heaven, who, as the myth very plainly characterizes it, brought her into being out of the black tempest-cloud, and amidst the roar and crash of a storm. Her character must therefore be regarded as forming in some way a complement to his. The purpose for which she was brought into existence must have been that she might do what he would plan, but as the supreme and impartial god, could not carry out. She is at once fearful and powerful as a storm, and in turn, gentle and pure as the warmth of the sky when a storm has sunk to rest and an air of new life moves over the freshened fields.

To express both these sides of her character—terrible and mighty as compared with open, gentle, and pure—she had the double name of Pallas-Athēnē: the former was applied to her function of goddess of storms—she who carried the ægis or storm-shield of her father. And further, as Pallas, she became the goddess of battle—valiant, conquering, frightening with the sight of her ægis whole crowds of heroes when they vexed her, and even driving Ares before her with her lightning spear. At the same time the soft, gentle, and heavenly side of her character took from her functions, as goddess of battle, that desire of confused slaughter and massacre which distinguished Ares, and formed the contrast we have already mentioned between the two deities of war. Pallas presides over battles, but only to lead on to victory, and through victory, to peace and prosperity.

When the war has been fought out, and that peace established which—whether it be amid the political life of nations here on earth, or whether it be amid the passions of individual men—is always the result of conflict and war, then it is that the goddess Athene reigns in all gentleness and purity, teaching mankind to enjoy peace, and instructing them in all that gives beauty to human life, in wisdom and art. If we observe and keep clearly before our minds these two sides of her character, the inseparable union of both, and their action and reaction upon each other, we shall see that this goddess, Pallas-Athēnē, is one of the most profound conceptions of a deep religious feeling—a being into whose hands the pious Greek could, with due reverence, commit his keeping.

The mutual relation of these two sides of her character is sufficiently obvious in the various myths relating to the goddess. The principal of these we shall proceed to narrate. But, first, we must call attention to this point, that Athēnē is represented in the myths as for ever remaining a virgin, scorning the affections which are said to have been frequently offered to her. Instead of suggesting her liability, in the smallest degree, to earthly passions and foibles, the myth shows admirably that she was a divine personification of mind, always unfettered in its movements; a personification, at the same time, of the origin of mind from the brain of the supreme Divine Being: a proof that mind is neither of a male nor of a female order, but a single and independent power at work throughout the whole of nature.

In the course of the war with the Giants Pallas rendered most valuable assistance to Zeus, both by advice and deed; being, in fact, the cause of his calling in the aid of Herakles, and thus completing successfully the subjugation of the rebels. Single-handed she overpowered the terrible giant Enkelados; but when Zeus' rule was at last firmly established, she took up the task of assisting and protecting those heroes on earth whom she found engaged in destroying the grim creatures and monsters upon it. In this capacity she was the constant friend of Herakles in all his hardships and adventures (see below), and of Perseus, whom she helped to slay the Gorgon Medusa, whose head she afterwards wore upon her ægis, and for this reason obtained the name of Gorgophone, or Gorgon slayer. Along with Hera she protected the Argonauts, while to her assistance was due the success with which Theseus (see below) overcame and slew monsters of all kinds. She stood by the Greeks in their war against Troy, which we shall describe afterwards, and devised the scheme by which, after ten years' duration, it was brought to a close.

But, in times of peace, her power as goddess in all kinds of skill and handicraft, of clearness like that of the sky, and of mental activity, was uniformly exercised, as has been said, for the general good and prosperity. The arts of spinning and weaving were described as of her invention. She taught how to tend and nurse newly-born infants; and even the healing art was traced back to her among other gods. The flute, too, was her invention. As became the goddess of war, it was her duty to instruct men in the art of taming horses, of bridling and yoking them to the war-chariot—a task which we find her performing in the story of Bellerophon, for whom she bridled the winged horse Pegasos; and in the story of Erichthonios, at Athens, the first mortal who learned from her how to harness horses to chariots. In a word, she was the protectress of all persons employed in art and industry, of those whose business it was on earth to instruct and educate mankind, and therefore to help forward the general happiness.

The principal scene of her influence and actions was Attica, that district of Greece which, according to the myth related above, she obtained as her special and peculiar province, after a contest for it with Poseidon, the god of the sea. There her worship and honour surpassed that of all other deities, and from her was named the chief town of the land. The visible proof and testimony of her guardianship of Attica was the olive on the Acropolis of Athens, which she created in the contest with Poseidon, and from which the Athenians believed all the olive trees of Attica to have spread. In the produce of the olives consisted the chief wealth of the land. Ancient writers relate a touching story concerning this olive tree on the Acropolis, which reveals how firmly the belief of their goddess was rooted in the minds of her people. When the Persians advanced with their overwhelming forces against Greece, it is said that Athēnē presented herself at the throne of her father, and begged for the preservation of her city. But fate had otherwise decreed: Athens must perish, in order that a better and nobler city might rise from its ruins, and accordingly Zeus was obliged to refuse the prayer of his beloved daughter. The Athenians took to their fleet, abandoning altogether the city, which the Persians then entered, and destroyed utterly with fire and sword, not even sparing the sacred olive of the goddess. But, lo! as a sign that she had not forsaken her city even in ruins, there sprang suddenly from the root which remained a new shoot, which, with wonderful quickness, grew to a length of three yards, and was looked on as an emblem of the regeneration of the city. With the aid of their goddess the Athenians fought foremost of all the Greeks in the famous sea-fight that ensued at Salamis, in which the Persian fleet, though vastly superior in numbers, was wholly destroyed, while the troops on the mainland were compelled to escape with shame and immense losses from Greece.

Among the great variety of her titles, some derived from her functions as a goddess, and others from the localities where her worship had a special hold on the people, we find Athene at Elis styled "mother," in consequence of her care over the nursing of children; in Athens and several other places, Polias, the "protectress of cities"; Sōteira, the "saviour"; Glaukopis, "blue-eyed goddess"; Parthenos, "the virgin"; Hippia, "tamer of horses"; Ergane, "mistress of industry"; Nike, the "victorious"; and Mechânitis, "ingenious." Every year a festival lasting several days, and called Panathenaea, was held in her honour at Athens, to commemorate the part she had taken in the war against the Giants: every fourth year—that is, every third year of the current Olympiad—it was celebrated with redoubled splendour. This festival is said to have been instituted by Theseus, or at least to have first derived its importance from him; in any case it was a festival of very great antiquity. Festal processions were formed, athletic games were held, while sacrifices and banquets took place on a large scale—all the Athenians, whether at home or abroad in colonies, having the privilege of taking part. The prizes in the games consisted of large painted earthenware vases filled with pure olive oil, the product of the tree sacred to Athene. Of these vases a small number have been preserved down to our times. On one side is painted a figure of the goddess striding forward in the attitude of hurling her spear, with a column on each side of her, to indicate the race course. On the reverse side is a view of the contest in which a particular vase was won. But perhaps the chief attraction of the festival was the procession in which a new robe or peplos, woven and embroidered for the goddess by a select number of women and girls in Athens, was carried through the town spread like a sail on a mast, placed on a wagon in the form of a ship. In this procession it appears as if the whole population of Attica took part, the youth of the nobility on horseback or in chariots, the soldiery in arms, and the burgesses with their wives and daughters in holiday attire. The new robe was destined for the very ancient statue of Athene which was preserved in the Erechtheum. This custom of placing actual drapery on statues appears to have been handed down from remote times, when the art of sculpture was unequal to the task of imitating the human figure, and it is not improbable that the statue of Athēnē, of which we are speaking, dated from that early time. The magistrates of Athens offered sacrifices to her at the commencement of spring. The services of her sanctuary were conducted by two virgins elected for the period of one year.

In Rome the worship of Minerva was conducted with as much zeal as that of Athēnē at Athens, her character as goddess of wisdom and serious thought being admirably calculated to attract a people like the Romans. She was the protectress of their arts and industries, of the domestic operations of spinning and weaving and embroidering, just as she was among the Greeks. In Rome she had several temples, one of the oldest of them being that on the Capitol. A festival which lasted from March 19th to 23d was annually held in her honour. But the object connected with her, which the Romans venerated above all things else, was the Palladium, or ancient figure of the goddess, the story of which was that it had originally fallen from heaven, and had thereupon become the property of the royal family of Troy, the possession of it being from that time always considered an assurance of the safety of that city. But in the course of the war between the Greeks and Trojans it was secretly carried off by Diomedes and Odysseus, upon which followed the capture of the town by means of the wooden horse. Another version of the story has it that Æneas took it with him when he fled from the city; and in consequence of this inconsistency in the story it happened in later times that more than one city claimed the possession of the real Palladium—as, for example, Argos, Athens, and Rome. Wherever it was believed to be, there the firm conviction existed that the endurance of the city depended on the possession of the image, and so it happened afterwards that the expression Palladium was employed in a wider sense to objects thought to be of similar importance; and when, for instance, we hear of the "Palladium of Freedom being carried off," we understand that the principal provision and security of freedom has been lost. The symbols of Athene were the owl, the cock, the snake, and the olive tree. (89–98)

POSEIDON, OR NEPTUNE

In the neighbourhood of Lerna, in the parched district of Argos, he had struck the earth with his trident, and caused three springs to well up for love of Amymone, whom he found in distress, because she could not obtain the water which her father Danaos had sent her to fetch. In Thessaly a stroke of his trident had broken through the high mountains, which formerly shut in the whole country and caused it to be frequently flooded with water. By that stroke he formed the pleasant vale of Tempē, through which the water collecting from the hills might flow away. A district well supplied with water was favourable to pasture and the rearing of horses, and in this way the horse came to be doubly his symbol, as god of the water of the sea and on the land. In Arcadia, with its mountainous land and fine streams and valleys, he was worshipped side by side with Demeter, with whom, it was believed, he begat that winged and wonderfully fleet horse Arion. In Bœotia, where he was also worshipped, the mother of Arion was said to have been Erinys, to whom he had appeared in the form of a horse. With Medusa he became the father of the winged horse Pegasos, which was watered at springs by Nymphs, and appeared to poets as the symbol of poetic inspiration. And again, as an instance of his double capacity as god of the sea and pasture streams, the ram, with the golden fleece for which the Argonauts sailed, was said to have been his offspring by Theophane, who had been changed into a lamb. Chief among his other offspring were, on the one hand, the giant Antaeos, who derived from his mother Earth, a strength which made him invincible, till Herakles lifting him in the air overpowered him, and the Kyklops, Polyphemos: on the other hand, Pelias, who sent out the Argonauts, and Neleus the father of Nestor.

To return to the instances of rebellious conduct on the part of Poseidon, it appears that after the conclusion of the war with the Giants a disagreement arose between him and Zeus, the result of which was that Poseidon was suspended for the period of a year from the control of the sea, and was further obliged during the time to serve, along with Apollo, Laomedon the King of Troy, and to help to build the walls of that city. Some say that the building of the walls was voluntary on the part of both gods, and was done to test the character of Laomedon, who afterwards refused to give Poseidon the reward agreed upon. Angry at this, the god devastated the land by a flood, and sent a sea-monster, to appease which Laomedon was driven to offer his daughter Hesione as a sacrifice. Herakles, however, set the maiden free and slew the monster. Thus defeated, Poseidon relented none of his indignation towards the Trojans, and would have done them much injury in after times, when they were at war with the Greeks, but for the interference of Zeus.

Though worshipped generally throughout Greece, it was in the seaport towns that the most remarkable zeal was displayed to obtain his favour. Temples in his honour, sanctuaries, and public rejoicings were to be met with in Thessaly, Bœotia, Arcadia, at Aegae, and Helike, on the coast of Achaea, at Pylos in Messenia, at Elis, in the island of Samos, at Corinth, Nauplia, Troezen, in the islands of Kalauria, Eubœa, Skyros, and Tenos, at Mycale, Taenarum, Athens, and on the Isthmus—that belt of land which connects Peloponnesos with the rest of Greece. In the island of Tenos an annual festival was held in his honour, at which he was worshipped in the character of a physician. People crowded to the festival from neighbouring islands, and spent the time in banquets, sacrifice, and common counsel. But chief of all the gatherings in his honour was that held on the Isthmus of Corinth in the autumn, twice in each Olympiad—a festival which had been established by Theseus, and in reputation stood next to the Olympian games, like them also serving the purpose of maintaining among the Greeks of distant regions the consciousness of their common origin. The Corinthians had the right of arranging and managing them, the Athenians having also certain privileges. It was in his double capacity of ruler of the sea and as the first to train and employ horses that the honours of this festival were paid to him. His temple, with other sanctuaries, stood in a pine grove, a wreath from which was the prize awarded to the victors. The prize had originally been a wreath of parsley. In this sacred pine grove was to be seen the Argo, the ship of the Argonauts, dedicated to Poseidon as a memorial of the earliest enterprise at sea; and there also stood the colossal bronze statue of the god, which the Greeks raised to commemorate the splendid naval victory gained over the Persians at Salamis. Horses and bulls were sacrificed to him, the method of performing the sacrifice being to throw them into the sea. It was the practice of fortunate survivors of shipwreck to hang up some memento of their safety in one of his temples.

The Romans, living mostly as herdsmen and farmers in early times, had little occasion to propitiate the god of the sea, and it was probably, therefore, rather as the father of streams that they erected a temple to Neptunus in the Campus Martius, and held a festival in his honour attended with games, feasting, and enjoyment like that of a fair. (52–54)

A GUIDE TO ARKADIA

Pausanias, a physician in Greece in the second century A.D., wrote up his extensive travels throughout Greece, paying particular attention to local legends, shrines to the gods, and religious rites. The following excerpt comes from his guide to Arkadia in Southern Greece. The excerpt includes references to Pelasgo (reputedly the first inhabitant of Arkadia), his son Lykaon, Tantalus (known for sacrificing his son Pelops to the gods), and Tantalus' daughter Niobe, whose children were killed by the gods before she was turned to stone because she had boasted that she had had more children than Leto, Zeus' consort and the mother of Apollo and Artemis. A griffin, which he mentions, is an animal with a lion's body and the head and wings of an eagle. Triton is a merman, with a fish tail. Pausanias' account is important in the study of *The Odyssey* for several reasons: it shows that even a man of science, living about a thousand years after Homer, retains a belief in the gods and myths, and it also shows that local mythology continues to evolve, even though Pausanias denies the veracity of later enlargements on the early stories.

FROM PAUSANIAS, *GUIDE TO GREECE*, BOOK VIII, TRANS. W.H.S. JONES

(London: William Heinemann, 1933)

Lykaon brought a human child to the altar of Lykaian Zeus, slaughtered it and poured its blood on the altar, and they say at that sacrifice he was suddenly turned into a wolf. And I believe this legend, which has been told in Arkadia from ancient times and has likelihood on its side. Because of their justice and their religion the people of that time entertained gods and sat at table with them, and the gods visibly rewarded their goodness with favour and their wickedness with wrath: and in those days certain human beings were turned into gods, and are still honoured.

...

So one may well believe that Lykaon was turned into a wild beast and Tantalos's daughter Niobe was turned to stone. But in my time when wickedness has increased to the last degree, and populates the whole world and all its cities, no human being ever becomes a god, except by a verbal convention and to flatter authority, and the curse of the gods is a long time falling on the wicked, and is stored away for those who have departed from the world. Those who have added so many constructions of lies on to truthful foundations have made a lot of things in the history of the world, things that happened in antiquity and things that will happen now, seem incredible to the majority of mankind. For example, they say that after Lykaian Zeus, someone was always turned into a wolf at the sacrifice of Lykaian Zeus, but not for his whole life, because if he kept off human meat when he was a wolf he turned back into a man after nine years, though if he tasted man he stayed a wild beast for ever. And they say Niobe on Mount Sipylos weeps in the summer. And there are other stories I have heard told: that griffins have spots like leopards and tritons speak in human voices, and some people say that blow through a pierced conch.

...

People who enjoy listening to mythical stories are inclined to add even more wonders of their own, and in this way they have done injuries to the truth which they have mixed up with a lot of rubbish. (vol. 3, 351, 353, 355)

MYTH AND CHILDREN'S EDUCATION

Plato, the most famous of Greek thinkers and the first to use the term *philosophy*, was born in 428 B.C. It was his purpose in *The Republic* to propose a government in which citizens could develop to their maximum potential. In a section of *The Republic* on the education of children, Plato, in the form of dialogue, considers the effect on young minds of mythic stories of Greece, using Homer's epics as his chief reference. At first he says that he is concerned about the detrimental effect on children of "untrue" stories, but then says that even if some stories are true, they may reflect immorality and provide children with bad examples, and thus should be censored. He refers specifically to Uranus (sometimes spelled Ouranos), who imprisoned and killed some of his children, and to his son Cronos, who castrated his father. Even if such stories are to be interpreted allegorically, they should be banned, Plato argues, because young children will take them literally. Plato also says that stories which show gods producing evil and show the afterlife as horrible, malign the gods and make cowards of children. It is one of the first iconoclastic views of the mythology inherent in *The Odyssey*, one that forces the reader to reconsider, and perhaps defend, Homer's presentation of the Heroic Age.

FROM PLATO, *THE REPUBLIC*, BOOKS II AND III, IN *THE DIALOGUES OF PLATO*, TRANS. BENJAMIN JOWETT

(New York: Charles Scribner and Co., 1871)

It seems, then, our first business will be to supervise the making of fables and legends, rejecting all which are unsatisfactory; and we shall induce nurses and mothers to tell their children only those which we have approved, and to think more of moulding their souls with these stories than they now do of rubbing their limbs to make them strong and shapely. Most of the stories now in use must be discarded.

What kind do you mean?

If we take the great ones, we shall see in them the pattern of all the rest, which are bound to be of the same stamp and to have the same effect.

No doubt; but which do you mean by the great ones?

The stories in Hesiod and Homer and the poets in general, who have at all times composed fictitious tales and told them to mankind.

Which kind are you thinking of, and what fault do you find in them?

The worst of all faults, especially if the story is ugly and immoral as well as false—misrepresenting the nature of gods and heroes, like an artist whose picture is utterly unlike the object he sets out to draw.

That is certainly a serious fault; but give me an example.

A signal instance of false invention about the highest matters is that foul story, which Hesiod repeats, of the deeds of Uranus and the vengeance of Cronos; and then there is the tale of Cronos's doings and of his son's treatment of him. Even if such tales were true, I should not have supposed they should be lightly told to thoughtless young people. If they cannot be altogether suppressed, they should only be revealed in a mystery, to which access should be as far as possible restricted by requiring the sacrifice, not of a pig, but of some victim such as very few could afford.

It is true: those stories are objectionable.

Yes, and not to be repeated in our commonwealth, Adeimantus. We shall not tell a child that, if he commits the foulest crimes or goes to any length in punishing his father's misdeeds, he will be doing nothing out of the way, but only what the first and greatest of the gods have done before him.

I agree; such stories are not fit to be repeated.

Nor yet any tales of warfare and intrigues and battles of gods against gods, which are equally untrue. If our future Guardians are to think it a disgrace to quarrel lightly with one another, we shall not let them embroider robes with the Battle of the Giants or tell them of all the other feuds of gods and heroes with their kith and kin. If by any means we can make them believe that no one has ever had a quarrel with a fellow citizen and it is a sin to have one, that is the sort of thing our old men and women should tell children from the first; and as they grow older, we must make the poets write for them in the same strain. Stories like those of Hera being bound by her son, or of Hephaestus flung from heaven by his father for taking his mother's part when she was beaten, and all those battles of the gods in Homer, must not be admitted into our state, whether they be allegorical or not. A child cannot distinguish the allegorical sense from the literal, and the ideas he takes in at that age are likely to become indelibly fixed; hence the great importance of seeing that the first stories he hears shall be designed to produce the best possible effect on his character.

Yes, that is reasonable. But if we were asked which of these stories in particular are of the right quality, what should we answer?

I replied: You and I, Adeimantus, are not, for the moment, poets, but founders of a commonwealth. As such, it is not our business to invent stories ourselves, but only to be clear as to the main outlines to be followed by the poets in making their stories and the limits beyond which they must not be allowed to go.

True; but what are these outlines for any account they may give of the gods?

Of this sort, said I. A poet, whether he is writing epic, lyric, or drama, surely ought always to represent the divine nature as it really is. And the truth is that that nature is good and must be described as such.

Unquestionably.

Well, nothing that is good can be harmful; and if it cannot do harm, it can do no evil; and so it cannot be responsible for any evil.

I agree.

Again, goodness is beneficent, and hence the cause of well-being.

Yes.

Goodness, then, is not responsible for everything, but only for what is as it should be. It is not responsible for evil.

Quite true.

It follows, then, that the divine, being good, is not, as most people say, responsible for everything that happens to mankind, but only for a small part; for the good things in human life are far fewer than the evil, and, whereas the good must be ascribed to heaven only, we must look elsewhere for the cause of evils.

I think that is perfectly true.

So we shall condemn as a foolish error Homer's description of Zeus as the "dispenser of both good and ill." We shall disapprove when Pandarus' violation of oaths and treaties is said to be the work of Zeus and Athena, or when Themis and Zeus are said to have caused strife among the gods. Nor must we allow our young people to be told by Aeschylus that "Heaven implants guilt in man, when his will is to destroy a house utterly." If a poet writes of the sorrows of Niobe or the calamities of the house of Pelops or of the Trojan war, either he must not speak of them as the work of a god, or, if he does so, he must devise some such explanation as we are now requiring: he must say that what the god did was just and good, and the sufferers were the better for being chastised. One who pays a just penalty must not be called miserable, and his misery then laid at heaven's door. The poet will only be allowed to say that the wicked were miserable because they needed chastisement, and the punishment of heaven did them good. If our commonwealth is to be well-ordered, we must fight to the last against any member of it being suffered to speak of the divine, which is good, being responsible for evil. Neither young nor old must listen to such tales, in prose or verse. Such doctrine would be impious, self-contradictory, and disastrous to our commonwealth.

I agree, he said, and I would vote for a law to that effect.

Well then, that shall be one of our laws about religion. The first principle to which all must conform in speech or writing is that heaven is not responsible for everything, but only for what is good.

I am quite satisfied.

Now what of this for a second principle? Do you think of a god as a sort of magician who might, for his own purposes, appear in various shapes, now actually passing into a number of different forms, now deluding us into believing he has done so; or is his nature simple and of all things the least likely to depart from its proper form?

I cannot say offhand.

Well, if a thing passes out of its proper form, must not the change come either from within or from some outside cause?

Yes.

Is it not true, then, that things in the most perfect condition are the least affected by changes from outside? Take the effect on the body of food and drink or of exertion, or the effect of sunshine and wind on a plant: the healthiest and strongest suffer the least change. Again, the bravest and wisest spirit is least disturbed by external influence. Even manufactured things—furniture, houses, clothes—suffer least from wear and tear when they are well made and in good condition. So this immunity to change from outside is characteristic of anything which, thanks to art or nature or both, is in a satisfactory state.

That seems true.

But surely the state of the divine nature must be perfect in every way, and would therefore be the last thing to suffer transformations from any outside cause.

Yes.

Well then, would a god change or alter himself?

If he changes at all, it can only be in that way.

Would it be a change for the better or for the worse?

It could only be for the worse; for we cannot admit any imperfection in divine goodness or beauty.

True; and that being so, do you think, Adeimantus, that anyone, god or man, would deliberately make himself worse in any respect?

That is impossible.

Then a god cannot desire to change himself. Being as perfect as he can be, every god, it seems, remains simply and for ever in his own form.

That is the necessary conclusion.

If so, my friend, the poets must not tell us that "the gods go to and fro among the cities of men, disguised as strangers of all sorts from far countries"; nor must they tell any of those false tales of Proteus and Thetis transforming themselves, or bring Hera on the stage in the guise of a priestess collecting alms for "the life-giving children of Inachus, the river of Argos." Mothers, again, are not to follow these suggestions and scare young children with mischievous stories of spirits that go about by night in all sorts of outlandish shapes. They would only be blaspheming the gods and at the same time making cowards of their children.

No, that must not be allowed.

But are we to think that the gods, though they do not really change, trick us by some magic into believing that they appear in many different forms?

Perhaps.

What? said I; would a god tell a falsehood or act one by deluding us with an apparition?

I cannot say.

Do you not know that the true falsehood—if that is a possible expression—is a thing that all gods and men abominate?

What do you mean?

This, I replied: no one, if he could help it, would tolerate the presence of untruth in the most vital part of his nature concerning the most vital matters. There is nothing he would fear so much as to harbour falsehood in that quarter.

Still I do not understand.

Because you think I mean something out of the ordinary. All I mean is the presence of falsehood in the soul concerning reality. To be deceived about the truth of things and so to be in ignorance and error and to harbour untruth in the soul is a thing no one would consent to. Falsehood in that quarter is abhorred above everything.

It is indeed.

Well then, as I was saying, this ignorance in the soul which entertains untruth is what really deserves to be called the true falsehood; for the spoken falsehood is only the embodiment or image of a previous condition of the soul, not pure unadulterated falsity. It is not so?

It is.

This real falsehood, then, is hateful to gods and men equally. But is the spoken falsehood always a hateful thing? Is it not sometimes helpful—in war, for instance, or as a sort of medicine to avert some fit of folly or madness that might make a friend attempt some mischief? And in those legends we were discussing just now, we can turn fiction to account; not knowing the facts about the distant past, we can make our fiction as good an embodiment of truth as possible.

Yes, that is so.

Well, in which of these ways would falsehood be useful to a god? We cannot think of him as embodying truth in fiction for lack of information about the past.

No, that would be absurd.

So there is no room in his case for poetical inventions. Would he need to tell untruths because he has enemies to fear?

Of course not.

Or friends who are mad or foolish?

No; a fool or a madman could hardly enjoy the friendship of the gods.

Gods, then, have no motive for lying. There can be no falsehood of any sort in the divine nature.

None.

We conclude, then, that a god is a being of entire simplicity and truthfulness in word and in deed. In himself he does not change, nor does he delude others, either in dreams or in waking moments, by apparitions or oracles or signs.

I agree, after all you have said.

You will assent, then, to this as a second principle to guide all that is to be said or written about the gods: that they do not transform themselves by any magic or mislead us by illusions or lies. For all our admiration of Homer, we shall not approve his story of the dream Zeus sent to Agamemnon; nor yet those lines of Aeschylus where Thetis tells how Apollo sang at her wedding:

> Boding good fortune for my child, long life
> From sickness free, in all things blest by heaven,
> His song, so crowned with triumph, cheered my heart.
> I thought those lips divine, with prophecy
> Instinct, could never lie. But he, this guest,
> Whose voice so rang with promise at the feast,
> Even he, has slain my son.

If a poet writes of the gods in this way, we shall be angry and refuse him the means to produce his play. Nor shall we allow such poetry to be used in educating the young, if we mean our Guardians to be godfearing and to reproduce the divine nature in themselves so far as man may.

I entirely agree with your principles, he said, and I would have them observed as laws.

So far, then, as religion is concerned, we have settled what sorts of stories about the gods may, or may not, be told to children who are to hold heaven and their parents in reverence and to value good relations with one another.

Yes, he said; and I believe we have settled right.

We also want them to be brave. So the stories they hear should be such as to make them unafraid of death. A man with that fear in his heart cannot be brave, can he?

Surely not.

And can a man be free from that fear and prefer death in battle to defeat and slavery, if he believes in a world below which is full of terrors?

No.

Here again, then, our supervision will be needed. The poets must be told to speak well of that other world. The gloomy descriptions they now give must be forbidden, not only as untrue, but as injurious to our future warriors. We shall strike out all lines like these:

> I would rather be on earth as the hired servant of another, in the house of a landless man with little to live on, than be king over all the dead;

or these:

> Alack, there is, then, even in the house of Death a spirit or a shade; but the wits dwell in it no more.

We shall ask Homer and the poets in general not to mind if we cross out all passages of this sort. If most people enjoy them as good poetry, that is all the more reason for keeping them from children or grown men who are to be free, fearing slavery more than death.

I entirely agree.

We must also get rid of all that terrifying language, the very sound of which is enough to make one shiver: "loathsome Styx," "the River of Wailing," "infernal spirits," "anatomies," and so on. For other purposes such language may be well enough; but we are afraid that fever consequent upon such shivering fits may melt down the fine-tempered spirit of our Guardians. So we will have none of it; and we shall encourage writing in the opposite strain.

Clearly.

Another thing we must banish is the wailing and lamentations of the famous heroes. For this reason: if two friends are both men of high character, neither of them will think that death has any terrors for his comrade; and so he will not mourn for his friend's sake, as if something terrible had befallen him.

No.

We also believe that such a man, above all, possesses within himself all that is necessary for a good life and is least dependent on others, so that he has less to fear from the loss of a son or brother or of his wealth or any other possession. When such misfortune comes, he will bear it patiently without lamenting.

True.

We shall do well, then, to strike out descriptions of the heroes bewailing the dead, and make over such lamentations to women (and not to women of good standing either) and to men of low character, so that the Guardians we are training for our country may disdain to imitate them.

Quite right.

Once more, then, we shall ask Homer and the other poets not to represent Achilles, the son of a goddess, as "tossing from side to side, now on his face, now on his back," and then as rising up and wandering distractedly on the seashore, or pouring ashes on his head with both hands, with all those tears and wailings the poet describes; nor to tell how Priam, who was near akin to the gods, "rolled in the dung as he made entreaty, calling on each man by name." Still more earnestly shall we ask them not to represent gods as lamenting, or at any rate not to dare to misrepresent the highest god by making him say: "Woe is me that Sarpedon, whom I love above all men, is fated to die at the hands of Patroclus." For if our young men take such unworthy descriptions seriously instead of laughing at them, they will hardly feel themselves, who are but men, above behaving in that way or repress any temptation to do so. They would not be ashamed of giving way with complaints and outcries on every trifling occasion; and that would be contrary to the principle we have deduced and shall adhere to, until someone can show us a better.

It would.

Again, our Guardians ought not to be overmuch given to laughter. Violent laughter tends to provoke an equally violent reaction. We must not allow poets to describe men of worth being overcome by it; still less should Homer speak of the gods giving way to "unquenchable laughter" at the sight of Hephaestus "bustling from room to room." That will be against your principles.

Yes, if you choose to call them mine.

Again, a high value must be set upon truthfulness. If we were right in saying that gods have no use for falsehood and it is useful to mankind only in the way of a medicine, obviously a medicine should be handled by no one but a physician.

Obviously.

If anyone, then, is to practise deception, either on the country's enemies or on its citizens, it must be the Rulers of the commonwealth, acting for its benefit; no one else may meddle with this privilege. For a private person to mislead such Rulers we shall declare to be a worse offence than for a patient to mislead his doctor or an athlete his trainer about his bodily condition, or for a seaman to misinform his captain about the state of the ship or of the crew. So, if anyone else in our commonwealth "of all that practise crafts, physician, seer, or carpenter," is caught not telling the truth, the Rulers will punish him for introducing a practice as fatal and subversive in a state as it would be in a ship.

It would certainly be as fatal, if action were suited to the word.

Next, our young men will need self-control; and for the mass of mankind that chiefly means obeying their governors, and themselves governing their appetite for the pleasures of eating and drinking and sex. Here again we shall disapprove of much that we find in Homer.

I agree.

Whereas we shall allow the poets to represent any examples of self-control and fortitude on the part of famous men, and admit such lines as these: "Odysseus smote his breast, chiding his heart: Endure, my heart; thou has borne worse things than these."

Yes, certainly.

Nor again must these men of ours be lovers of money, or ready to take bribes. They must not hear that "gods and great princes may be won by gifts."

No, that sort of thing cannot be approved.

If it were not for my regard for Homer, I should not hesitate to call it downright impiety to make Achilles say to Apollo: "Thou has wronged me, thou deadliest of gods; I would surely requite thee, if I had but the power." And all those stories of Achilles dragging Hector round the tomb of Patroclus and slaughtering captives on the funeral pyre we shall condemn as false, and not let our Guardians believe that Achilles, who was the son of a goddess and of the wise Peleus, third in descent from Zeus, and the pupil of the sage Chiron, was so disordered that his heart was a prey to two contrary maladies, mean covetousness and arrogant contempt of gods and men.

You are right.

TOPICS FOR ORAL AND WRITTEN DISCUSSION

1. Write an essay on an instance in *The Odyssey* when the actions of the gods merely reflect human character.
2. Discuss why it is to be expected that Athena, of all the deities, chooses to champion Odysseus.
3. Have a class committee of five people construct a Jeopardy game on the subject of the Homeric gods.
4. Using the material in this chapter, augmented with your own independent research, make a report on the subject of the failure of the gods to act admirably.
5. Research the extent to which one of the mythic narratives referred to in *The Odyssey* has been the inspiration for subsequent works of art—painting, sculpture, opera, drama, poetry, or fiction. Construct a program on your subject, using videotapes, slides or other audiovisual materials.
6. Write an essay on any two family relationships in Greek myth. Speculate on what aspects of the story caused it to achieve mythic stature, and to endure and inspire subsequent literature.
7. Using Bulfinch's description, draw a map of the world of the Olympian gods.
8. Write a research paper on the Delphic Oracle.
9. Study Murray's accounts of Athena and Poseidon. Are there any further clues in his examination of the view of these two gods that would further explain their attitude toward Odysseus?
10. Write an essay on Plato's view of the power of Homer in *The Republic*.

SUGGESTIONS FOR FURTHER READING

Guthrie, W.K.C. *The Greeks and Their Gods.* Boston: Beacon Press, 1955.
Harnsberger, Caroline Thomas. *Gods and Heroes.* New York: Whitson, 1977.
Huffington, Arianna. *The Gods of Greece.* Toronto: McClelland and Stewart, 1983.
Long, Charlotte. *The Twelve Gods of Greece and Rome.* New York: E.J. Brill, 1987.
Meagher, Robert E. *Helen.* New York: Continuum Press, 1995.
Scully, Stephen. *Homer and the Sacred City.* Ithaca, NY: Cornell University Press, 1990.
Sissa, Giulia. *The Daily Life of the Greek Gods*, trans. Janet Lloyd. Palo Alto, CA: Stanford University Press, 2000.
Stroud, Joanne H., ed. *The Olympians.* Dallas: Dallas Institute, 1995.

3

The Geography of *The Odyssey*

Even for a twentieth- or twenty-first-century observer—one of the soldiers in the guerrilla band behind the lines in the Greek mountains during World War II, or even a present-day tourist standing on the shores of Greece looking out to the vast Mediterranean—the importance of *place*—Greece's location and terrain—becomes graphically, emotionally felt. And the geography of Greece was no less crucial for Odysseus' world. Therefore, to have an understanding of *The Odyssey*, it is essential to know something of the stunning geography of the Mediterranean world. To that end the following discussion (1) locates Greece on the map of Europe; (2) identifies and situates areas within Greece pertinent to *The Odyssey*; (3) maps where Odysseus probably traveled in his voyage home; and (4) considers how the terrain and winds of those areas affect the action of the story. It will be useful for the reader to refer closely to the maps at the beginning of this chapter as you proceed.

LOCATION OF GREECE

Greece, the tail end of the Balkan Peninsula in the southeastern portion of Europe, located between 36 and 42 degrees latitude, is an extension of land and outlying islands surrounded on three sides by bodies of water. To the west is the Ionian Sea; to the east is the Aegean Sea, near the Dardenelles (a strait between Europe and Asian Turkey), and to the south is the Mediterranean Sea. To the north, it shares borders with what is now (from west to east) Albania, Macedonia, Bulgaria, and Turkey. Troy, the extinct city that a loose federation

A map of the Mediterranean area showing areas mentioned in *The Odyssey*, and areas where scholars believe Odysseus may have traveled.

of Greeks attacked, destroyed, and plundered in Homer's *Iliad*, lies directly across the Aegean, in what is now Turkey. Across the Ionian Sea to the west of Greece lie southern Italy and Sicily. To the south, across the Mediterranean Sea, lie what is now, from west to east, Libya and Egypt, in northern Africa.

TERRITORY COMPRISING GREECE

Greece itself is composed of a variety of different landmasses:

Mainland Greece, adjoining Europe to the north.

A long, narrow island called Euboea that runs close along the east coast of the mainland.

A southern landmass called the Peloponnese, which is separated from mainland Greece by the narrow Gulf of Corinth.

Many large islands and collections of small islands that comprise one-fifth of the landmass of Greece:

- Cythera, located close to the southern shore
- Rhodes, located off the southern coast of Turkey

Map of the Greek region.

- Crete, south of Greece, separated from southern Greece by the Sea of Crete.
- Lesbos, Samos, Samothrace, Chios, and Lemnos, in the Aegean Sea within sight of Turkey.
- Smaller groups, called the Sporades and Cyclades, in the Aegean.
- Smaller groups in the Ionian Sea that include Odysseus' home, Ithaca, and the possible home of King Alcinoos, Corfu.

Sites in Greece and the Mediterranean Pertinent to *The Odyssey*

Mount Olympus: located in east central Greece, the highest peak in Greece, rising 9,576 feet and usually cloud-covered, the mythical home of the Olympian gods.

Ithaca: a small, rugged island, in the Ionian Sea northwest of the Greek mainland, the home of Odysseus and the place where *The Odyssey* begins and ends.

Pylos: on the southwest coast of southern Greece, the home of King Nestor, whom Telemachos visits to receive news of his father, Odysseus.

Sparta: in the south central portion of southern Greece, home of King Menelaos and Helen, whom Telemachos visits for news of his father.

Mycenae: located in the east central portion of southern Greece, home of King Agamemnon, leader of the Greek forces against Troy, whose murder in Mycenae is told repeatedly in *The Odyssey*.

Nestor, in his conversation with Telemachos, mentions several names of places where various Greek warriors sailed in attempting to get home or where they went to plunder before going home:

Crete: island in the Mediterranean Sea, south of Greece, home of King Idomeneos, a Greek warrior whose return home is related to Telemachos by Nestor.

Tenedos: island in the Aegean off the coast of Troy, in what is now Turkey, where Nestor and Menelaos made sacrifices to the gods after victory over Troy. They have left Agamemnon behind.

Lesbos: large island south of Tenedos that Nestor and Menelaos pass.

Chios: an island south of Lesbos that Nestor and Menelaos pass.

Euboea: long island along the coast of the Greek mainland, where Nestor and Menelaos intend to sail to escape the wrath of Zeus.

Geraetus: community on south Euboea where they spend the night and sacrifice to the gods.

Sunion: headlands of Athens on southeast coast of the Greek mainland where Menelaos, stopping to bury his dead pilot, parts company with Nestor.

Argos: city on the east central coast of southern Greece where Diomedes, a Greek warrior, returns.

Maleia: island of sheer cliffs in the Aegean where Menelaos stops briefly

Cydonia: city in Crete where some of Menelaos' crew stop

Egypt: Menelaus' ships that survive reach Egypt, where he stays to collect much gold to take home

Odysseus, in telling his story to the Phaeacian court, mentions the following places, identifiable by name, in recounting his journey home:

Ismaros in the Ciccones: peoples sympathetic with the Trojans, located north of Troy, where Odysseus and his men "sacked the city and its men" after the fall of Troy.

Malea and Cythera: Malea in the southernmost tip of Greece, Cythera an island just south of Greece. North winds blow Odysseus far past Cythera for nine days.

Theories on the Rest of Odysseus' Journey

Excepting Ithaca, the other places on Odysseus' journey do not have names now in use, and have been matters of frequent conjecture. The question is asked, "What actual places did Odysseus visit on his long trip home?" Bernard Knox in his "Introduction" to Robert Fagles' translation, *Homer. The Odyssey* (New York: Penguin Books, 1996), writes that attempts to locate the actual places where Odysseus sailed is a "wild-goose chase" (23), and that Homer's own geography, even of mainland Greece, was unreliable. Homer has Telemachos, for example, travel from Pylos to Sparta by horse-drawn carriage at a time when there were no roads between the two sites, which were separated by inaccessible mountains. But other scholars have continued to speculate on the real places in Odysseus' travels. One of the most unusual ideas is that Odysseus traveled to the Baltic Sea and the coasts of Finland and Norway. Others, including Tim Severin, who tried to re-create Odysseus' voyage and published the result in *The Ulysses Voyage. Sea Search for Odysseus* (New York: E.P. Dutton, 1987), argues that Odysseus' adventures confined him to the seas around Greece. But most scholars have for some time argued that Odysseus' voyage home took place largely in and off the coasts of Italy and Sicily. The following are the places where Odysseus is presumed to have gone, according to the generally accepted theory:

Land of the Lotus-Eaters: likely the northern coast of Africa.

Land of the Cyclopes: possibly Sicily

Aeolia: Malta, an island south of Sicily

Land of the Lestrygonian Giants: western tip of Sicily

Land of Circe: area between Rome and Naples

Entrance of Hades: lake near Naples

Land of the Sirens: Bay of Naples, under Mount Vesuvius

Scylla and Charybdis: Straits of Messina, between Italy and Sicily

Island of the Sun: Sicily

Ogygia, Land of Calypso: island of Gozo, north of Malta

Phaeacia, Land of Nausicaa and King Alcinoos: island of Corfu, in the Ionian Sea north of Ithaca.

Certain physical features of Greece, the seas surrounding Greece, and the Mediterranean area around Italy also enlarge on our understanding of Odysseus' journey.

MOUNTAINS OF GREECE

Greece is composed of rugged, craggy mountain ranges, running from northwest to southeast. The highest, most inaccessible peaks, extensions of the Alpine system, are in the northwest of mainland Greece. The highest mountains in this area reach 8,136 feet (Mount Pindus), and 9,576 feet (Mount Olympus). Although the mountains in the south do not reach such heights, the terrain is rugged in the Peloponnese as well, with a pattern of tall mountain ranges separated by long, narrow valleys. Many of the islands, some of which are extensions of mountain ranges that rise here and there above the water, also are craggy and contain few good harbors. Corfu, where Odysseus finally is swept into a river from the ocean, has only one good harbor in an otherwise forbidding coast line.

Results of Mountainous Terrain

The seas that surround Greece on three sides provided an arduous way of trading within the country, at least with coastal areas. But the terrain, making travel overland and communication from area to area extremely difficult even in such a relatively small land area, isolated centers of population from one another. Sometimes the only way of reaching an area was by walking or by using pack animals. But oxcarts, for example, which could be used for carrying heavy loads in Homer's day, had no rotating axles for turning corners. The total area of Greece, including the islands, is only 50,949 square miles, about 8,000 square miles smaller than the entire state of Georgia in the United States. Nevertheless, Telemachos and others living in Ithaca have known nothing of their father and king Odysseus, or the fates of the other warriors since the Trojan War. Although we see that some stories of the Trojan War have reached the court of Alcinoos in nearby Corfu, the fate of Agamemnon is news to Telemachos. Nestor and Menelaos also have details about Odysseus that Telemachos is unaware of. Nestor tells him all he knows, and advises him to visit Menelaos at Sparta to gather further information.

The rugged terrain also lent itself to the development of small, relatively isolated city-states, rather than one unified country. Thus, Ithaca, Pylos, Sparta, Mycenae, Crete, and Phaeacia, all of which were part of Greece, were kingdoms unto themselves with their own independent rulers. The war with Troy marked a significant turn of events in that the separate kingdoms united in a common cause.

Natural Resources

The soil of Greece was generally very poor except in a few coastal plains in the east, on the Aegean Sea. Cultivation of crops was made difficult elsewhere by the dearth of topsoil. Solid rock lay on or near the surface of much of the land. Furthermore, the long, hot, arid summers did not provide enough moisture for rich cultivation of crops. Some olives, grapes, peas, beans, barley, and nuts were grown on the sparse fertile plains, but foodstuffs were scarcely plentiful, and there was a shortage of grass and fodder for raising the animals most suitable for Greece, like the pigs, goats, and sheep mentioned in Ithaca. Even today, only 19 percent of land in Greece is arable. This scarcity of crops and fodder lends credence to Telemachos' fear that the suitors will soon deplete his father's estate.

Greece, which is surrounded by water on three sides, has the reputation for being a fishing area. But even here, the edible species of fish, except possibly tuna, are not abundant.

INVASION, COLONIZATION, AND TRADE

Greece's scarcity of natural resources likely contributed not only to its development of trade but also to its history of invasion and colonization of other countries such as Troy. It was not fishing, but colonization and exploration, often in search of plunder, that made the Greeks, like Odysseus, sailors. Note how often Odysseus, Menelaos, and Agamemnon are in search of treasure outside Greece, either received as gifts or stolen from other areas and brought back home to Greece. All the warriors plunder the conquered Troy. In addition, after the war is over, Odysseus steals from the Ciccones and from Polyphemos. His men try to steal cattle from the Island of the Sun. As scholars point out, "Sacker of Cities," the name often given Odysseus, is meant to be a compliment, not a criticism. Menelaos also brings home gold he has likely plundered from the Egyptians.

THE AEGEAN AND MEDITERRANEAN SEAS

The currents, winds, and the lack of winds in the doldrums of the seas around Greece and Italy where Odysseus probably sailed are important for an understanding of *The Odyssey*. For instance, Odysseus encounters a strong north wind in the Aegean Sea shortly after leaving Troy. As he is sailing for the island of Cythera, tumultuous waves and winds in the Aegean send him off course, all the way to Africa. Indeed, sailing north in the mid-Aegean in summer was an impossibility.

Later, the winds carry him safely within sight of Ithaca in the Ionian Sea, before a destructive west wind drives the ship back to the middle of the Mediterranean. Still later, he is stuck for many days at the Island of the Sun, probably in Sicily, because of the complete absence of wind. Immediately upon leaving there, however, a horrific south wind blows Odysseus back to Scylla and Charybdis, and eventually to Calypso's island. When he finally sets to sea again and nears Phaeacia (probably Corfu, in the Ionian Sea), a huge storm so buffets his raft that he has to abandon it, and is then dashed against the rocky coast and taken back out to sea.

All these misfortunes with storms and tempestuous winds are attributed in *The Odyssey* to the wrath of Poseidon and the god from the Island of the Sun, but these conditions are consistent with the winds that prevail in the areas he traveled. The winds in the Aegean and Ionian seas are often unpredictable and fierce, in part caused by the warming of the sea air by the sun. Along the shores of the Aegean, strong currents flow to the north, and probably assisted Odysseus in making a side trip to loot the Ciccones, north of Troy, after the war. But in the middle of the Aegean Sea, away from shore, strong currents from the Black Sea in the north, which is higher than the Aegean, rush in and are likely what took Odysseus from the coast of Greece to the Lotus-Eaters in North Africa.

The trouble that Menelaos and Nestor encounter near the shores of eastern Greece is also typical of the experience of Greek sailors, in that the rivers, gulfs, islands, and cliffs create treacherous currents all around the Greek coast.

The Mediterranean Sea was even more perilous for Odysseus' craft, for it is a sea of fierce and sudden storms. In this sea, hot, dry winds from the Sahara, blowing up from the south, collide with cold winds blowing down from the mountains in the north. This collision of hot and cold winds in an inland sea produce the tumultuous and unpredictable weather that posed continual hazards for Odysseus on his long journey home.

The first of the documents included in this chapter, an excerpt from Max Cary's 1949 geography, provides the reader of *The Odyssey* with some sense of why sea travel, like that made by Odysseus, developed largely as a response to the configuration and topography of Greece. The second, by ancient Greek geographer Strabo, supports the widely held theory that many of Odysseus' adventures on his way home from Troy took place in and around Sicily, where volcanic activity made both land and sea dangerous. The third excerpt, from the Greek historian Thucydides, paints a picture of the piracy of Greek sailors, not unlike that of Odysseus and his fellow warriors, an accepted practice at the time and one of which Homer writes. The final excerpt is from Tim Severin's 1984 attempt to re-create the voyage of Odysseus. His conclusion, radically different from that of most scholars, is that the voyage was solely within the waters of Greece.

GEOGRAPHY AS BACKGROUND TO HISTORY

Although English scholars like Professor Cary had been interested in the classics since the Renaissance, when they looked to Homer and the Greek tragedians for their models, the discipline of geography and its place in the study of the classics did not emerge until the 1930s. At this time, scholars began to notice the extent to which geography affected the way cultures develop. In the following excerpts from Cary's book, one finds reference to the Greeks' isolation by mountains from the rest of Europe, a situation that forced them to look to the seas that surrounded them on three sides. His account of the importance of the islands and the danger of the sea with which Greeks had to contend throws light on Odysseus' orientation to the sea, why the Greek warriors went home by sea rather than by land, and why their returns home took almost as much time as fighting the war itself.

FROM MAX CARY, *THE GEOGRAPHIC BACKGROUND OF GREEK AND ROMAN HISTORY*

(Oxford: Clarendon Press, 1949)

No other country of the Mediterranean presents a more tumbled surface than Greece: it is estimated that not much more than 20 percent of the land is level. (40)

...

While Greece is almost closed to the European continent, it lies wide open on its sea fronts. The territory of the Greek mainland is one-third that of Italy and one-sixth that of the Spanish peninsula, yet its coastline (2,600 miles) is longer than that of the two larger peninsulas. ... No point of Central Greece lies farther than 40 miles from the sea, and none in the Peloponnese is distant more than 32 miles.

The seas that encompass Greece are as typically Mediterranean as the Greek lands themselves. In winter-time the southern Adriatic is a storm-centre with an irregular play of currents; and the north Aegean is infested until late in spring with a gusty north wind. ... Occasional fall-winds may swoop down from a coastal range: their force and frequency off Cape Malea at the south-eastern tip of Peloponnese gave this headland a particularly bad reputation. Long stretches of the seaboard are lined with sheer cliffs. (45)

...

The surrounding seas accordingly remained closed to all Greeks in winter and to some Greeks at almost any season. (46)

...

[T]he obstacles to easy travel within the Greek mainland are even greater than a mere glance at the map, showing its high relief, would suggest. The irregular strike of the mountain system leaves no room for long corridors running parallel to well-defined ranges. In Greece, cross-country journeys in almost any direction are like trips on a switchback railway, and since many of the mountain passes are at a height of 3,000 feet or over, they are snow-bound for at least part of the winter. (47)

AN ANCIENT ACCOUNT OF GREEK GEOGRAPHY

Strabo, a Greek who lived from 64 B.C. to A.D. 25, is known as the father of geography. His writings on the ancient Mediterranean world consist primarily of the location of distinct areas and cities rather than detailed descriptions of their terrain and climate. Still, the following passage provides some description of Sicily, where classicists, even from the time of Strabo, located much of the action of *The Odyssey*. Strabo's account of volcanic action on Sicily gives some credence to Homer's perception that violent giants and Cyclopes might inhabit the island.

The passage also makes specific reference to a chasm in the sea around Sicily, a chasm called Charybdis, and Strabo places the land of Aeolios, king of the winds, in Sicily. The most widely accepted modern theory places the Charybdis that Odysseus faces in the Strait of Messina, between Italy and Sicily, and the land of Aeolios in Malta, an island just south of Sicily. In *The Odyssey*, Odysseus is initially treated hospitably by King Aeolios. The unpredictable winds and high seas that surround Sicily and smaller, nearby islands, as they are described by Strabo, are very like those experienced by Odysseus when his men release the bag of west wind, incurring the wrath of King Aeolios.

The proper names mentioned in the selection include Aetna, in Sicily, the highest volcano in Europe, now usually spelled "Etna"; the Nebrodes Mountains, a range in northwest Sicily; Palici, an area in southeast Sicily; Mataurus, an area in western Sicily known as Mazzara; the Liparaean (Lipari) Islands, a group of islands north of Sicily, of which Lipara is the largest (an island north of Lipara was known as Aeolia); Cnidians, Greek immigrants to Sicily by way of Asia Minor; Thermessa, the island closest to Sicily; "the Strait," the Strait of Messina, between Sicily and Italy, leading from the Tuscan or Tyrrhenian Sea to the Ionian Sea; "the Poet" refers to Homer, who, despite many reservations about Homer's geography, Strabo believed was the first and best of all geographers.

FROM STRABO, *THE GEOGRAPHY OF STRABO*, VOL. 3, TRANS. HORACE LEONARD JONES

(London: William Heinemann, 1917)

Over against Aetna rise the Nebrodes Mountains, which, though lower than Aetna, exceed it considerably in breadth. The whole island is hollow down beneath the ground, and full of streams and of fire. ... [T]he island has at many places springs of hot waters which spout up. ... The territory of Palici has craters that spout up water in a dome-like jet and receive it back again into the same recess. The cavern near Mataurus contains an immense gallery through which a river flows invisible for a considerable distance, and then emerges to the surface ... which sinks into the chasm (called Charybdis)... . Phenomena akin ... to those in Sicily are to be seen about the Liparaean Islands and Lipara itself. The islands are seven in number, but the largest is Lipara (a colony of the Cnidians) which, Thermessa excepted, lies nearest to Sicily. ... [B]y some they are called the Islands of Aeolus. ... [The] whole island is rocky, desert, and fiery, and it has three fire blasts, rising from three openings which one might call craters. From the largest the flames carry up also red-hot masses, which have already choked up a considerable part of the Strait. From observation it has been believed that the flames, both here and on Aetna, are stimulated along with the winds and that when the winds cease the flames cease too. And this is not unreasonable, for the winds are begotten by the evaporations of the sea and after they have taken their beginning are fed thereby; and therefore it is not permissible for any who have any sort of insight into such matters to marvel if the fire too is kindled by a cognate fuel or disturbance. ... Now if the south wind is about to blow ... a cloud-like mist pours down all round the island, so that not even Sicily is visible in the distance; and when the north wind is about to blow, pure flames rise aloft from the aforesaid crater and louder rumblings are sent forth; but the west wind holds a middle position, so to speak, between the two; but though the two other craters are like the first in kind, they fall short in the violence of their spoutings; accordingly, both the difference in the rumblings, and the place whence the spoutings and the flames and the fiery smoke begin, signify beforehand the wind that is going to blow again three days afterward; at all events, certain of the men in Lipara, when the weather made sailing impossible, predicted ... the wind that was to blow, and they were not mistaken; from this face, then, it is clear that the saying of the Poet which is regarded as most mythical of all was not idly spoken, but that he hinted at the truth when he called Aeolus "steward of the winds." (Book VI, 91–99)

WHY PIRACY?

The paucity of natural resources in Greece and the Greeks' orientation to the sea were two of the main reasons for the rise of piracy, not only by professional pirates but also by men like Odysseus, who often plundered for food and treasure on his way home from Troy. Thucydides, in writing of the "ancient customs," enlarges on the practice of piracy in the following excerpt. Note that "Hellenes" was another name for the Greeks that, according to Thucydides, came into being only after the Trojan War somewhat unified the country. Thucydides' statement that hosts often matter-of-factly asked their visitors if they were pirates refers to lines in book 3 of *The Odyssey* when King Nestor of Pylos asks Telemachos, who has come only for news of his father, if he is "one of those reckless wanderers of the sea, like those corsairs who risk their lives to prey on other men?"

FROM *THUCYDIDES, THE HISTORIES*, VOL. 1, TRANS. BENJAMIN JOWETT

(Oxford: Clarendon Press, 1900)

For in ancient times both the Hellenes, and those Barbarians, whose homes were on the coast of the mainland or in islands, when they began to find their way to one another by sea, had recourse to piracy. They were commanded by powerful chiefs, who took this means of increasing their wealth and providing for their poorer followers. They would fall upon the unwalled and straggling towns, or rather villages, which they plundered, and maintained themselves chiefly by the plunder of them; for, as yet, such an occupation was held to be honourable and not disgraceful. This is proved by the practice of certain tribes on the mainland who, to the present day, glory in piratical exploits, and by the witness of the ancient poets, in whose verses the question is invariably asked of newly-arrived voyagers, whether they are pirates; which implies that neither those who are questioned disclaim, nor those who are interested in knowing censure the occupation. ... For the piratical tribes plundered, not only one another, but all those who, without being seamen, lived on the sea-coast. (4, 6)

A RE-CREATION OF ODYSSEUS' VOYAGE

In 1984 Tim Severin and his crew made a voyage on a replica of a Greek galley ship, similar to the one on which Odysseus sailed, in order to re-create the events in Homer's epic. Severin was impressed upon visiting the site of Troy, now in Turkey, at how Homer had exaggerated the scale and grandeur of that city. This caused him to believe that Homer had, in the manner of the epic, exaggerated in his description of Odysseus' voyage home—making the distances far greater and making the seas and places on shore far more dangerous. This led him to doubt the established theory that Odysseus had many of his experiences in Italy, Sicily, and the far west waters of the Mediterranean. Severin attributes this widely accepted older theory to the ancient Greek geographer Strabo, who was influenced by Greek colonization of Sicily that occurred long after Odysseus' voyage. Instead, Severin posits the theory that Odysseus never left the waters around Greece itself. He bases this on his belief that at the time of Odysseus' voyage home, the world west of Greece was totally unknown to the Greeks.

In the first sentence below, he mentions Wilhelm Dorpfeld, Carl Blegen, and Heinrich Schliemann, all archaeologists of Homer's ancient world.

FROM TIM SEVERIN, *THE ULYSSES VOYAGE*

(New York: E.P. Dutton, 1987)

But what emerges is that although an actual Troy, whether Dorpfeld's or Blegen's, certainly existed on the spot where Schliemann had dug, it is nothing like the great city that Homer pictures for us. (42)

...

Homer and the bands were not deliberate liars, they were describing the place as poets. The magic of their words took a minor citadel and turned it into a stupendous stronghold immortalized by their descriptions. This is a credit to poetic imagination, but it was another warning. If Homer could treat Troy like this, would he not also have done the same for the places in the *Odyssey*? Might he not have similarly inflated the locations that Ulysses visited in their size and grandeur to embellish his tale? ...

He inflates ordinary places so as to make them seem vast and impressive. As I walked around the ruins of Troy I realized that we would have to apply the same law of the epic while we were searching for the locations of the adventures of the *Odyssey*. (43)

...

The *Odyssey*'s myths and folktales go back to a much earlier and more primitive time, to a world that believed in monsters and witches and the notion of a small habitable landmass surrounded by the all-encircling world river. To the east the Greeks looked across the Aegean Sea and knew of Asia Minor, southward they were in contact with Crete and with Egypt. But the west was terra incognito. The unknown began at the very fringe of Greece itself. (244)

...

This was the lesson we had learned from our own odyssey as *Argo* retrieved the story of Ulysses from the disarray of hyperbole, doubts, and contradictions. In the end it proved very straightforward—*Argo* had brought the *Odyssey* back to Greece. (242–245)

QUESTIONS FOR ORAL AND WRITTEN DISCUSSION

1. Construct a wall-sized map of the Mediterranean area and draw lines plotting Odysseus' journey, using the most widely accepted theory.
2. Choose one of the adventures on Odysseus' journey, describe it in detail, and research arguments about where it may be located on the map, and why.
3. Research the physical character of Mount Olympus. For what reasons would believers have located the home of the gods there?
4. Reread *The Odyssey* for hints about the types of agriculture carried on in the locations mentioned there. What do Odysseus and his crew regard as valuable agriculture? Compose your findings in an essay.
5. Research the characteristics attributed to Zeus. How is his character connected to climate, and why?
6. With close reference to the epic as well as research on where Odysseus actually went, have a debate on two different theories.
7. Using your own close reading of *The Odyssey*, write an essay on Odysseus as pirate.

SUGGESTIONS FOR FURTHER READING

Avery, Catherine, ed. *The New Century Handbook of Classical Geography*. New York: Appleton-Century-Crofts, 1972.

Braudel, Fernand. *Memory and the Mediterranean*. New York: Alfred A. Knopf, 2001.

Dueck, Daniela. *Strabo of Amasia: A Greek Man of Letters in Augustan Rome*. London: Routledge, 2000.

Horden, Peregrine. *The Corrupting Sea*. Malden, MA: Blackwell, 2000.

Jones, Peter V. *The World of Athens*. Cambridge: Cambridge University Press, 1984.

King, Russell, ed. *Geography, Environment and Development in the Mediterranean*. Brighton, UK: Sussex Academic Press, 2001.

Meijer, Fik. *A History of Seafaring in the Classical World*. London: Croom Helm, 1986.

Oren, Eliezer D. *The Sea Peoples and Their World: A Reassessment*. Philadelphia: University of Pennsylvania Press, 2000.

4

Archaeological Excavations Pertinent to Homer's Epics

Archaeological excavations, which began to be conducted in the late nineteenth century, are the chief sources of historical information available about the places and times of which Homer wrote.

The major relevant areas of excavation include the following:

- Troy, at the site of Hissarlik in Anatolia (now part of Turkey), across the Aegean Sea from mainland Greece
- Knossos, on the island of Crete, south of mainland Greece
- Mycenae, Sparta, and Pylos in the Greek Peloponnese.

The most important archaeologists are the following:

Heinrich Schleimann—Troy and Mycenae
Wilhelm Dorpfeld—Troy
Chresos Tsountas—Sparta and Mycenae
Minos Kalokairinos—Crete
Arthur Evans—Crete
Carl Blegen—Pylos, Troy
Alan Wace—Pylos
Michael Ventris—translator of Linear B.

The following include some of the landmarks in Greek and Anatolian archeology:

The royal tombs at Mycenae, excavated by Heinrich Schliemann and thought by him to be the resting place of King Agamemnon and Cassandra, who were killed by Aegisthus and Agamemnon's wife, Clytemnestra, upon their return to Mycenae after the Trojan War. Here Schliemann found many solid gold artifacts, including the most famous—what he called the mask of Agamemnon. *Source:* Schliemann, Henry. *Mycenae.* New York: Charles Scribner's Sons, 1880, p. 125.

1742, 1750   British classicist Robert Wood visits the Aegean area, including Anatolia (part of what is now Turkey), searching for Troy.

1769   Wood publishes *Essay... on the Original Genius of Homer*, in which he argues that the topography of Troy was markedly different from what it was in Homer's day, having been altered by rivers that had changed course. He also contends that Homer's epics were delivered orally before they were written down.

1785   Jean Baptiste Lechevalier explores the topography of Anatolia by walking over the area between the Dardenelles and Mount Ida. He comes to believe that Troy had been located inland on a river, at a site called Bunarbashi.

1791   Lechevalier argues that because there was ample evidence that the Greeks had continually laid siege to Anatolia throughout 1200 B.C., it was entirely plausible that a Trojan War actually occurred.

Skeptics, notably Jacob Bryant, counter that Lechevalier was wrong: there is insufficient evidence to support the existence of Troy and a Trojan War.

1795   John Morritt, an Englishman, seeks out a spot in Myceanae, on the Greek Peloponnese, that local tradition marks as the palace of Agamemnon. There he finds exposed above ground a massive "Lion's Gate" and a great room called the Treasury of Atreus.

Early 1800s Many Europeans interested in archaeology (and/or plunder) visit Myceanae to study the treasures exposed above ground.

1802 Thomas Bruce, Lord Elgin, visits Myceanae and takes stone ornamentation from the site back to England. At about the same time Elgin removed the famous "Elgin Marbles" from the Parthenon and sent them back to England, where they are in the British Museum.

1830 William Leake publishes *Travels in the Morea* (London: J. Murray), one of the most thorough books on the topography around Mycenae.

1850s The Calverts, a family of Englishmen who had lived in Turkey for several generations, have long had an interest in finding the site of the city of Troy and have published their findings in popular magazines. Frank Calvert, one of the three brothers, at first believes Troy was at Bunarbashi.

1862 After much investigation, Frank Calvert announces that he has changed his mind. He now believes Troy to be at Hissarlik, considerably west of Bunarbashi.

1863 Charles Maclaren, a scholar, publishes *A Dissertation on the Topography of the Plain of Troy* (Edinburgh: A. and C. Black). He theorizes that the ancient city of Troy is located at New Ilium or Hissarlik, closer to the Aegean Sea than Bunarbashi, Lechevalier's choice for the site of Troy. He arrives at his conclusions without ever having been to Anatolia.

Calvert hopes to begin excavations at Hissarlik, supported with funds provided by the British Museum, but the museum bungles the opportunity and Calvert has no funds to proceed with a full-scale excavation.

1864 Bunarbashi is excavated by a team of Germans, who decide it is not the site of Troy.

1865 Even without the British Museum's help, Frank Calvert is able to begin limited excavation at the Hissarlik site, discovering a temple to Athena and an ancient city wall.

1868 German entrepreneur Heinrich Schliemann visits Turkey and is convinced by Calvert that the city of Troy lies beneath Hissarlik. With a growing interest in Homer, he also visits Mycenae.

1870 Schliemann secures permission from the government of Turkey to begin excavations at Hisarlik, agreeing to share any treasure he finds and to use all precautions necessary to avoid destroying buildings on the site. Schliemann will break both provisions of this contract. With Calvert's help, he begins excavation in April of this year and exposes cities on top of cities.

1873 Schliemann claims to have found a vast amount of gold ornaments and jewelry. The most famous find, an elaborate gold necklace, he called "Jewels of Helen." These treasures Schliemann spirited out of Turkey. Held in Berlin, most of them disappeared in 1945, at the end of World War II. Some reputedly surfaced in Russia in the last years of the twentieth century. Some scholars doubt Schliemann's finds and accuse him of planting artifacts on the site.

1876 Schliemann returns to Mycenae, where he finds five grave shafts in which nineteen men and women and two babies are buried. Their graves are filled with artifacts made of gems and gold. The three men buried in the last tomb he excavates have massive gold masks on their faces. One of these men, Schliemann concludes, is Agamemnon; his mask, the most magnificent artifact to come out of Greece, was called "the Mask of Agamemnon." Later tests determined that these graves were from a period around 1600 B.C., not the period between 1200 and 1300 B.C., the time of the Trojan War.

1878–1881 Schliemann finds four distinct cities of Troy on Hissarlik and identifies the second city as Homer's Ilium or Troy because it had been totally devastated, as if in a war.

In the same year, excavation is begun at Knossos on Crete by Minos Kalokairinos, a local archaeologist.

1886 Schleimann visits Knossos, talks to Kalokairinos, and views his collection of artifacts. He is convinced that Mycenaean civilization had its beginnings here but eventually decides to work elsewhere.

1888 Schliemann looks without success for the palace of King Nestor of Pylos and the palace of Menelaos in Sparta near Menelaion Hill.

1889 The Greek archaeologist Chresos Tsountas finds evidence of Mycenaean Age relics at Menelaion Hill.

Schliemann returns to Troy with the archaeologist Wilhelm Dorpfeld. Dorpfeld discovers that Schliemann's second Troy is not the Troy of the Trojan War but is 1,000 years older than the Trojan War.

1893 Dorpfeld goes back to Troy, financed by the German kaiser and Schliemann's widow. He excavates the southern side of the hill and finds a grander city than had previously been exposed and that fits the description given by Homer in his epics. Further, the discovery here in Anatolia of Mycenaean pottery, of a sort that was produced in mainland Greece during the time of Agamemnon, strongly suggests that mainland Greeks had had contact with the Troy that eventually came to be identified as level VIIa.

1894 The Greek archaeologist Kalokairinos shows Arthur Evans, an Englishman, around the Knossos site.

1898 Kaloikairinos' vast collection of artifacts from his excavations of Knossos are destroyed during Crete's war to achieve liberation from Turkey.

1900 Evans begins excavation at Knossos, finding an advanced civilization including a lost palace, the date of which coincides with the Trojan War and the reign of King Idomengas of tradition. He finds a throne room, a complex system of aqueducts, and frescos. He also finds Mycenaean artifacts and vast numbers of tablets inscribed in two languages. The tablets with a type of language designated as Linear A, largely confined to Crete, are found at archaeological levels dating from around 1750 to 1400 B.C. Linear B, in a cursive style, is found at a level dated around 1400 B.C. Although these will remain uncoded and untranslated for over fifty years, Evans continues to insist that both Linear A and Linear B are Minoan. To prevent erosion at the site, to reach further buried areas, and to reconstruct rooms, Evans makes drastic changes to the site. Al-

Archaeological Excavations Pertinent to Homer's Epics

though the discovery is spectacular, Evans' conclusions, on which he continues to insist vehemently, are seriously flawed. Basically, he argues that Homer's tales were not in a Greek language and did not originate from mainland Greece, but were Minoan Crete.

1920s Two archaeologists of note, Alan Wace, an Englishman, and Carl Blegen, an American, explore a site thought to be King Nestor's Pylos.

1933–1938 At the Troy site, Carl Blegen uncovers new information about Troy VIIa—that it had first been destroyed by earthquake and afterward had suffered a long siege. The evidence of Troy having been sacked was strong. The findings lead the team to the conclusions that this was the Troy, weakened by a major earthquake, and thereafter easily conquered and sacked by the mainland Greeks in the 1200s B.C.

1939 Blegen and the Greek archaeologist K. Kourouniotis explore Pylos and begin excavations there. They find it similar to the Mycenaean culture throughout Greece in the 1200s B.C. and uncover some 1,000 Linear B tablets, discoveries that put in doubt the theory that Linear B tablets were Minoan. They suggest that Proto Greeks had arrived in mainland Greece around 2000 B.C.

1940–1951 World War II and the civil wars, especially in Greece, that followed it, completely halt all archaeological work in the area.

1952 Fifty tablets of Linear B, dating around 1250 B.C., are discovered at Mycenae.

For many years it has been assumed that since the Linear B scripts were Minoan, this meant that Cretan civilization had somehow impinged upon that of the mainland. Then British archeologist Michael Ventris, having access to the Linear B tablets taken from earlier digs at Knossos, Pylos, and other excavations on the mainland, cracked the code and translated the fragments, proving, counter to Evans' theory, that the language employed was not Minoan but Greek, an ancient form that ultimately developed into the language of classical Greece, somewhat the same way Anglo-Saxon developed into English. This opened the way for speculation that the mainland Mycenaeans had somehow influenced Crete, rather than the other way around.

The translation also opened up a complex array of information about life in the Bronze Age world dominated by Mycenae, for here household and government records were preserved in minute detail.

1964 Twenty Linear B scripts dated around 1320 B.C. are found in Thebes.

1970s A team of British archaeologists excavates a site near Menelaion Hill in Sparta, uncovering a palace with a date in the 1200s B.C., and thus creating the possibility that it could have been the palace of the legendary King Menelaos and Helen of Troy.

The following documents are reports by three outstanding archaeologists who revolutionized the history of the Aegean. Each of these men was inspired by the work of Homer. Furthermore, Homer became their chief guide in uncovering the past. First, there are the reports of Sir Arthur Evans of excavations in Crete, that island that Odysseus describes to Penelope as an enchanted isle in a wine-dark sea. Second is a report of the man many call the father of archaeology, Heinrich Schliemann, who thought, using Homer as a guide, that he had found the tomb of Agamemnon. Third is the report of a Greek archaeologist, Chrestos Tsmountas, who laid bare fabulous palaces like those that play a major role in *The Odyssey*.

KNOSSOS AND THE PALACE OF MINOS

Sir Arthur Evans was a British archaeologist who revolutionized the study of classical Greece. His most famous excavations were made in Crete, whose city of Knossos once ruled the Aegean world. Although the site of the city had been located and explored earlier, by other scholars, Evans is considered the discoverer of ancient Crete. In March 1900, Evans began his excavations of what turned out to be the palace of the king. He was able to locate the throne room, a grand staircase, intricate corridors, and an complex series of baths and pipes. Some of his findings included artifacts going back to 4000 B.C., at the time assumed to be much older than anything that had been located on the mainland of Greece.

The following excerpts are descriptions of two of Evans' observations and discoveries. The first indicates the setting of the ancient city of Knossos, which was not built on a hill and surrounded like a fortress, as were Troy and Mycenae, but was, according to Evans, "cradled amidst the surrounding hills," giving it a magical aura, much like that described by Homer.

The second excerpt gives some indication of just what an advanced civilization existed in Crete, so many years before the Mycenaean culture in the Peloponnese rose to prominence. In the palace in Knossos, Evans found evidence of an elaborate system of baths that included hot running water and drains. The custom of elaborate baths, taken frequently as a rite of renewal and offered as hospitality to the weary traveler, is one of the aspects of Cretan civilization that Evans was convinced had transferred to the mainland culture—rituals to which Homer makes frequent reference in *The Odyssey*, especially in the courts of Nestor, Menelaos, and Alcinoos, and in Odysseus' own household.

FROM SIR ARTHUR EVANS, *THE PALACE OF MINOS*, VOL. 2

(London: Macmillan, 1928)

[On the location of the greatest city in Crete, Knossos]

In considering the site of Knossos and the part it played in the early history of the East Mediterranean basin we are continually struck with the apparent inferiority of its position as compared with that of other great centres in the same geographical region. … It stands back, moreover, from the river-mouth and harbour and it is only its uppermost terrace that catches the merest glimpse of sea. To the visitor approaching the site by the high road from Candia its remains come suddenly into view, cradled amidst the surrounding hills.

The explanation is to be sought in the special circumstances of its origin. In the case of so many other ancient centres of human habitation the deliberate designs of warlike chiefs seem to have played a leading part in the choice of position, and the town arose within the walls or under the shadow of a fortified acropolis of native rulers. But the beginnings of Knossos were of a quite different order. It seems to have taken its rise in remote antiquity simply because it was a spot suitable for the needs of primitive man. So far, indeed, from starting as a hill stronghold it may be said to a great extent to have formed its own hill. ... [T]he hill of Kephala on which the great Palace afterwards rose is itself essentially a "Tell" such as we find in Egypt or the East, built up out of the debris and deposits formed by successive stages of occupation going back without a break to the earliest Neolithic phase of which we have any record in the Island. The residence of native dynasts was ultimately fixed here because the site had been a centre of population from immemorial time. (2, 3)

[*On the advanced system of running water in the palace at Knossos*]

The foot-washing basin already mentioned occupies the compartment of the building immediately West of the Pavilion, the wall of which on that side is common to the two. As in the case of the Pavilion, the bath could be freely entered from the yard, in this case by a descent of three steps, while on the South side a flight of five steps, equally open, led down to its upper margin from what seems to have been an interior Court on that side. The public nature of the bath was made evident, and for those approaching the inner Court by this avenue, foot-washing seems to have been obligatory. ... [T]he water would have reached to the knees of the average Minoan man who could also have easily used it as a hip-bath. ...

The water system connected with the bath for supply, overflow, and waste was most elaborate. Above the steps leading down to it from the South, and descending beneath their upper edge, were three elongated limestone blocks channeled for the passage of water. ...

In the N.W. corner of the basin, very accurately cut so as to be traversed immediately above by the last described duct, was the overflow channel of the bath embedded in the masonry and crossing the angle of the wall diagonally. A projecting slab with the continuation of its channel shows that it must have been in communication with a drain running in a N.W. direction across the yard and forming a junction, near the presumed course of the Minoan roadway, with the drain or conduit that conveyed the superfluous water from the neighbouring Spring Chamber.

...

One quite exceptional feature that was noted in the waste duct or drain on this side was that its interior channel was blackened, as by the passage of carbonized particles in the water. As there was no trace in the spring water here of any substance like peroxide or iron or manganese that might have produced such an effect, the presumption is almost inevitable that it stood in connexion with some heating apparatus in the area immediately West. If water had been heated there in some such large bronze cauldron as those found at Tylissos, sooty particles from the wood-fire below might easily have settled on its surface and the waste water that found its way into the drain may also have partly washed the blackened exterior of the cauldron itself. (116, 118, 119, 120, 123)

SCHLIEMANN AND THE TOMBS AT MYCENAE

The German archaeologist Heinrich Schliemann (who began calling himself Henry after taking up residence in the United States) is considered to have discovered the various cities of Troy and much of the splendor of Mycenae, the ancient civilization in Greece and the general locale for much of the action of *The Odyssey*. The king of Mycenae was traditionally thought to be Agamemnon, and Schliemann claimed to have discovered the tomb of Agamemnon, though subsequent studies have shown that the tomb he found was of a date too early to be that of this Mycenaean king.

In the first excerpt, Schliemann describes the physical setting of the walled city of Mycenae. The acropolis that he mentions here is a high, fortified area. Note that, in contrast to Knossos, Mycenae is on a high hill and is protected not only by gorges and cliffs but also by thick walls that, in Schliemann's time, were still in evidence. This suggested that these cities were often under siege by outsiders.

The second excerpt indicates Schliemann's determination to find the tombs of prominent Mycenaeans and his subsequent belief that he had found the resting place of Agamemnon, Cassandra, and others killed by Aegisthus at the same time. His argument that one grave is that of Agamemnon and his party is that in this grave he found a group of noble individuals who had all died at the same time. Another argument is that over this particular grave, citizens of the area in classical times had erected a holy altar. Schliemann also actually claimed to have found vast treasures of gold and jewels in these tombs, the most famous of which was the Mask of Agamemnon, a huge artifact fashioned of solid gold.

What is interesting here is how Schliemann and other archaelogists used Homer's epics in conjunction with their science to uncover and identify artifacts. Though he was later proven wrong in assuming this to be the tomb of Agamemnon, he uses Homer's story of Agamemnon's murder to reach his conclusions about who is buried here. Although Schliemann became a figure of controversy, and some of his findings were proven faulty, his contributions to archaeology in Greece and at Troy are immeasurable.

FROM HENRY (HEINRICH) SCHLIEMANN, *MYCENAE*

(New York: Charles Scribner's Sons, 1880)

The situation of Mycenae is beautifully described by Homer, "In the depth of the horse-feeding Argos," because it lies in the north corner of the plain of Argos, in a recess between the two majestic peaks of Mount Euoea, whence it commanded the upper part of the great plain, and the important narrow pass. ... The acropolis occupied a strong rocky height, which projects from the foot of the mountain behind it in the form of an irregular triangle slope to the west. This cliff overhangs a deep gorge, which protects the whole south flank of the citadel. Through the abyss below winds the bed of a torrent usually almost dry, because it has no other water than that of the copious fountain Perseia, which is about half a mile to the north-east of the fortress. This gorge extends first from east to west, and afterwards in a south-westerly direction. The cliff also falls off precipitously on the north side into a glen, which stretches in a straight line from east to west. Between these two gorges extended the lower city. The cliff of the citadel is also more or less steep on the east and west side, where it forms six natural or artificial terraces.

The Acropolis is surrounded by Cyclopean walls, from 13 to 35 feet high, and on an average 16 feet thick. Their entire circuit still exists, but they have evidently been much higher. They are of beautiful hard breccia, with which the neighbouring mountains abound. They follow the sinuosities of the rock, and show three different kinds of architecture.

...

Homer gives to Mycenae the epithets "well-built city," "with broad streets," and "rich in gold." The second of these epithets can only apply to the wide street which led from the Lion's Gate, along the ridge, through the enclosed town, to the bridge over the torrent of the ravine; for all the remaining part of the town as well as the suburb being on slopes, the other streets must have been more or less steep, and cannot have been alluded to by the epithet. Regarding the third epithet ... , we have the great authority of Thucydides that Mycenae had immense wealth under the domination of the Pelopids.

...

[*Searching for the tombs of Agamemnon; his concubine captured in battle, Cassandra; his charioteer, Eurymedon; his daughter Electra; Aegisthus, who murdered him; and his wife Clytemnestra*]

In February, 1874, therefore, I sank there thirty-four shafts in different places, in order to sound the ground and to find out the place where I should have to dig for them. The six shafts which I sank on the first western and south-western terrace gave very encouraging results, and particularly the two which I dug within 100 yards south of the Lion's Gate; for not only did I strike two Cyclopean house-walls, but I also found an unsculptured slab resembling a tombstone, and a number of female idols and small cows of terra-cotta. I therefore resolved at once on making extensive excavations at this spot, but I was prevented by various circumstances which I need not explain here, and it is only now that I have found it possible to carry out my plan.

I began the great work on the 7th August, 1876, with sixty-three workmen, whom I divided into three parties. I put twelve men at the Lion's Gate, to open the passage into the Acropolis.

. . .

I now proceed to discuss the question, whether it is possible to identify these sepulchers with the tombs which Pausanias, following the tradition, attributes to Agamemnon, to Cassandra, to Eurymedon, and to their companions. ... I never doubted that a king of Mycenae, by name Agamemnon, his charioteer Eurymedon, a Princess Cassandra, and their followers had been treacherously murdered either by Aegisthus at a banquet "like an ox at the manger," as Homer says, or in the bath by Clytemnestra, as the later tragic poets represent; and I firmly believed in the statement of Pausanias, that the murdered persons had been interred in the Acropolis. ...

My firm faith in the traditions made me undertake my late excavations in the Acropolis, and led to the discovery of the five tombs, with their immense treasures.

. . .

I have not the slightest objection to admit that the tradition which assigns the tombs in the Acropolis to Agamemnon and his companions, who on their return from Ilium were treacherously murdered by Clytemnestra or her paramour Aegisthus, may be perfectly correct and faithful. I am bound to admit this so much the more, as we have the certainty that, to say the least, all the bodies in each tomb had been buried simultaneously. ...

The identity of the mode of burial, the perfect similarity of all the tombs, their very close proximity, the impossibility of admitting that three or even five royal personages of immeasurable wealth, who had died a natural death at long intervals of time, should have been huddled together in the same tomb, and finally, the great resemblance of all the ornaments, which show exactly the same style of art and the same epoch—all these facts are so many proofs that all the twelve men, three women, and perhaps two or three children, had been murdered simultaneously and buried at the same time.

. . .

The site of each tomb was marked by tombstones, and when these had been covered by the dust of ages and had disappeared, fresh tombstones were erected on the new level, but precisely over the spot where the ancient memorials lay buried. Only on the large fourth sepulcher with the five bodies, instead of new tombstones, a sacrificial altar of almost circular form was built. (28–29, 57, 61, 62, 334, 335, 337)

MYCENAEAN PALACES

In 1887, Chrestos Tsountas, a Greek archaeologist, was given a commission by the government of Greece to excavate Mycenaean sites and to take his study well beyond Heinrich Schliemann's exploration of "Agamemnon's tomb." Tsountas ended up uncovering the complex and extensive household of a Mycenaean king. As is indicated in the preface to his volume written by Professor J. Irving Manatt, Tsountas "laid bare the old Archaean capital in its great enduring features, and ... revealed to modern eyes the typical Acropolis of the Heroic Age" (1). What Tsountas found is consistent with Homer's description of the palaces of Nestor, Menelaos, Alcinoos, and Odysseus in *The Odyssey*.

FROM CHRESTOS TSOUNTAS, *THE MYCENAEAN AGE*

(Boston: Houghton, Mifflin, 1897)

Thus far we have recovered in various stages of preservation at least three Mycenaean palaces, viz., at Tiryns, Mycenae, and Gha (or Arne), not to mention the scanty remains on the Athenian acropolis or the palace of the second city on the hill of Hissarlik (Troy) which is now known to be indefinitely earlier than the Mycenaean age. Of all these the palace at Tiryns is far the best preserved and most certain in its groundplan. We shall therefore study it in detail before proceeding to the palace at Mycenae, with which Time and the destroyer have dealt more ruthlessly.

The palace of Tiryns, brought to light by Dr. Schliemann in 1884, occupies the highest of the three plateaus composing the acropolis. To reach it you ascend the great ramp under the eastern wall, pass through the open entrance, traverse the high-walled approach and enter the inner fortress by the great gate. From this the road leads up to a large court, closed on the east by the circuit wall which here bears a covered colonnade opening on the interior of the fortress. Over against this colonnade is the outer gate of the palace. It is a spacious and stately portal—about 46 feet wide—composed of a middle wall, pierced by folding-doors and covered by an outer and an inner portico.

...

This inner gateway opens into the chief courtyard of the palace, the Men's Court—a quadrangle, measuring 52 by 66 feet. This court is almost surrounded by colonnades; but, as in the propylaea and the fore-court, only the stone bases remain, the wooden pillars having perished. Midway along the south side of the court before the portico stands a quadrangular block of masonry (measuring 8 by 10 2/3 feet), with a central circular cavity some 4 feet in diameter but less than 3 feet deep.

...

The Great Hall incloses an area of about 1235 square feet. Its roof was suppported in part by four wooden pillars, whose stone bases are still in place. . . . In the centre of the space defined by these pillars was the great circular hearth, now unfortunately destroyed, although we can still clearly distinguish its position.

In the west wall of the vestibule, as already noted, is a door opening into a narrow corridor which leads by several zigzags to a small square chamber. The floor of this chamber is made of one great limestone block, measuring about 13 by 11 by 2 1/4 feet, with an estimated weight of some 25 tons. . . . there is a square gutter cut in the flooring-block at the north-east corner of the chamber and connecting with a stone pipe which reaches through the eastern wall. These arrangements prove beyond a doubt that we have here found that indispensable appointment of the Homeric palace,—the bath-room. Fortunately, too, we have found fragments sufficient to determine the pattern, material and decoration of the bath-tub.

...

The palace is composed of two main suites, one for the men, the other for the women, each with a court of its own. Both quarters communicate directly with the outer court, though their communication with each other is only by narrow and winding passages. In easy reach from the men's hall is the bath-room, to which by Homeric custom the guest was conducted on his arrival. Adjoining the women's hall is the Royal Bedchamber, and disposed about the same quarter of the palace are lodgings for the rest of the household, storerooms and the like. (42–45, 48, 49, 50)

PROJECTS RELATING TO ARCHAEOLOGY

1. As a class, locate a sufficient open space, say in a nearby park, to measure off the dimensions of rooms in the Mycenaean palace uncovered by Tsountas.
2. By consulting with a museum or an archaeologist in a college or university near you, locate a site near you that the class can visit. Write reports on the methods used to study the site and the findings of the excavators.
3. Research and write an essay on one of the more prominent archaeologists of the Aegean area.
4. Do a Web search to ascertain whether any archaeological excavations are currently being conducted in Greece.

SUGGESTIONS FOR FURTHER READING

Calder, William, and David Traill, eds. *Myth, Scandal, and History*. Detroit: Wayne State University Press, 1986.

Catling, H.W. *Some Problems in Aegean Prehistory*. Oxford: Leopard's Head Press, 1989.

Etienne, Roland. *The Search for Ancient Greece*. New York: Harry N. Abrams, 1992.

Fagan, Brian M. *The Adventure of Archaeology*. Washington, D.C.: National Geographic Society, 1985.

Shanks, Michael. *Classical Archaeology of Greece*. London: Routledge, 1996.

Snodgrass, Anthony M. *An Archaeology of Greece*. Berkeley: University of California Press, 1987.

Wilkie, Nancy C., and William Coulson, eds. *Contributions to Aegean Archaeology*. Dubuque, Iowa: Kendall-Hung, 1985.

Wood, Michael. *In Search of the Trojan War*. New York: Facts on File, 1985.

5

The Historical Context of *The Odyssey*

The Greeks of the classical period looked to Homer's epics for a record of Greece's mythological history in which, as we have seen in chapter 2, the sequence of events in human history are direct consequences of the personal lives of the gods. The voyage of Odysseus is steeped in the Greek history that Homer knew from oral traditions. Our own more scientific understanding of ancient Greek history has been sharpened and expanded by nineteenth- and twentieth-century archaeologists and scholars whose discovery of artifacts and fragmentary documents have allowed them to piece together a history—sometimes educated speculations rather than definite conclusions—about Greece up to the time of Homer. That history, however inexact, enlarges our understanding of Odysseus and his voyage.

The following discussion proceeds roughly chronologically according to major periods, beginning with the early periods of prehistory, whose agricultural character reverberates in *The Odyssey*, and moving to the proto-Greek invasions of Greece that brought the language and culture adopted by Homer; the age of Minoan Crete, whose developments contributed to the mainland culture of which Homer was a part; the Mycenaean Age that dominates *The Odyssey*; and the so-called Dark Ages, which also resonate in *The Odyssey*.

EARLY PREHISTORY

About twelve thousand years ago in the Near East cradle of civilization, an agricultural revolution occurred: humans stopped wandering and began to settle down. They learned to cultivate the land with simple tools and, some time later, to herd animals such as sheep and goats. By 7000 B.C., people in the Near East had learned to fire pottery. Some time later (ca. 4000–3800 B.C.) they invented the wheel and began to smelt copper. By 3000 B.C., they had learned the use of bronze. To till the soil, they used simple tools like the hoe, for the plow had not yet been invented. Women were more likely than men to use the plow in these early days, to do little more than scratch the soil, a type of agriculture that resembled limited horticulture rather than massive farming. With their agriculture, the basis of Western civilization was established.

Around 6200 B.C., early migrants crossed the Aegean Sea from the Near East and settled in the Aegean islands, the Greek mainland, and ultimately the Greek Peloponnese, bringing with them this basic agricultural civilization. On Crete, the large, grand island to the south, they settled mainly in the east, where the weather was pleasant, although characteristically dry. The city of Knossos on Crete was settled somewhere between 5500 and 6100 B.C.; the Cycladic islands in the Aegean, around 4000 B.C.

At the same time, other peoples crossed to Europe from the east: to the north at the Bosporus, proceeding westward along the Danube into central Europe, and thence from Macedonia southward into Greece. European settlers introduced more advanced agricultural practices, maintaining the agricultural village and using sound farming practices, possibly even crop rotation. In addition to farming, these Europeans made pottery without a wheel, built brick houses on stone foundations, and developed a complex system of gods and goddesses who accounted for natural phenomena and human experiences, causing ill or bad luck (which prompted people to try to pacify or bribe them in order to improve everyday human life). The people of this period, whose deities were agricultural, produced great numbers of squat female statuettes that presumably had great significance as earth goddesses.

Many of the people in Greece at this time lived in caves. For about 500 years, their villages had no fortifications, presumably an indication that they felt no need to defend themselves from warring tribes.

The metals, especially copper, found on Crete and other islands, led the islanders to develop the critical skill of working metal (an art that seems to have come from the Near East). In these skills islanders were in advance of mainland peoples, and dominated trade in metal goods for many years.

By 2700 B.C. weapons began to appear. Significantly, although stone tools were as good as copper for farming, copper was distinctly better for the making of weapons. The demand for copper was immense, and this to a large extent determined areas where trade flourished and greater power was wielded. The Bronze Age (or Bronze *Ages*—for this was a skill that developed at different times in different places) was ushered in with the invention of bronze (a mixture of 10 percent tin and 90 percent copper). The introduction of bronze increased the trade in tin as well as bronze. By comparison, the Sumerians, an important Near Eastern civilization, developed these skills by about 2500 B.C.

By this time, too, all aspects of flourishing commerce had evolved as great trade routes developed across the Greek islands of the Aegean and along the valleys and mountains of the north. Traders crossed mountain valleys and sailed the seas, not only to trade but also to create colonies.

By 3000 B.C., communities with sophisticated governments were present throughout the area. One of the special functions of government was the regulation of local laws pertaining to farming. At the same time, the government was involved in matters that went beyond village borders. Military power became increasingly important as intense competition for all the elements of power—especially for the copper, tin, and bronze to make weapons—typically produced a fiercely competitive imperialism based on conquest. With the scramble for power, a great gulf began to separate the rich and the poor. There were increasing displays of royal magnificence by rulers of powerful nations or city-states—the kind of world displayed in *The Iliad* and *The Odyssey* (although the epics were set at a later time). For the common man, for the slaves, miners, soldiers, common laborers, and other "losers" in a hierarchical society—in fact as well as in epic adventures—life was desperate and hard; it was more than a little nasty, brutish, and short.

Another aspect of an emerging civilization was the detailed keeping of records—on tablets of clay and on papyrus. The clay tablets, softened so they could be used again and again, were originally designed to be temporary, while permanent records were kept on papyrus; ironically, however, as a result of fires, volcanic explosions, and violent destructions of cities, many of the clay tablets were baked and became hard, while papyrus, being more fragile, largely vanished.

In the northwest corner of Anatolia, across the Aegean Sea from Greece, significant trade in those early years produced a place (founded ca. 3600 B.C.), both a city and a fortress, situated near the Hellespont, with at least close proximity (as the bird flies) to trade from all directions: from the east, from the west, from the Black (Euxine) Sea, and from the Aegean. Even though the inhabitants were blocked by mountain ranges to the east and had no practical outlet to the Black Sea, they prospered. Originally a Neolithic settlement, it rapidly grew to great power and achieved commercial importance, while at the same time attracting the envy of casual raiders and others interested in loot and slaughter. It ultimately came to be called Troy. And it became one of the most famous cities in history, while its demise, or at least the demise of one of its many incarnations, became one of the most influential disasters.

Historically, it was a small city on a windy hill overlooking the sea, at its height measuring 200 yards by 150 yards, as long as two football fields and as wide as one and a half placed end to end; a place hardly worth a tourist's extra trip. Poetically, it was the subject of Homer's poem. And it assumed a splendor beyond all power of description.

PROTO-GREEK INVASIONS

Toward the end of the third millennium, new immigrants or invaders came from somewhere beyond the Caucasus. These were proto-Greek-speaking tribes who were part of a larger and restless Indo-European series of movements. They began descending into the Balkan Peninsula (now Greece) and probably into Anatolia (now Turkey) on the eastern shores of the Aegean, bringing with them a culture of conquest and war: first came the Ionians (ca. 2000 B.C.); then the Achaians (ca. 1580 B.C.) and probably the Aeolians; and last the Dorians (ca. 1200 B.C. or later—after the fall of Troy). They brought with them a new language, new gods, new customs, and patriarchal, warlike values. In time, over a period of centuries, they completely conquered, dominated, or fused with the local populations. The ideals of a war culture thus replaced the largely agricultural way of life, while the gods and the myths of the invaders replaced or dominated the local gods and goddesses. The older language vanished except in place-names and a number of ancient references obviously not of Greek origin.

From the first, the Ionians brought with them a militaristic social structure, along with new kinds of crafts and a feudalistic system, and, for a time at least, disrupted Mediterranean trade. One of their most important contributions was to introduce into Greece an animal that would revolutionize history, and especially was to transform the techniques of warfare. This animal was the horse. Just as at a later time the introduction of the horse to the American continent by Cortez would transform the life of the Plains Indians, so it revolutionized life in Greece. Thus, Homer notes that Hector, the great Trojan hero, was a "tamer of horses." And the horse became not just a necessary, utilitarian animal; at times it assumed godlike grandeur in the myths and in the epics. The horse and the war chariot are extremely important in *The Iliad*. A divinely inspired horse even speaks in *The Iliad*. In book II of *The Odyssey*, Troy is distinguished as a place that abounds in horses. And in book III, Nestor directs that the nimblest horses should be given to Telemachos for his journey. In book IV Helen in her conversation with Telemachos speaks of the area of Argos in the Greek Peloponnese as "horse-nourishing" and also tells him of the story of the Trojan Horse, a huge structure in which Greek soldiers hid to get within the walls of Troy, a ruse conceived by Odysseus. In book VIII Odysseus, who has not yet announced his identity in Phaeacia, asks the singer Demodocos to sing the story of the Trojan Horse.

MINOAN CRETE

In 1900, the English archaeologist Arthur Evans, following the spectacular success of Heinrich Schliemann, the first archaeologist to explore Greece and Troy, dug up and analyzed remains of a civilization at Knossos Crete that so electrified the world, that it was called, along with the discovery of ancient Troy, the archaeological find of the modern world. Evans called it "Minoan Crete" in honor of King Minos, who in legend kept the Minotaur (literally meaning "Bull of Minos"), a creature that was half bull and half man, who slaughtered unwelcome foreign guests until Theseus killed it.

Crete was considered a brilliant, glittering culture that, it has been thought, might have inspired the legend of the Golden Age, that Eden-like time in Greek myth that was undisturbed by war, strife, or the need to work. Having towns without fortification, a navy that traded to the edges of the world while protecting the home island from invasion or conquest, and artisans and artists who produced grand, distinctive pottery and resplendent frescoes, the Cretans produced a civilization thought to have been unsurpassed in the ancient world; and it existed on an island looking out upon a seascape of unsurpassed beauty. In the times of brutality and conquest that followed—that is, the world of Homer's Greeks and the last days of the Mycenaean Age—Crete might well have loomed in the popular imagination as an age of gold, a time of peace, ease, beauty, and benevolence.

However, certain facts intrude rudely on the ideal. Cretans also, as Michael Wood points out in [*In Search of the Trojan War,*] practiced human sacrifice and ritual cannibalism. Particularly dangerous, even brutal sports were popular in Crete, including bull-vaulting, in which both boys and girls also participated.

Minoan civilization began about 3000 B.C., more than a thousand years before proto-Greek tribes descended into Greece. It ended, definitively, about 1100 B.C., a time when all Aegean civilizations collapsed and the Dark Ages began. The great period of Crete lasted from about 2200/2000 to 1450 B.C., after which it was superseded by the mainland culture dominated by Mycenae.

The reason for this sudden collapse of Crete has long been a matter of debate. One of the most plausible speculations cites a violent volcanic explosion on the isle of Thera in 1500 B.C. It is estimated to have been ten times more powerful than Krakatoa in the modern world. As a result of this explosion, great tidal waves washed the coastal shores of Crete, destroying cities and disrupting all phases of its civilization. The cities were rebuilt, some of them magnificently. But shortly thereafter mainland forces assumed control of Crete between about 1475 and 1400 B.C. Crete still managed to prosper for a time, but around 1400 B.C., a Mycenaean invasion from the Greek Peloponnese destroyed its great city, Knossos, and the dominance of Minoan Crete came to a sudden and violent end.

While ancient Crete does not play a direct part in *The Odyssey*, it is, in the tales of Odysseus and the mind of Homer, a distinct echo of a not-quite-faded splendor. In fact, Evans mistakenly believed that all of Homer's epics, and his Mycenaean world, were but echoes of Crete's magnificence. One of the Greek warriors against Troy was the Cretan king, Idomeneos, who plays a major role in Homer's *The Iliad*. Crete is also mentioned by name in book III of *The Odyssey*, when King Nestor tells Telemachos about the wreck of some of Menelaos' ships on the coast of Crete on their way home after the Trojan War. In spinning the story of his voyage to King Alcinoos and his court (book XI), Odysseus reports meeting the daughter of the mythical King Minos in hell. In book XIX of *The Odyssey*, Odysseus, in constructing one of his many false identities, tells Penelope that he is the brother of King Idomeneos of Crete, and that he was born and reared in Crete. Odysseus' lines in book XIX of *The Odyssey*, as translated by S.H. Butcher and Andrew Lang, captures something of how the grandeur of Crete remained in collective memory:

> There is a land called Crete in the midst of the wine-dark sea, a fair land and a rich, begirt with water, and therein are many men innumerable, and ninety cities. And all have not the same speech, but there is confusion of tongues; there dwell Achaeans and there too Cretans of Crete, high of heart, and Cydonians there and Dorians of waving plumes and goodly Pelasgians. And among these cities is the mighty city of Cnosus, wherein Minos when he was nine years old began to rule. (*The Complete Works of Homer*. New York: Modern Library, 1935, 297, 298)

THE MYCENAEAN AGE

Following the domination of the Aegean world by the island Crete, mainland Greece rose to the fore, to become the most powerful area in the Aegean world, led by Mycenae—Homer's Golden Mycenae. By 1600 B.C., the Mycenaeans had totally superseded the Minoan world of Crete, though Mycenae took from Crete many advances, including the formation of cities, the art of record keeping, and much more. The period of Mycenae's dominance was between 1600 and 1200 B.C.

For some two and a half centuries of savage but brilliant supremacy, the Mycenaeans conducted a flourishing trade with the Mediterranean world, built luxurious palaces and fortresses for their rulers, and achieved a powerful and vigorous civilization by brutal means: slavery, casual acts of cruelty, and random raids against other settlements and against each other.

About 1250 B.C., the Mycenaeans sailed for a war, supposedly with Troy, the small but now spectacular and wealthy city on the northwest corner of Anatolia (a subject to be explored in chapter 6). The Greek warriors of Homer's epics were, of course, Myceanean; and—though several hundred years separate the singer from the subject of his song, and though discrepancies along with twisted or distorted memories occur over the years as oral poets repeat and adapt the same body of material—Homer is still the closest direct source to the Mycenaean Age, and there is, in both of his epics, enough valid representation of people, motivation, and events to throw light upon Mycenaean power and demise.

In *The Odyssey* the reader is provided with descriptions of the small, independent kingdoms like those of Greece in the Mycenaean Age: Nestor in Pylos, Menelaos in Sparta, and, above all, Agamemnon in Mycenae. We are provided with vivid details of life in these kingdoms: the food and drink, the luxurious baths, the extravagant entertainments and athletic contests, and the system of courtiers and servants. And Homer gives the reader a sense of the prevailing customs, of both piracy and hospitality, and of the exchange of gifts and riches.

THE DARK AGES

At some time between 1200 and 1100 B.C., the Mycenaean world, like the Cretan civilization before it, totally collapsed, and the so-called Dark Ages ensued, lasting until about the eighth century, shortly before the time of Homer. These years are called the Dark Ages not only because of the barbarism into which Greece lapsed at this time, but also because so little is known, even now, about this period. Civilization stopped. Knowledge of writing ceased, and chaos set in. The total collapse of Mycenae has especially tantalized professional observers. Although the immediate cause is shrouded in mystery, scholars assume that it was the result of war of some kind, somewhere, with somebody. It may also have been due to internal decay and corruption: the gradual diminution of power too brutally and too mercilessly wielded over many generations. Homer himself may provide some clues in *The Iliad* and *The Odyssey* as to the reasons for Mycenae's collapse. Who can doubt the certain fate of the destroyers of Troy—the casual burning of cities, the betrayals, the generations of people they had brutalized by turning them into slaves or corpses, the countless numbers of women stolen and raped? They have (these heroes) violated every possible code of humane behavior. With the decline of powerful leaders, whoever cheered got a sad, if ultimate, revenge.

Between 1200 and 1100 B.C., after the Mycenaean civilization lost its vigor, the Dorians—a tribe said to be even more brutal and more destructive than others—seized control of the mainland. This is often referred to as an *invasion* from outside Greece, but the Dorians may well have already been present in Greece in significant numbers, and have assumed power in what some scholars call a class upheaval. Whatever their origin, however, the Dorians were even more violent, brutal, and despotic than the Mycenaeans. They completely wiped out Mycenaean civilization, and destroyed temples and palaces, works of art, fortifications, and written records, none of which were replaced. The creation of art virtually ceased. This included the intricate clay pots on which the story of Greece had been told, and which had been so thoroughly a part of the culture. Trade, which had joined Greece to the rest of the Mediterranean world, came to a virtual halt. Under the Dorians, slavery, class distinctions, lower-class suffering, and despotic privilege grew like a plague. The Dorians were even more warlike than their predecessors, an attitude encouraged by their adoption of the relatively new skill of iron production. Iron, as a killing tool, is no more effective than bronze, but it is distinctly cheaper and more available to the common fighter, thus presenting fewer barriers to warlike behavior. In their perpetual wars, the Dorians either killed or enslaved the people they conquered.

One consequence of the Dorian sovereignty in Greece was the creation of masses of refugees fleeing from the mainland and the Peloponnese. From Thessaly and other areas where the Aeolian dialect was spoken, people fled to northern Anatolia, that area across the Aegean Sea from Greece in what is now Turkey. Inhabitants of the Peloponnese fled to the outlying Aegean islands and mid-Anatolian coast.

Eventually, around 1100 B.C., the Dorians seemed to abandon their domination of all of Greece and concentrate their residence in the very area, Sparta and its environs, where, according to legend, Menelaos and Agamemnon had held sway in the Mycenaean Age. This is one explanation for the continuation in Sparta of a fairly harsh system of slavery and caste after those practices had been greater modified or abandoned elsewhere.

In the wake of the Dorian conquest, other areas of Greece assumed types of governments that appeared guaranteed to forestall the rise of tyrants like the Dorians. In some areas, especially in the early years just after the demise of the Dorians, tribal leaders emerged who were also leaders of local armies. In these early periods, such men were called kings. Although the title might imply a position of absolute power, these areas were ruled not just by the king but also by groups of local warriors, of whom the king was the most important. The position was roughly equivalent to that of Agamemnon in the Trojan War: he is described as an equal among equals, but still the commander of the Achaean army.

But the power of the kings shortly began to be eroded, and communities, still harboring in memory the detestation of Mycenaean and then Dorian tyrants, began to form more representative governments, whereby cities or areas were ruled by groups of citizens rather than by any single individual. By the end of the Dark Ages, Greece had instituted government by a council of the "best people" (the *aristoi*) and by executives appointed by the council; an association of warriors met to carry out the will of the council. In all probability the older periods of domination led, in Athens at least, to an inherent distaste for despots. It has even been suggested that in the long run the Dorian invasion was actually a good thing because it led ultimately to the determination of Greeks to find better ways to solve mankind's problems, and was the impetus that led them to reject despots and struggle for democracy.

Just what part of the Dark Ages is represented by the political situation in Ithaca in *The Odyssey* is debatable. On the one hand, we might locate the chaos to which Odysseus comes home with the suitors terrorizing and depleting his household (as well as the disruption in Agamemnon's homeland), in the early years of the Dark Ages, when anarchy beset most of Greece. Aegisthus, who assumed Agamemnon's household and country and then killed him, can be seen as the prototype of the Dorian takeover. Indeed, many Dorians seemed to be native to the area and settled in that area.

On the other hand, our picture of Ithaca in *The Odyssey* may well be located in the post-Dorian years of the Dark Ages, when kingship dwindled and communities were beginning to be governed by assemblies. Note that Odysseus is supposed to be king of Ithaca, but when he goes off to the Trojan War and then wanders around for years, he is not replaced as king. Telemachos, his grown son, does not have the power of a king, nor does anyone else. Ithaca seems to be ruled instead by an assembly, to which Telemachos fruitlessly appeals for relief from the atrocities of the suitors (see book II). In book XXIV the assembly meets again, to decide to attack Odysseus for killing their sons. The ringleaders are subsequently dispatched, but there is still the understanding that Odysseus will not be able to prevail without the support of the important men in the community.

Also pertinent to *The Odyssey* is another consequence of the savagery born of both pre-Dorian anarchy and Dorian domination: the great desire, even necessity, for heroes in such times, men who could rise above all others to fight off roaming predators. Without such men in savage times, community vanished. Thus, singers like Homer honored and immortalized heroes like Troy's Hector and Greece's Odysseus. Such men, who could at least give their all in warding off invasion, as Hector tried to do, or keep anarchy at bay, as Odysseus tried to do, were worshiped as gods, immortalized in schools, sung to in the Olympic games, and used as inspiration by craftsmen and playwrights. Homer's epics are constructed of these heroic legends, necessitated near the end of the Dark Ages, and they perpetuated these legends for the emerging civilization, called classical Greece, that followed the Dark Ages.

The following excerpts present different aspects of Greek history from the perspective of different times. The first provides a picture of pre-historic Greece and the Heroic Age of Odysseus and Agamemnon from the perspective of Thucydides, a citizen of classical Greece. The second excerpt, also on communities in the Heroic Age, is from the perspective of a modern historian, Charles Freeman, who has the knowledge provided by many archaeological excavations. The third excerpt, from the work of classicist John Bagnell Bury, is a detailed picture of the systems of government in the time of Odysseus. The final section, by a modern historian, Robin Osborne, uses archaeology to characterize the collapse of the society of which Odysseus was a part.

HELLAS

The great historian of Greece, Thucydides, writes of the history of Greece, called Hellas. He describes its early inhabitants as well as its period of powerful tribes—those who advanced on Troy in their first united effort. Finally he brings the reader to the decline of Hellas after the Trojan War, when internal fighting and invasions brought on the Dark Ages.

The early settlements consisted of individual tribes who usually regarded each other with suspicion, and poor land was often a protection against invasion. Areas richer in resources came to be more powerful and attracted strong tribal leaders. Gradually, tribes occasionally would seek help from one another to fend off a common enemy. Only with the Trojan War did this collaborative effort of self-defense develop into a united effort to attack an adversary on the basis of common interests.

Thucydides notes the power of King Minos of Crete, who ruled the Aegean world before the tribes on the Greek mainland became rich and strong. Greece's historical link with the sea can be seen in this passage.

His mention of the infighting that arose after the Trojan War can be seen in *The Odyssey* in both Agamemnon's household and Odysseus' household.

FROM *THUCYDIDES, THE HISTORIES*, VOL. 1, TRANS. BENJAMIN JOWETT, SECOND EDITION, REVISED

(Oxford: Clarendon Press, 1900)

The country which is now called Hellas was not regularly settled in ancient times. The people were migratory, and readily left their homes whenever they were overpowered by numbers. There was no commerce, and they could not safely hold intercourse with one another either by land or sea. The several tribes cultivated their own soil just enough to obtain a maintenance from it. But they had no accumulations of wealth, and did not plant the ground; for, being without walls, they were never sure that an invader might not come and despoil them. Living in this manner and knowing that they could anywhere obtain a bare subsistence, they were always ready to migrate; so that they had neither great cities nor any considerable resources. The richest districts were most constantly changing their inhabitants; for example, the countries which are now called Thessaly and Boeotia, the greater part of the Peloponnesus with the exception of Arcadia, and all the best parts of Hellas. For the productiveness of the land increased the power of individuals; this in turn was a source of quarrels by which communities were ruined, while at the same time they were more exposed to attacks from without. Certainly Attica, of which the soil was poor and thin, enjoyed a long freedom from civil strife, and therefore retained its original inhabitants. And a striking confirmation of my argument is afforded by the fact that Attica through immigration increased in population more than any other region. For the leading men of Hellas, when driven out of their own country by war or revolution, sought an asylum at Athens. ...

The feebleness of antiquity is further proved to me by the circumstance that there appears to have been no common action in Hellas before the Trojan War. And I am inclined to think that the very name was not as yet given to the whole country, and in fact did not exist at all before the time of Hellen, the son of Deucalion; the different tribes, of which the Pelasgian was the most widely spread, gave their own names to different districts. But when Hellen and his sons became powerful in Phtiotis, their aid was invoked in other cities, and those who associated with them gradually began to be called Hellenes, though a long time elapsed before the name prevailed over the whole country. Of this Homer affords the best evidence; for he, although he lived long after the Trojan War, nowhere uses this name collectively, but confines it to the followers of Achilles from Phtiotis, who were the original Hellenes; when speaking of the entire host he calls them Danaans, or Argives, or Achaeans. Neither is there any mention of Barbarians in his poems, clearly because there were as yet no Hellenes opposed to them by a common distinctive name. Thus, the several Hellenic tribes (and I mean by the term Hellenes those who, while forming separate communities, had a common language, and were afterwards called by a common name), owing to their weakness and isolation, were never united in any great enterprise before the Trojan War. And they only made the expedition against Troy after they had gained considerable experience of the sea.

Minos [of Crete] is the first to whom tradition ascribes the possession of a navy. He made himself master of a great part of what is now termed the Hellenic sea; he conquered the Cyclades, and was the first colonizer of most of them, expelling the Carians and appointing his own sons to govern in them. Lastly, it was he who, from a natural desire to protect his growing revenues, sought, as far as he was able, to clear the sea of pirates. ...

After Minos had established his navy, communication by sea became more general. For, he having expelled the marauders when he colonized the greater part of the islands, the dwellers on the sea-coast began to grow richer and to live in a more settled manner; and some of them, finding their wealth increase beyond their expectations, surrounded their towns with walls.

...

Even in the age which followed the Trojan War, Hellas was still in process of ferment and settlement, and had no time for peaceful growth. The return of the Hellenes from Troy after their long absence led to many changes: Quarrels too arose in nearly every city, and those who were expelled by them went and founded other cities. ... In the eightieth year after the war, the Dorians led by the Heraclidae conquered the Peloponnesus. A considerable time elapsed before Hellas became finally settled; after a while, however, she recovered tranquillity and began to send out colonies (1–4, 6, 9, 10)

MYCENAE REVEALED THROUGH ARCHAEOLOGY

Charles Freeman, an archaeologist, classicist, and prolific writer about Egypt, Greece, and Rome, uses the historical information uncovered by archaeology to characterize the world of Odysseus and Agamemnon when Agamemnon's Mycenae was at its height. Note the development of resources, the cultivation of trade, and the rise to power of a single ruler in each region. Despite the wealth and power of the ruler, it is obvious that he could keep his status only by remaining aware of the desires of the whole community.

FROM CHARLES FREEMAN, *THE GREEK ACHIEVEMENT*

(New York: Penguin Books, 1999)

There is no obvious explanation as to how and why a group of chieftains in mainland Greece should have elevated themselves above their fellows and gained access to goods from across the eastern Mediterranean. Mycenae, for instance, is no richer in resources than the rest of Greece and has no immediate access to the sea. However, Greece was on the edge of the thriving Minoan trading empire and it can only be assumed that determined individuals were able to exploit the opportunity to trade any surplus produce they could squeeze from their locality, grain, hides, wool woven into textiles, timber, oil, even slaves, for the riches and other resources of the east. It has been argued that the real driving force of Aegean trade was the search for the constituents of bronze, copper and tin. Copper was relatively plentiful, in Crete and Cyprus, for instance. Tin, essential for hardening copper into an effective metal compound, was more elusive. The main source was probably Anatolia but the Mycenaeans may have been involved in passing copper and tin into the Aegean from Europe.

By 1500 there is growing evidence that the local elites of the Greek mainland were forging closer links with each other and producing a more coherent culture. There was now a typical Mycenaean stronghold, a ruler's citadel on a low hill in an area where the land was reasonably fertile and the water supply good.

...

Mycenaean rulers have left the impression that they dominated their people through showy displays of their power, partly perhaps through the ownership of exotic goods but even more so through the effective use of stone for imposing fortifications and tombs....

There is evidence of an effective administration able to coordinate the raising of extra supplies and organizing defense at times of crisis.... (31, 32, 33)

POLITICAL ORGANIZATION IN THE HEROIC AGE

John Bury, one of an earlier school of distinguished Irish classical scholars, bases his most famous work, on the history of Greece, on archaeological findings in the late nineteenth and early twentieth centuries. The following excerpt details the political organization of Greece in what is known as the Heroic Age, when kings prominent in *The Odyssey*—particularly Nestor, Agamemnon, and Menelaus—presumably ruled. Most of these kings, even though they were presumed to be descended from gods, came to have very limited power, needing always to look to community leaders for support even if those leaders were friends or members of their extended families. Bury believes that the eventual overthrow of these Mycenaean rulers made it more possible for democracy to develop in the period we know as classical Greece.

FROM JOHN BAGNELL BURY, *A HISTORY OF GREECE*

(New York: Modern Library, 1927)

The Basileus or King

The king was the chief priest, the chief judge, and the supreme war-lord of the tribe. He exercised a general control over religious ceremonies, except in cases where there were special priesthoods; he pronounced judgment and dealt out justice to those who came to his judgment-seat to have their wrongs righted, and he led forth the host to war. He belonged to a family, which claimed descent from gods themselves. His relation to his people was conceived as that of a protecting deity; "he was revered as a god in the deme." The kingship passed from sire to son, but it is probable that personal fitness was recognized as a condition of the kingly office, and the people might refuse to accept a degenerate son who was unequal to the tasks that his father had fulfilled. The sceptered king had various privileges—the seat of honour at feasts, a large and choice share of booty taken in war and food offered at sacrifices. A special close of land was marked out and set apart for him as a royal domain, distinct from that which his family owned.

The Bule or Council/Class of nobles

The royal functions were vague enough, and a king had no power to enforce his will if it did not meet the approval of the heads of the people. He must always look for the consent and seek the opinion of the deliberative Council of Elders. Strictly, perhaps, the members of the council ought to have been the heads of all the clans, and they would thus have represented the whole tribe, or all the tribes if there were more than one. But we must take it for granted, as an ultimate fact, which we have not the means of explaining, that certain families had come to hold a privileged position above the elders—had, in fact, been marked out as noble, and claimed descent from Zeus; and the Council was composed of this nobility. In the puissant authority of this Council of Elders lay the germ of future aristocracy.

Agora, or Gathering of the Folk/The Army Is the Assembly

More important than either King or Council for the future growth of Greece was the Gathering of the people, out of which democracy was to spring. All the freemen of the tribe—all the freemen of the nation, when more tribes had been united—met together, not at stated times but whenever the king summoned them, to hear and acclaim what he and his councilors proposed. To hear and acclaim, but not to debate or propose themselves. As yet Gathering of the folk for purposes of policy had not been differentiated from the Gathering for the purposes of war. . . . The Assembly was not yet distinguished as an institution from the army; and if Agamemnon summons his host to declare his resolutions in the plain of Troy, such a gathering is the Agora in no figurative sense, it is not mere military assembly formed on the model of a political assembly; it is in the fullest sense the Assembly of the people. . . .

The King's Companions

The king was surrounded by a body of Companions, or retainers, who were attached to him by personal ties of service, and seem often to have abode in his palace. The Companions are the same institution as the thanes of our English kings. And if kingship had held its ground in Greece, the Companions might possibly, as in England, have developed into a new order of nobility, founded, not on birth, but on the king's own choice for his service.

Survival of Old Form of Monarchy in Macedonia/Alexander the Great

Though the monarchy of this primitive form, as we find it reflected in Homeric lays, generally passed away, it survived in a few outlying regions which lagged behind the rest of the Hellenic world in political development. Thus the Macedonian Greeks in the lower valley of the Axius retained a constitution of the old Homeric type till the latest times—the royal power continually growing. At the close of the tale of Greek conquest and expansion, which began on the Cayster and ended on the Hyphasis, we shall come back by a strange revolution to the Homeric state. When all the divers forms of the rule of the few and the rule of the many, which grew out of the primitive monarchy, have had their day, we shall see the Macedonian warrior, who is to complete the work that was begun by the Achaean conquerors of Troy, attended by his Companions like Agamemnon or Achilles, and ruling his people like an Achaean king of men.

THE DARK AGES

Robin Osborne, a lecturer in ancient history at the University of Oxford and author of three volumes on ancient Greece, writes from the perspective of a classicist who is in command of the archaeological findings of the last half of the twentieth century. In the following excerpt he comments on the Dark Ages, which separated Odysseus from Homer, the author of *The Odyssey*. Evidence makes clear that the world of Odysseus and Agamemnon completely collapsed after the Trojan War. What took place in the Dark Ages that ensued is, he argues, not only unknown to the modern world but also probably was unknown to Homer as well, thus allowing Homer and other poets to create their own past to embody the ideals apparent in the character of Odysseus.

FROM ROBIN OSBORNE, *GREECE IN THE MAKING*

(London: Routledge, 1996)

The Mycenaean world ended with a bang *and* a whimper. Around 1200 B.C. several of the major Mycenaean centres in the Peloponnese and in central Crete show signs of violent destruction, fire, or abandonment.

...

But there can be little doubt that all over the Greek world, and in Cyprus too, earlier settlements were abandoned, and where we can trace later settlements they are often not long-lived.

...

The general impression that we get is of contracted horizons: no big buildings, no multiple graves, no impersonal communication, limited contact with a wider world. ... By the eleventh century everything which depended directly or indirectly on organization at more than an individual level seems to have become impossible to sustain. Hence the gloom: the slate was rubbed all but clear of the traces of earlier organization and the products of that organization.

None of our earliest literary records from archaic Greece ... knows anything about, or shows any concern with, the Dark Age.

...

As we have already seen, material remains suggest that after the end of the Mycenaean palaces the whole social and economic organization broke up. ...

In the face of this, and of the silence of Homer and Hesiod, we are obliged to conclude that the Greeks of the archaic period *knew* nothing about the Dark Age. Indeed, one might say that for them ignorance was bliss, for upon the clean slate they could, and did, write their own beginnings, creating for themselves the past for which contemporary realities and desires for the future made them wish. They could, and did, invent themselves. (19, 30, 33, 37)

TOPICS FOR ORAL AND WRITTEN DISCUSSION

1. Reread *The Odyssey* carefully to find references to farm animals and vegetation that may link Odysseus to prehistoric agriculture. Write an essay on your findings.

2. Some scholars have speculated that Odysseus' account of the land of the Cyclopes reads like that of a traveler looking for lands that can be colonized by Greece. Reread accounts of several areas written about by Homer and, imagining that you are scouting for prospective lands for Greece to colonize, write reports assessing the areas. What are the area's assets? What are its dangers?

3. Review mentions of piracy in *The Odyssey*. Write an essay on Homer's apparent attitude toward piracy. Does he condone it or condemn it? Be sure to take into account the attitude and actions of the gods.

4. Examine the details Homer provides about the households of the kings mentioned in *The Odyssey*. What elements are common to them and might be used to generalize on the life of the nobility in the Mycenaean era?

5. Given what you have learned about the geography of Greece, write an essay on how the introduction of the horse may have changed life in Greece.

6. The decline of Mycenaean civilization during which Nestor, Menelaos, and Agamemnon supposedly ruled is said to have begun after the Trojan War. Are there hints of the unraveling of stability, evidence of anarchy, in *The Odyssey?* Write an essay on the subject.

7. Write an essay comparing the government revealed in *The Odyssey* with the political landscape described by the classicist Bury.

SUGGESTIONS FOR FURTHER READING

Andrewes, Antony. *The Greeks*. New York: Knopf, 1967.

Baker, Rosalie F., and Charles F. Baker III. *Ancient Greeks. Creating the Classical Tradition*. New York: Oxford University Press, 1997.

Boardman, John et al. eds. *The Oxford History of Greece and the Hellenistic World*. Oxford: Oxford University Press, 1991.

Chadwick, John. *The Mycenaean World*. Cambridge: Cambridge University Press, 1976.

Cutling, H.W. *Some Problems in Aegean Prehistory*. Oxford: Leopard's Head Press, 1989.

Dickinson, Oliver Thomas. *The Aegean Bronze Age*. New York: Cambridge University Press, 1994.

Fine, John V.A. *The Ancient Greeks. A Critical History*. Cambridge, MA: Belnap Press of Harvard University Press, 1983.

Flensted-Jensen, Pernelle, et al., eds. *Polis and Politics: Studies in Ancient Greek History*. Copenhagen: Museum Tusculanum Press, 2000.
Grant, Michael. *The Founders of the Western World.* New York: Scribner's, 1991.
Hooker, J.T. *The Coming of the Greeks.* Claremont, CA: Regina Books, 1999.
Vivante, Bella. *Events That Changed Ancient Greece.* Westport, CT: Greenwood, 2000.

6

The Trojan War of Myth and Legend

> Is this the face that launched a thousand ships
> And burnt the topless towers of Ilium?
>   Christopher Marlowe, *Doctor Faustus*

The Trojan War, the cataclysmic armed conflict between the kingdom of Troy and a loose federation of Greek kingdoms, was arguably the most renowned war in Western culture. Although the Trojan War has already occurred when the action of *The Odyssey* takes place, this armed conflict is the fundamental event from which every action in *The Odyssey* flows, and a firm grasp of the events in the Trojan War is essential for a full understanding of Homer's epic. The Trojan War propels both *The Iliad* and *The Odyssey*. The battles themselves—the psychological ones between Greek or Achaean warriors and the siege of Troy by the Greeks—is the actual subject matter of *The Iliad*. *The Odyssey* is an account of what happened to the warriors—Odysseus, Agamemnon, Achilles, Nestor, and Ajax, in particular—as a consequence of the Trojan War. And into Odysseus' journey are woven many tales of the war.

    Homer's *The Iliad* is, of course, one version of the story of the Trojan War. For the classical Greeks, the Trojan War was an important, accepted page of Greek history. For them, there was no difference between the myth and the history of the Trojan War. The following is intended to be the mythic, legendary account of the Trojan War as the classical Greeks and Homer understood it. At the end of this discussion of the Trojan War of legend, there will be a consideration of how the war is now regarded by historians.

An etching of the legend of the Trojan Horse. Armed Greek soldiers are climbing out by ladder and rope, and a figure, perhaps the Trojan princess Cassandra, is sounding the alarm from the wall. *Source:* Hill, G.F. *Illustrations of School Classics.* London: Macmillan, 1903, 111.

THE BEAUTY CONTEST

Strangely enough, the Trojan War, this conflict of epic proportions and enduring influence, began with a seemingly mundane, frivolous event—a beauty contest, on a rural hillside, among three women who had chosen as their judge a naive shepherd boy. Despite its deceptive simplicity, this was the most notorious beauty contest in history because the contestants, as it is described in chapter 2, were three goddesses and the judge was Paris, abductor of Helen of Troy.

THE TROJAN WAR BEGINS

With Paris' abduction of Helen, the Trojan War began. Menelaos naturally wanted his wife back, and he was lucky enough to have the support of Helen's many suitors before her marriage, men who had taken a vow (at the suggestion of Odysseus) that if the happy couple were ever in trouble, the others would all come to the rescue. So when Paris abducted Helen, the Greeks decided to wage war on Troy.

MAJOR CHARACTERS IN THE TROJAN WAR

Troy

The walled city of Troy, also known as Ilium, was located across the Aegean Sea from Greece in Anatolia, in what is now Turkey. The Trojans were also called, at different times, Teucrians or Dardanians.

Priam—king of Troy
Hecuba—his queen
Cassandra—Priam's daughter, taken as a slave by Agamemnon
Paris Alexander—Priam's son, seducer of Helen, and skilled warrior on the Trojan side
Hector—Priam's son and Troy's chief heroic warrior, who is killed by Achilles

Greeks

The Greeks were also called, at different times, Achaeans, Danaans, Argives, and Mycenaeans.

Agamemnon—leader of the forces from Mycenae
Clytemnestra—his wife, and sister of Helen of Troy
Iphigenia—his daughter
Orestes—his son
Menelaos—his brother, husband of Helen, and leader of Sparta
Idomeneos—leader of Knossos on Crete
Nestor—king of Pylos
Odysseus—leader of Ithaca
Penelope—his wife
Telemachos—his son
Achilles—warrior from Phthia
Ajax—warrior from Salamis

The Greek Army

Agamemnon

Ultimately a great invasion fleet was organized under the leadership of Agamemnon, the brother of Menelaos. Agamemnon's irresponsibility, arrogance, and ineptitude continually placed the Greeks in jeopardy throughout the war that followed. His actions caused a delay in their embarking from Greece, his daughter's death, and the withdrawal of the best Greek warrior from battle. But, despite the fact that Agamemnon was not a great warrior, he was designated the "commander" and "first among equals."

Odysseus

Odysseus, who was king of Ithaca, had also been one of Helen's suitors and so was obliged, by the old agreement to protect her, to join Agamemnon in war against Troy. But he had his own family by now, and had no interest in putting his life on the line in a war. He tried to get out of his sworn duty to rescue Helen by pretending insanity: he began uselessly plowing the seashore; but when a clever colleague put Odysseus' infant son Telemachos on the shore in front of the plow, Odysseus carefully moved the plow around the boy, thus proving to their satisfaction that he was perfectly sane.

Odysseus, as he is portrayed in Homer's *Iliad*, while being a great warrior, was also a man of deception and trickery, one who could never be completely trusted. He was also a man of clear vision who recognized that "fairness" and "war" are contradictory terms, a kind of fantasy designed for people who do not know any better, and that in a genuine war, the only object is to win. He is often referred to as the "man of many wiles," to use one of the many epithets that Homer contrives—inclined to solve his problems by using his brain, by inventing schemes or adopting disguises and telling false tales in order to survive. In the nineteenth century, English Victorians found in Odysseus a perfect symbol of one who always strives, who constantly tries to learn, and who uses his mind not merely for slaughter (although he can do that well enough) but also for the achievement of light and human progress.

Achilles

Once Odysseus had been recruited to fight the Trojans, he in turn helped to recruit Achilles, whose mother, Thetis, was doing her best to see that he escaped military service. She insisted that he hide in disguise among a group of handmaidens. But Achilles was also outwitted when Odysseus put out a display of feminine articles along with a display of arms. And like iron filings to a magnet, all the girls went to the former and Achilles went to the latter. Thus he, along with other Greek kings and warriors, joined the invading forces and became the unbeatable warrior of the Greek world. Being from Thrace, one of the farthest outposts of the Greek world, Achilles was in many ways a "country boy"; a teenager when the war began, he was one of the youngest of the soldiers. But inside the country youth was a skilled and ferocious soldier. He had an emotional, impulsive, and hot-tempered personality, but was at times kind and generous as well. As a master of the skills expected of a young nobleman, his chief aim always was to be superior in all things. Because of this, he was, along with Odysseus, typical of the Greek heroic ideal.

Ajax

Among the Achaean warriors at Troy, Ajax was big, powerful, a giant of a man, second only to Achilles in battle. He was also supremely confident of his own ability—so confident, in fact, that he scorned the help of the gods, believing that he was sufficiently capable without them. For instance, in one scene, in the heat of battle, he even wounds one of the gods. He is known not only for his oversupply of cockiness but also for his undersupply of intelligence. Despite his failings, a duel with the Trojan warrior Hector ends in a draw, with Ajax perceived as being the better fighter.

Nestor

Nestor was the grand old man of the Greek army, a great warrior in his youth and now recognized as a man of wisdom. He is a garrulous talker as well; once he gets started, he never knows when to stop. Nevertheless, he is kindly and wise, a font of wisdom treated with respect and kindness, but also a verbose old codger who provides a suggestion of comic relief. If Homer's audience was composed generally of young and vigorous people, as it no doubt was, there were undoubtedly many among them who would remember such old men as Nestor from their own lives and look upon them, in memory, with both favor and condescension. Nestor is a bit like Shakespeare's Polonious in *Hamlet*.

THE DELAY AT AULIS

It took two years for the great fleet to gather at Aulis in preparation for an invasion of Troy. Even with the army assembled, however, there was another delay. The virgin goddess Artemis refused to allow them to sail because their commander, Agamemnon, had deeply offended her. The monstrous deed that Agamemnon committed to appease the goddess and secure favorable winds for the departure was the sacrifice of his virgin daughter, Iphigenia.

THE TEN-YEAR SIEGE OF TROY LEADING UP TO THE ACTION OF *THE ILIAD*

The Greek siege of Troy lasted for ten years. They ravaged the countryside. Soldiers found death where they had only looked for sleep, in a foreign land where frost encrusted their hands and faces. The Trojans defended their land against the Greek invasion behind impregnable city walls. The Olympian gods personally took part in daily military actions while Zeus looked on from afar, and weighed the scales of Destiny.

Major Trojan Warriors

The two prominent Trojan warriors were Hector and Paris, both sons of King Priam but opposite in every way. Hector was the noble fighter, the devout family man, the person of honor. Paris, who bore the major responsibility for causing the war, was, in legend, strong in the Trojans' battle against the Greeks, but in Homer's *Iliad* Paris is a shirker who avoids battle, ignores his responsibility, spends most of his time with his mistress Helen, and in general deserves the reprimands of the Trojan warrior Hector.

Rage in Homer's Account of the Trojan War

The Iliad, the title of Homer's account of the Trojan War, means the "story of Ilium," or Troy—but, ironically, *The Iliad* is not the story of Troy at all. It is the tale of the tenth and final year of a long and destructive war, which in the end destroyed both the victor and the vanquished. It begins with an occasion of childish pique ("rage") on the part of its greatest warrior and with the irresponsible, blundering incompetence and pride of his commander-in-chief, Agamemnon. The first word of *The Iliad* is "rage" or "wrath."

After arriving on the outskirts of Troy, Agamemnon, the commander-in-chief of this loose federation of Greek warriors, again offended the gods by taking as his prize Chriseis, the daughter of the priest Chrises. This again placed the entire Achaean expedition in jeopardy. Unless he relinquished her, all would be lost. So he was forced to give up his concubine, in the process losing face and being humiliated. To assuage his injured dignity, he demanded that he be given the girl Briseis, whom Achilles had captured as his own prize in battle. This outrage not only offended Achilles, it sent him into an unimpeded fury.

Achilles could easily have slaughtered his commander on the spot. Instead, he decided to withdraw from battle, to let Agamemnon and the Achaeans see, through bloody experience, how much they needed him and how much he should be truly honored. So he sulked in his tent while the battle went on. He played his lyre, passed the time with his intimate friend Patroclus, and watched from the sidelines as the Trojan warriors under Hector, the great leader and protector of Ilium, dominated the field, breached the defensive walls of the Achaeans, and finally stormed the last defense, the ships themselves. Achilles observed, among other things, the numerous deaths of his own Myrmidons, dying in battle because he was not there. He was so angry that when Agamemnon offered to restore the girl Briseis (still "untouched," Agamemnon says) and to give Achilles many treasures and privileges, Achilles still refuses.

So far, it might be noted, according to the Greek codes of honor and protocol, Achilles had been justified in his resentment of Agamemnon's humiliating treatment of him; but now, in his refusal of this crucial offer of total restitution and unsurpassed honors, he was considered "wrong," unsympathetic, and childish in allowing his fellow warriors to die as he sulked in his tent.

The Death of Patroclus

With Achilles retired from the battle, the situation for the Achaeans became desperate. Under the circumstances, Patroclus sought and received permission to go into battle using Achilles' armor. For the sight of Achilles' armor on the field was, in itself, enough to inspire terror in the hearts of the enemy and cause them to flee. After some initial success, Patroclus was killed and dishonored, his armor taken from him by the great Trojan hero Hector.

Death of Hector

The death of Patroclus brought Achilles raging in fury and grief from his tent, onto the battlefield again. His terrible war cry, as he stood alone on a parapet, even without armor, evoked chills of fear and terror in the Trojan fighters on the field. Many of them fled at the sound of his voice. He entered the field like an insane man, a killing machine, violating all sense of propriety and all traditions of honor.

As William Tecumseh Sherman, an American general of the Civil War, was to say of battle many years later, "War is hell." On this occasion Achilles determined to avenge his friend's death by making hell for the Trojans in a bloody orgy. The entire episode was regarded by the Greeks of the fifth century B.C., who virtually deified Homer and his epic heroes, as a fatal lapse in the great hero. This did nothing, however, to detract from their perception of his greatness: Achilles remained for them, along with Odysseus of the Many Wiles, the defining national hero, faults and all.

In the final scene of battle, between Achilles and Hector, the noble Hector faces his slayer, but at the crucial moment, panic seizes him and he runs. Achilles chases him three times around the walls of Troy. Then, in one of the brilliant scenes of literature, the Trojan warrior screws up his courage, stops, and stands to face his maddened nemesis, calmly and heroically. He overcomes his own sense of mindless fear, a feat that requires incalculable courage and power of will, and prepares to fight with all his strength. Achilles wins with the help of the gods after they have deserted Hector.

While Trojans watch from the impregnable walls of their city, Achilles dishonors the slain Trojan hero, drags his body around the walls of Troy behind his carriage, and in every way possible screams dishonor and hate. When at last the anger of Achilles has been assuaged (in part, at least), and the gods themselves have shown their displeasure by perfectly preserving the body of Hector, Achilles accepts a visit from the dead Trojan's mourning father. He is still the mad killing machine he always was; he has not softened in the least; but he recognizes something in the old man that strikes a responsive chord. And so, at last, he agrees to permit the Trojans to mourn and to bury their dead hero.

Death of Achilles

When Achilles ruthlessly pursued Hector on the plains of Troy, with only brutal death in mind, he knew, from the inviolable prophecy told him by his immortal mother, that if he killed Hector, his own death would follow closely. However, he never hesitated in any action, either from common sense or fear, and did not faltered in his pursuit. By killing Hector, he sealed his doom, choosing a short and glorious life rather than a long and peaceful one.

According to legend (to which Homer makes no reference), when Achilles was an infant, his mother, Thetis, dipped him in the River Styx to make him invincible over most of his body. But she had to hold him by his heels, leaving this part of his anatomy vulnerable. Achilles met death shortly after he killed Hector at the hand of Paris, who killed him with an arrow that pierced the heel.

The Trojan Horse

Troy finally falls because of a stroke of genius—the brainchild of Odysseus. The Greeks built an enormous wooden horse, left it on the beach, entered their ships, and sailed. The Trojans, thinking that this was somehow a Greek gift to the gods, dragged it inside the walls of Troy. As Helen of Troy relates in *The Odyssey*, she is taken to the horse to entice whatever warriors might be hidden in it to emerge by imitating the voices of their wives. When the ruse fails, the Trojans assume that the wooden edifice is harmless. But when night falls, Greek warriors climb down out of the huge device, open the gates of the city, and in turn ravish, burn, kill, or enslave all of its inhabitants.

The Sacking of Troy

When Troy falls, the victorious Achaeans destroy the city, slaughtering whatever males are still within reach and taking the women as slaves. Holy Ilium, or Troy, is no more. By also defiling the temples and violating accepted customs, they enrage the gods. As a consequence of the anger of the gods, all the returning Greek leaders are punished for their deeds. After a period of about three or four hundred years, during the classical period in the fifth century B.C., when Athens was engaged in the war that would mean the end of their independence, and after Athenian forces had sacked and destroyed the city of Melos, the Athenian playwright Euripides, in his play *The Trojan Women*, made use of the Trojan War to express the horror of postwar pillage, suggesting a warning to his contemporaries. In his play, the god Poseidon looks down on the wild and senseless slaughter of Troy and says, in effect, "How blind you are, you who destroy cities and lay waste tombs, the ancient resting places of the honored dead—your own time will come."

Hector's Funeral

The last line of *The Iliad* is devoted to the Trojan hero Hector: "And so they celebrated the funeral of Hector, tamer of horses," a reminder that the introduction of horses was comparatively recent. Here Homer's *The Iliad* ends, with reference not to Achilles but to the son of King Priam of Troy, a Trojan hero who, in the absence of Achilles, had been the greatest warrior on the field, and who emerges, by modern standards, as the most humane and noble character in this cast of military characters.

A CURRENT HISTORICAL VIEW OF THE TROJAN WAR

Was there a Troy? Did a war between Trojans and Greeks actually take place?

Even as early as classical Greece, many Greeks quietly doubted the roles that the gods like Zeus and Athena were said to play in human affairs, including the Trojan War, but the war itself was still considered a historical event. As early as the eighteenth century, scholars of classical history began to doubt the existence of Troy, there being no actual place identifiable as Troy, and the historical reality of a Trojan War.

Many people searched for Troy, but the question of whether Troy existed seemed to be settled once and for all by the excavations of Heinrich Schliemann, the nineteenth-century German archaeologist who was convinced that Troy had been situated in what was then Turkey. His extensive searches for the ancient cities of Troy, begun in 1870, led him to believe, and to convince most of the scientific world, that he had found the Troy of legend.

Schliemann and the German archaeologist Wilhelm Dorpfeld had found at the site of Troy at least nine cities, one on top of the other. All evidence pointed to a cataclysmic destruction of the city at level VI, at about the time Myceanaean culture was at the height of its aggression. The historian-archaeologist Carl Blegen's theory, that the city was destroyed by an earthquake, is indisputable. However, it is also argued that one reason Troy fell to the marauding Greeks is that they attacked after Troy had been weakened by the earthquake. Documents unearthed in Myceanae suggest that Trojan women lived there as slaves. The logical conclusion is that they were taken after the defeat of Troy. Thus there is widespread historical agreement that, yes, there was a Trojan War, waged and won on Trojan soil (in Anatolia) by mainland Greeks.

Subsequent excavations by Schliemann and others on mainland Greece also have led to the conclusion that Mycenae was a strong, warlike civilization intent on controlling its own enslaved populations by terror, and on plundering and colonizing the rest of the Aegean to retain their wealth and power. It is entirely probable, scholars argue, that Mycenaean warriors decided to attack Troy, an act that would have been, the historian Michael Wood writes, "in the very nature of Mycenaean society and kinship." (*In Search of the Trojan War*, 249).

Schliemann's conviction that he had found absolute proof of the existence of Agamemnon, his palace, and his tomb was not shared universally by scholars. But the worldwide practice of preserving the names of ancient kings in epics and legends has led scholars to entertain the possibility that Agamemnon and Priam, king of Troy, existed.

What about a historical Helen? Did the abduction of Helen cause the Trojan War? Although history does not provide evidence of a woman named Helen, it is true that women, especially beautiful women, were frequently kidnapped at this time and that war was often waged against the kidnappers in order to retrieve the women, and perhaps treasure stolen at the same time. So, even though ancient historians, like Herodotus, doubted that any war would be fought over a woman, records recovered in archaeological digs indicate that it is a distinct possibility that war could be provoked by the abduction of a woman, especially if she were a king's wife and the sister-in-law of the most powerful man in Greece at the time.

It is even plausible that the Trojan Horse could have played a part in the war. It could well have been used as a battering ram to break down the gates of Troy to allow the Greeks entry. It also could have been an image built to honor the god Poseidon, often associated with horses, but also associated with earthquakes, one of which had made Troy vulnerable to capture by the Greeks! (See Michael Wood's *In Search of the Trojan War*, 250, 251.)

DOCUMENTS

Historical documents included here shed further light on the background of *The Odyssey:* an excerpt from the ancient Greek historian Herodotus reveals one of many accounts of Helen of Troy that varies from Homer's, and shows how Homer shaped his material for dramatic effect; the excerpt from Greek historian Thucydides reveals the political realities behind the Trojan War; the accounts of the turn-of-the-twentieth-century Irish scholar John Bagnell Bury, and of America's pioneer archaeologist of the Aegean, Carl Blegen, indicates that archaeological discoveries reinforced the actual validity of the Homeric material.

HERODOTUS ON PARIS' ABDUCTION OF HELEN

Herodotus, the Greek writer whose approximate dates are 484 B.C. to 428 B.C., has been called the father of history. He collected his information by extensive interviews conducted during his travels throughout Macedonia, Thrace, Scythia, Asia Minor, Phoenicia, Syria, Babylonia, Egypt, Libya, and Greece. He was hampered by the paucity of extant records and his need to rely on translators in countries other than Greece. Nor did he always clearly separate legend and historical fact, leading modern scholars to classify him more as an artist than as a historian.

In the following excerpts from his history, Herodotus reports what he has learned about Paris Alexander's abduction of Helen, chiefly from his interviews with Egyptian priests. Note that he believes that Paris (to whom he refers by his second name, Alexander) ended up in Egypt with Helen and the treasure he had stolen from Menelaos. Herodotus is told by the priests that the Egyptians, learning of Paris Alexander's misbehavior, forced him to return to Troy, leaving behind Helen and the property of Menelaos. According to the many legends, Helen never went to Troy; Menelaos retrieved her from Egypt. Also, Herodotus believes that Homer knew this story to be true, but altered the facts to make a better story.

FROM HERODOTUS, *THE HISTORY OF HERODOTUS*, TRANSLATED BY GEORGE RAWLINSON

(New York: Lincoln MacVeagh, 1928)

In the next generation afterwards, according to the same authorities, Alexander the son of Priam, bearing these events in mind, resolved to procure himself a wife out of Greece by violence, fully persuaded, that as the Greeks had not given satisfaction for their outrages, so neither would he be forced to make any for his. Accordingly he made prize of Helen; upon which the Greeks decided that, before resorting to other measures, they would send envoys to reclaim the princess and require reparation of the wrong. Their demands were met by a reference to the violence which had been offered to Medea, and they were asked with what face they could now require satisfaction, when they had formerly rejected all demands for either reparation or restitution addressed to them.

Hitherto the injuries on either side had been mere acts of common violence; but in what followed the Persians consider that the Greeks were greatly to blame, since before any attack had been made on Europe, they led an army into Asia. Now as for the carrying off of women, it is the deed, they say, of a rogue; but to make a stir about such as are carried off, argues a man a fool. Men of sense care nothing for such women, since it is plain that without their own consent they would never be forced away. The Asiatics, when the Greeks ran off with their women, never troubled themselves about the matter; but the Greeks, for the sake of a single Lacedæmonian girl, collected a vast armament, invaded Asia, and destroyed the kingdom of Priam. Henceforth they ever looked upon the Greeks as their open enemies. For Asia, with all the various tribes of barbarians that inhabit it, is regarded by the Persians as their own; but Europe and the Greek race they look on as distinct and separate.

Such is the account which the Persians give of these matters. They trace to the attack upon Troy their ancient enmity towards the Greeks.

...

The priests, in answer to my inquiries on the subject of Helen, informed me of the following particulars. When Alexander had carried off Helen from Sparta, he took ship and sailed homewards. On his way across the Aegean a gale arose, which drove him from his course and took him down to the sea of Egypt; hence, as the wind did not abate, he was carried on to the coast, when he went ashore, landing at the Salt-Pans, in that mouth of the Nile which is now called the Canobic. At this place there stood upon the shore a temple, which still exists, dedicated to Hercules. If a slave runs away from his master, and taking sanctuary at this shrine gives himself up to the god, and receives certain sacred marks upon his person, whosoever his master may be, he cannot lay hand on him. This law still remained unchanged to my time. Hearing, therefore, of the custom of the place, the attendants of Alexander deserted him, and fled to the temple, where they sat as suppliants. While there, wishing to damage their master, they accused him to the Egyptians, narrating all the circumstances of the rape of Helen and the wrong done to Menelaus. These charges they brought, not only before the priests, but also before the warden of that mouth of the river, whose name was Thônis.

As soon as he received the intelligence, Thônis sent a message to Proteus, who was at Memphis, to this effect: "A stranger is arrived from Greece; he is by race a Teucrian, and has done a wicked deed in the country from which he is come. Having beguiled the wife of the man whose guest he was, he carried her away with him, and much treasure also. Compelled by stress of weather, he has now put in here. Are we to let him depart as he came, or shall we seize what he has brought?" Proteus replied, "Seize the man, be he who he may, that has dealt thus wickedly with his friend, and bring him before me, that I may hear what he will say for himself."

Thônis, on receiving these orders, arrested Alexander, and stopped the departure of his ships; then, taking with him Alexander, Helen, the treasures, and also the fugitive slaves, he went up to Memphis. When all were arrived, Proteus asked Alexander, "who he was, and whence he had come?" Alexander replied by giving his descent, the name of this country, and a true account of his late voyage. Then Proteus questioned him as to how he got possession of Helen. In his reply Alexander became confused, and diverged from the truth, whereon the slaves interposed, confuted his statements, and told the whole history of the crime. Finally, Proteus delivered judgment as follows: "Did I not regard it as a matter of the utmost consequence that no stranger driven to my country by adverse winds should ever be put to death. I would certainly have avenged the Greek by slaying thee. Thou basest of men,—after accepting hospitality, to do so wicked a deed! First, thou didst seduce the wife of thy own host—then, not content therewith, thou must violently excite her mind, and steal her away from her husband. Nay, even so thou were not satisfied, but on leaving, thou must plunder the house in which thou hadst been a guest. Now then, as I think it of the greatest importance to put no stranger to death, I suffer thee to depart; but the woman and the treasures I shall not permit to be carried away. Here they must stay, till the Greek stranger comes in person and takes them back with him. For thyself and thy companions, I command thee to begone from my land within the space of three days—and I warn you, that otherwise at the end of that time you will be treated as enemies."

Such was the tale told me by the priests concerning the arrival of Helen at the court of Proteus. It seems to me that Homer was acquainted with this story, and while discarding it, because he thought it less adapted for epic poetry than the version which he followed, showed that it was not unknown to him.

. . .

I made inquiry of the priests, whether the story which the Greeks tell about Ilium is a fable, or no. In reply they related the following particulars, of which they declared that Menelaus had himself informed them. After the rape of Helen, a vast army of Greeks, wishing to render help to Menelaus, set sail for the Teucrian territory; on their arrival they disembarked, and formed their camp, after which they sent ambassadors to Ilium, of whom Menelaus was one. The embassy was received within the walls, and demanded the restoration of Helen with the treasures which Alexander had carried off, and likewise required satisfaction for the wrong done. The Teucrians gave at once the answer in which they persisted ever afterwards, backing their assertions sometimes even with oaths, to wit, that neither Helen, nor the treasures claimed, were in their possession,—both the one and the other had remained, they said, in Egypt; and it was not just to come upon them for what Proteus, king of Egypt, was detaining. The Greeks, imagining that the Teucrians were merely laughing at them, laid siege to the town, and never rested until they finally took it. As, however, no Helen was found, and they were still told the same story, they at length believed in its truth, and despatched Menelaus to the court of Proteus.

So Menelaus travelled to Egypt, and on his arrival sailed up the river as far as Memphis, and related all that had happened. He met with the utmost hospitality, received Helen back unharmed, and recovered all his treasures. After this friendly treatment Menelaus, they said, behaved most unjustly towards the Egyptians; for as it happened that at the time when he wanted to take his departure, he was detained by the wind being contrary, and as he found this obstruction continue, he had recourse to a most wicked expedient. He seized, they said, two children of the people of the country, and offered them up in sacrifice. When this became known, the indignation of the people was stirred, and they went in pursuit of Menelaus, who, however, escaped with his ships to Libya, after which the Egyptians could not say whither he went. The rest they knew full well, partly by the inquiries which they had made, and partly from the circumstances having taken place in their own land, and therefore not admitting of doubt.

Such is the account given by the Egyptian priests, and I am myself inclined to regard as true all that they say of Helen from the following considerations:—If Helen had been at Troy, the inhabitants would, I think, have given her up to the Greeks, whether Alexander consented to it or no. For surely neither Priam nor his family, could have been so infatuated as to endanger their own persons, their children, and their city, merely that Alexander might possess Helen. At any rate, if they determined to refuse at first, yet afterwards when so many of the Trojans fell on every encounter with the Greeks and Priam too in each battle lost a son, or sometimes two, or three, or even more if we may credit the epic poets, I do not believe that even if Priam himself had been married to her he would have declined to deliver her up, with the view of bringing the series of calamities to a close. Nor was it as if Alexander had been heir to the crown, in which case he might have had the chief management of affairs, since Priam was already old. Hector, who was his elder brother, and a far braver man, stood before him, and was the heir to the kingdom on the death of their father Priam. And it could not be Hector's interests to uphold his brother in his wrong, when it brought such dire calamities upon himself and the other Trojans. But the fact was that they had no Helen to deliver, and so they told the Greeks, but the Greeks would not believe what they said—Divine Providence, as I think, so willing, that by their utter destruction it might be made evident to all men that when great wrongs are done, the gods will surely visit them with great punishments. Such, at least, is my view of the matter. (2, 118, 119, 120, 121)

THUCYDIDES ON THE TROJAN WAR

Thucydides was a Greek general and military historian who lived from approximately 465 B.C. to 399 B.C. Whereas Herodotus was known as the father of history, Thucydides, whom Herodotus inspired, brought accuracy, objectivity, the scientific method, and respectability to the discipline. In the following excerpts from his history, he examines the power and motives of Agamemnon in launching the war against Troy, the nature of the forces that left Greece for Troy, the reasons for their inability to conquer Troy for ten years, and the effect of the war on the Greeks who returned home.

FROM *THUCYDIDES, THE HISTORIES*, VOL. 1, TRANS. BY BENJAMIN JOWETT, SECOND EDITION, REVISED

(Oxford: Clarendon Press, 1900)

The love of gain made the weaker willing to serve the stronger, and the command of wealth enabled the more powerful to subjugate the lesser cities. This was the state of society which was beginning to prevail at the time of the Trojan War.

I am inclined to think that Agamemnon succeeded in collecting the expedition, not because the suitors of Helen had bound themselves by oath to Tyndareus, but because he was the most powerful king of his time.

Rise of the Pelopidae: the wealth and power which Agamemnon inherited from Atreus and Eurystheus enabled him to assemble the chiefs who fought at Troy.

...

The greatness of cities should be estimated by their real power and not by appearances. And we may fairly suppose the Trojan expedition to have been greater than any which preceded it, although according to Homer, if we may once more appeal to his testimony, not equal to those of our own day. He was a poet, and may therefore be expected to exaggerate; yet, even upon his showing, the expedition was comparatively small. For it numbered, as he tells us, twelve hundred ships, those of the Boeotians carrying one hundred and twenty men each, those of Philoctetes fifty; and by these numbers he may be presumed to indicate the largest and the smallest ships; else why in the catalogue is nothing said about the size of any others? That the crews were all fighting men as well as rowers he clearly implies when speaking of the ships of Philoctetes; for he tells us that all the oarsmen were likewise archers. And it is not to be supposed that many who were not sailors would accompany the expedition, except the kings and principal officers; for the troops had to cross the sea, bringing with them the materials of war, in vessels without decks, built after the old piratical fashion. Now if we take a mean between the crews, the invading forces will appear not to have been very numerous when we remember that they were drawn from the whole of Hellas.

Homer's account of the number of the forces.

The cause of the inferiority was not so much the want of men as the want of money; the invading army was limited, by the difficulty of obtaining supplies, to such a number as might be expected to live on the country in which they were to fight. After their arrival at Troy, when they had won a battle (as they clearly did, for otherwise they could not have fortified their camp), even then they appear not to have used the whole of their force, but to have been driven by want of provisions to the cultivation of the Chersonese and to pillage. And in consequence of this dispersion of their forces, the Trojans were enabled to hold out against them during the whole ten years, being always a match for those who remained on the spot. Whereas if the besieging army had brought abundant supplies, and, instead of betaking themselves to agriculture or pillage, had carried on the war persistently with all their forces, they would easily have been masters of the field and have taken the city; since, even divided as they were, and with only a part of their army available at any one time, they held their ground. Or, again, they might have regularly invested Troy, and the place would have been captured in less time and with less trouble. Poverty was the real reason why the achievements of former ages were insignificant, and why the Trojan War, the most celebrated of them all, when brought to the test of facts, falls short of its fame and of the prevailing traditions to which the poets have given authority.

Considerations respecting the Trojan War.

Even in the age which followed the Trojan War, Hellas was still in process of ferment and settlement, and had no time for peaceful growth. The return of the Hellenes from Troy after their long absence led to many changes, quarrels too arose in nearly every city, and those who were expelled by them went and founded other cities. Thus in the sixtieth year after the fall of Troy, the Boeotian people, having been expelled from Arnè by the Thessalians, settled in the country formerly called Cadmeis, but now Boeotia: a portion of the tribe already dwelt there, and some of these had joined in the Trojan expedition. In the eightieth year after the war, the Dorians led by the Heraclidae conquered the Peloponnesus. A considerable time elapsed before Hellas became finally settled. (6, 8, 9, 10)

POLITICAL POWER AND TERRITORIAL EXPANSION

John Bagnell Bury, an Irishman, was a translator of ancient Greek and Roman texts as well as a historian and professor of history at Trinity College, Dublin. His major work was *A History of Greece*, first published in 1900. In 1913 he revised his history on the basis of excavations on Crete made by the archeologist Sir Arthur Evans in 1900. Evans' discoveries caused Bury to make major changes in his view of the Trojan War. In his 1913 revised edition, Bury presents the Trojan War as a historical occurrence rather than myth.

In the following excerpt from chapter 1 of the 1913 edition, Bury outlines the political power in the Aegean enjoyed by Troy, and the interest of the Achaeans, or Greeks, in expanding their territory eastward, where Troy held sway. Bury presents Priam of Troy and Agamemnon of Mycenae as historical military figures.

His footnote 35 shows that he entertains the possibility of an actual abduction of Helen by Paris, though he makes plain that such an event would not have been the real or major reason for the attack on Troy by the Greeks.

FROM JOHN BAGNELL BURY, *A HISTORY OF GREECE*

(New York: The Modern Library, 1927)

The policy of Troy was to levy a toll upon all the traffic which converged on the Hellespontine shores. It has been conjectured that there was held a great yearly market in the Trojan plain, to which traders from all quarters came by sea or land with their merchandise, an arrangement which was exceedingly profitable to the Trojan king who received the market dues. But there is no evidence for such a yearly international gathering at Troy.[34]

But while, in the absence of any positive evidence, we cannot accept this particular theory, it is clear that a strong power, entrenched at the entrance of the Dardanelles, could interfere with the free access of other powers to the Propontis and the Euxine. That Troy had been found to be an obstacle to Greek enterprise in those seas may well be reflected in the legend of the sack of Troy by Heracles, which was connected with the story of the Argonauts. Heracles embarked at Iolcus with the other heroes in the Argo, and leaving the ship during the voyage destroyed Troy, of which Laomedon, Priam's father, was king.

Troy was the strongest power on the west coast of Asia Minor, and it was to the interest of Troy in the north, and of Lycia in the south, to oppose attempts of the Achaeans to expand eastward. That they desired to make settlements on the Asiatic coasts and adjacent islands is shown by the fact that such settlements began soon after the fall of Troy.

It was probably at the beginning of the twelfth century that the Achaeans made ready a great expedition to exterminate the power which was the chief obstacle to eastward expansion.[35] It is uncertain how far the Greek states of the time can be described as a federation or an empire, but most of them recognised the supremacy of Mycenae, and there seems no reason to doubt that the Achaean king of Mycenae, whose name was Agamemnon, son of Atreus, succeeded in enlisting the co-operation of the chief kings and princes of northern as well as southern Greece; it looks, indeed, as if the Achaean lords of Phthia and Thessaly—the country from which the Argo sailed—had a particular interest in the enterprise. All sailed to the plain of Troy. The peoples of the west coast of Asia, including the Lycians, all rallied to the help of Priam. It was a war between both sides of the Aegean Sea. According to the tradition of the poets the siege lasted nine years; and, however it came about, Priam's city was destroyed. Its fall was the necessary prelude to the opening of the Propontis and the Euxine sea to Greek enterprise, and Greek colonisation on the eastern coasts and islands of the Aegean would soon begin. The hill of Troy would be again inhabited, but it would be of small importance, little more than a place of famous memories.

Sect. 5. The Homeric Poems

The later period of the heroic age, its manners of life, its material environment, its social organisation, its political geography, are reflected in the Homeric poems. Although the poets who composed the *Iliad* and the *Odyssey* probably did not live before the ninth century, they derived their matter from older lays which must have belonged to the generations immediately succeeding the Trojan War. After the age of bronze had passed away, and the conditions of life and the political shape of the Greek world had been utterly changed, it would have been impossible for any one, however imaginative,—unless he were a scientific antiquarian with abundance of records at his command,—to create a consistent picture of a vanished civilisation. And the picture which Homer presents is a consistent picture, closely corresponding, in its main features and in remarkable details, to the evidence which has been recently recovered from the earth and described in the foregoing pages. (41–42, 43)

NOTES

34. It is to be observed that in the Trojan War the various peoples whose merchandise came to the Hellespont appear to have been the allies of Troy.
35. It is quite possible that the motive which the poets assigned for the Trojan War—to recover Helen, the wife of Menelaus, king of Sparta, carried off by Paris, son of Priam—had some historical basis; but if such an incident occurred, it served only as a pretext for the war.

LEVEL VIIA AT HISSARLIK AS THE SITE OF THE TROJAN WAR

Carl W. Blegen, the first prominent American archaeologist of the Aegean area, received support from the Cincinnati Archaeological Expedition to direct excavations at Troy from 1932 to 1938.

The following excerpt from the book in which Blegen collected his reports of the expedition indicates the reasons for his conclusions that level VIIa on Hissarlik was the site of the Trojan War, and that the date of the war should be revised to around 1260 B.C.

His evidence rests on what he found at the site: skeletons, in many places, of people who had met with violent deaths; the wholesale storage of supplies that suggested a siege; and the evidence of forcible entries and burned buildings.

The history supported by archaeology, he concludes, is more compatible with the myth of the Trojan War than had been earlier supposed. Here was evidence of what a man like Odysseus and his fellow warriors had perpetrated: slaughter and pillage that had provoked the gods to thwart them at every turn in their attempts to return home.

FROM CARL W. BLEGEN, *TROY AND THE TROJANS*

(New York: Frederick A. Praeger, 1963)

The overthrow of Settlement VIIa must surely have been brought about by 1250 B.C., if not a decade or two earlier.

Whatever the precise date, the destruction was undoubtedly the work of human agency, and it was accompanied by violence and by fire. A great mass of stones and crude brick, along with other burned and blackened debris, was heaped up over the ruined houses as well as in the street. ... On the western slope of the hill outside the acropolis wall ... a skeleton was found. ... The skull had been crushed and the lower jaw broken away. Were these the remains of a victim, either an attacker or a defender, who was killed in the struggle that preceded the capture of the town? ...

In any event the cumulative evidence seems to me to be sufficient to demonstrate that fighting and killing must have accompanied the destruction of Troy VIIa. ... The fire-blackened wreckage and ruins of the settlement offer a vivid picture of the harsh fate that was regularly meted out to a town besieged, captured and looted by implacable enemies, as is so graphically described in the accounts of marauding expeditions in the Homeric poems, when the men were ruthlessly slain and the women and children carried off into slavery.

Here, then, in the extreme northwestern corner of Asia Minor—exactly where Greek tradition, folk memory and the epic poems place the site of Ilios—we have the physical remains of a fortified stronghold, obviously the capital of the region. As shown by persuasive archaeological evidence, it was besieged and captured by enemies and destroyed by fire, no doubt after having been thoroughly pillaged, just as Hellenic poetry and folk-tale describe the destruction of King Priam's Troy. (160–162)

TOPICS FOR DISCUSSION AND EXPLORATION

1. Write a paper on each of the references to the Trojan War in *The Odyssey* and the context in which the reference occurs.
2. Can Athena's actions in *The Odyssey* be partially explained as the result of the beauty contest? Discuss fully.
3. Examine references to Helen in both *The Iliad* and *The Odyssey*. Stage a debate on the following proposition: Helen of Troy is personally blameless in the story of the Trojan War.
4. Write a paper on the complex motivation of Clytemnestra in the killing of Agamemnon. Don't forget to consider the fates of Iphigenia and Cassandra.
5. Why do you suppose Homer makes no mention of Iphigenia in his epics?
6. Write an essay on Achilles' remarks to Odysseus in the Land of the Dead. How does what we know of him in the Trojan War intensify the impact of his comments?
7. What effect is achieved by Homer's ending *The Iliad* with reference to Hector rather than one of the Greeks? By doing additional research, contrast Achilles and Hector.
8. How does the part Odysseus plays in negotiating an agreement with Helen's suitors, his part in securing the services of Achilles as a warrior, and his part in contriving the wooden horse underscore the characteristics he displays in *The Odyssey*?
9. What parts of the story of the Trojan War are clearly supernatural rather than historical?
10. How does the language of Herodotus reveal what he thinks of Paris Alexander?
11. Investigate the way in which classical Greek dramatists interpreted the Trojan War by having different class members read relevant Greek tragedies and report on them: *Agamemnon* and *Choëphoroe* by Aeschylus; *Ajax* and *Electra* by Sophocles; and, especially, *Andromache, Hecuba, The Trojan Women, Iphigenia in Tauris, Electra, Helena*, and *Iphigenia in Aulis* by Euripides.

SUGGESTIONS FOR FURTHER READING

Burgess, Jonathan S. *The Tradition of the Trojan War in Homer and the Epic Cycle.* Baltimore: Johns Hopkins University Press, 2001.

Erskine, Andrew. *Troy Between Greece and Rome.* New York: Oxford University Press, 2001.

Foxhall, Lin, and John K. Davies, eds. *The Trojan War: Greenbank Colloquium.* Bristol, UK: Bristol Classical Press, 1984.

Owen, E.T. *The Story of the Iliad.* New York: Oxford University Press, 1947.

Quintas, Smyrnaeus. *The Fall of Troy.* Trans. Arthur S. Way. Cambridge, MA: W. Heineman, 1962.

Redfield, James M. *Nature and Culture in the Iliad.* Durham, NC: Duke University Press, 1994.

Whitman, C.H. *Homer and the Homeric Tradition.* Cambridge, MA: Harvard University Press, 1958.

Wood, Michael. *In Search of the Trojan War.* Berkeley: University of California Press, 1998.

Woodford, Susan. *The Trojan War in Ancient Art.* Ithaca, NY: Cornell University Press, 1993.

7

Supporting Players in *The Odyssey*: The Underclasses

Homer's epics focused on the exploits of heroes—men of such noble birth that some of them were presumed to be the descendants of gods. The central characters of both *The Iliad* and *The Odyssey* are rulers who live in vast, luxurious palaces and have fleets of ships at their disposal. But constantly in the background, and sometimes in the foreground, of *The Odyssey* are the Greek underclasses who make the lives of the heroes possible: servants, farmers, entertainers, and artisans, many of whom are slaves bought or captured from other countries.

The world of Odysseus was fundamentally militaristic, and society was rigidly organized along the lines of military rank. At the head of the class hierarchy of the Mycenaean society, as it is portrayed in *The Odyssey*, were the kings. All the great warriors of Homer's *The Iliad*, including those who surface in *The Odyssey*, were kings of different Greek communities. The kings were supported by young noblemen, most of whom formed the military. These kings and noblemen invariably had confiscated all of the good land, in a country where most of the land was extremely poor. Below the nobles were the *damos*, meaning the common people. In this class were doctors, bureaucrats, scribes, bakers, carpenters, potters, weavers, merchants, and blacksmiths. (But even many who performed these specialized jobs were not free men and women, but slaves.) The scorn with which noblemen regarded the merchants is found in book VIII of *The Odyssey* when a member of King Alcinoos' court taunts and insults Odysseus by saying that he suspects Odysseus isn't the kind

Etching on a silver vase of the Mycenaean period showing the siege of a city by warriors attacking with bows and spears. On the wall a group of women, who will likely be carried away as slaves if the siege is successful, are seen waving their arms in distress or in supplication to the gods. *Source:* Hill, G.F. *Illustrations of School Classics.* London: Macmillan, 1903, 359.

of person capable of performing athletics feats expected of the high born, but is just a greedy merchant who oversees cargoes.

Beneath the common people were the peasants, mainly farmers in the employ of noblemen or owners of small plots of their own land. Below the peasants were the slaves, who usually were attached to a household. No matter what their occupation or their personal status, slaves were not regarded as real people. They were property, like cattle or pieces of armor. And even lower than the slaves were the *thetes*, wandering laborers who were unattached to any house or place. As time passed and hard times came, the rich landowners became richer and the poor became poorer, freemen often becoming slaves or virtual slaves to the landowners as a result of contracts that gave wealthy landowners four-fifths of their produce.

Servants are mentioned in what emerges as a pattern of duties in the households of Odysseus/Telemachos, Nestor, Menelaos, and Alcinoos. In each case,

Supporting Players in *The Odyssey*: The Underclasses

heralds, a seemingly higher level of servants, attend the kings. Handmaidens constantly accompany and serve the mistress of the household. A crew of servants, mostly female, prepare meals, pour the wine, serve the bread, and pour water for washing hands. Serving maids also bathe the nobility and their guests, rub them with oil, and adorn them with clothes. At night, they prepare the beds of their masters and guests of the court. Telemachos' lifelong servant puts him to bed and hangs up his clothes. Homer tells us that both Odysseus and King Alcinoos have at least fifty serving maids in their households. In addition, a number of women in the household are responsible for the growing of grain and the making of bread. Women servants are also occupied full time in spinning and weaving cloth. Records from Pylos, home of King Nestor of *The Odyssey*, suggest that women who participated in the making of cloth, and in the growing and grinding of grain for the palace household, may have numbered in the hundreds.

Men servants took care of horses, pigs, and goats. The court singers were also servants in the various courts. Rarely mentioned specifically in *The Odyssey* were the men conscripted to fight the battles of the kings, but it stands to reason that not all of the hundreds of Greek warriors who fought in the Trojan War were of noble birth. Although the abduction of Helen probably had nothing to do with the lives of most of the men, many across class lines obviously perished as cannon fodder on the plains of Troy and on the treacherous trip home. Odysseus, who commanded many ships in the Trojan War, lost every one of his men. He alone survived to return to Ithaca.

The reader sees some evidence of the community's resentment of Odysseus in taking away their men for this battle in which they had little interest. To make matters worse, Odysseus' own arrogance and intellectual curiosity had cost many of those lives. The brutal class system of the ancient Greek military is validated by Homer's *The Iliad* when Achilles, in his childish pique, allows his men, the Myrmidons, to be sent into battle without himself leading them, thereby condemning them to be slaughtered on the battlefield. Achilles even appeals to the gods that all his fellow *Achaians* may die in great numbers, to prove to them his own invincibility as a leader.

A considerable portion of servants in the households are slaves, stolen from other countries or bought from sailors trafficking in slaves. Excavations of palaces and burial sites, and tablets inventorying their goods, provide ample evidence that Greek kings had insatiable appetites for luxurious furnishings and high living, felt compelled to memorialize themselves by constructing colossal graves, and continually waged wars and mounted raids, not only to steal greater treasures but also to enhance their reputations. Moreover, in upper-class Greek society, war was glorified, leisure was idealized, and work was demeaned. Such lives could be supported only by armies of slaves who had to be continually replenished by raiding parties. The main purpose of the pirate raids on other countries was to steal treasure and to procure slaves who would become part of the workforce in the huge households of the aristocracy.

Our first hint of this in *The Odyssey* is from the mouth of Telemachos, who declares that he will be lord "over the servants that Odysseus *won* for me" (italics added). When Telemachos visits the court of Nestor, seeking information about his father, Nestor tells him of taking treasure and women in their ships after the defeat of Troy, and Odysseus later tells the court of King Alcinoos that he and his men took women and many possessions when they sacked Ismaros after leaving Troy. Passing references are also made to Cassandra, daughter of Troy's King Priam, who is taken forcibly as a concubine by Agamemnon after the Trojan War. Although a few male slaves were purchased from slave traders, most of the slaves were females captured in wars. Men defeated in battle were invariably killed. Records from Pylos and other cities indicate that slaves were provided rations of about twenty-four liters a month of wheat and figs. This is equivalent to about twenty-five quarts of food a month.

One category in the social hierarchy was on an even lower level than the slave. The *thes* was at the very bottom of the social strata because he or she was not connected to any particular household in the performance of regular work. The *thes* was similar to a hobo or a migrant worker. There are two noteworthy mentions of *thetes* or a *thes* in *The Odyssey*. The first is when Achilles, in the Land of the Dead, tells Odysseus that he would rather work on earth as the lowest *thes* for a poor man than to be an honored, noble hero in the Land of the Dead. The second mention occurs after Odysseus has returned to Ithaca as a stranger, and one of the suitors taunts him with an offer of work as a *thes*. Odysseus and others present view this as an unforgivable, mortifying insult.

Several episodes in *The Odyssey* humanize those who must live by serving others. They actually have names and stories, and often are important to the action of the epic. Homer names Pheneios and Demodocos, both singers like himself. Others receive passing mention by name: Eteoneos and Asphalion are servants of Menelaos; Adreste, Alcippe, and Phylo are servants of Helen; Medon and Dolios are servants in the house of Odysseus; Eurymedousa, an old woman who was stolen as a prize when she was young, is the chambermaid of Arete, wife of King Alcinoos; and Pontonoos is the herald of King Alcinoos.

The two servants most central to the action of the epic are also those whose origins are related by Homer. Eurycleia, an aged woman who reared both Odysseus and Telemachos, was in her youth bought for twenty head of cattle by Laertes, Odysseus' father. Laertes has made a point of saying that he never lay with her, as if sexual relations with female slaves was a commonly expected practice. It is she who puts Telemachos to bed, she in whom he confides about his trip to find out about his father, and she who washes Odysseus at Penelope's request and recognizes him from a scar he received as a child. Odysseus also depends upon her to keep his secret and to help him in identifying those servants who have been disloyal by fraternizing with the suitors.

The swineherd Eumaeos also has a major place in the action. In book XV, he enlarges on his origins, revealing the ironical domino effect of slavery as it was practiced. Once he was the princely young son of a father who ruled two cities on the island of Syria. The boy's maidservant was a Phoenician slave, kidnapped from home and sold. She agrees to steal treasure, as well as the son of the king, and turn them over to Phoenician sailors in return for passage to her homeland. She loses her life en route, and the Phoenicians bring the boy, Eumaeos, to Ithaca, where they sell him to Laertes. Although Eumaeos has long since given up hope of ever seeing his homeland and parents, he has not ceased grieving for them. The twist on the subject of slavery continues as we learn that Eumaeos himself has a slave named Mesaulios, "bought from the Taphians with his own resources" (book XIV).

Odysseus, in a curious false tale he contrives for Eumaeos, claims that he is the son of "a bought mother, a concubine," and that he was captured by a Phoenician and sold by him as a slave for an immense price (book XIV).

When Odysseus lands at Ithaca, those he seeks out and trusts are his slaves Eumaeos and Eurycleia, and his son, Telemachos. He makes no appeal for assistance to anyone else. While these servants are shown to be trustworthy people of character, others are painted as disloyal and are, as a consequence, treated brutally. The twelve serving women whom Eurycleia identifies as having dishonored the household are made to clean the hall and clear it of the corpses of the suitors, and then are hanged. Melanthios, the goatherd who had insulted and challenged Odysseus, has his nose and ears lopped off, his genitals torn off and fed to the dogs, and his hands and feet chopped off.

The following documents are excerpts from Hesiod's *Works and Days*, Hesiod providing the only written record of life in Homeric Greece other than Homer; Michael Wood's summation of archaeological materials on the capture of slave women by Greeks; and Aristotle's arguments in defense of slavery in his *Politics*.

LIFE AND WORK IN ANCIENT GREECE

Most of what we know about the ancient world of Greece comes from two sources: Homer, who wrote of the lives and battles of the aristocratic warrior kings, and Hesiod, who lived shortly after Homer and gives us our only picture of the common people in *Works and Days*. Hesiod, born in Boeotia, the son of a sea merchant and farmer, was a poet who earned his living as a hardworking farmer.

Works and Days is addressed to his shiftless brother Perses, who died in poverty despite having bribed a judge to award him a greater share of their father's inheritance, and despite Hesiod's brotherly advice.

Selections from *Works and Days*, which probably was written in the middle of the ninth century B.C., contain a view of life and work in Greece that is contrary to that of Homer's warrior kings like Odysseus. Here the focus is on the independent farmer, the merchant, and the artisan rather than the warrior/ruler. Even the characters here, however, are assumed, like the king, to own slaves and servants. The real difference appears to be in the work ethic recommended for the common man.

FROM HESIOD, *WORKS AND DAYS* IN *HESIOD*, TRANS. HUGH G. EVELYN-WHITE

(Cambridge, MA: Harvard University Press, 1914)

Perses, lay up these things in your heart, and do not let that Strife who delights in mischief hold your heart back from work, while you peep and peer and listen to the wrangles of the court-house. Little concern has he with quarrels and courts who has not a year's vituals laid up betimes, even that which the earth bears, Demeter's grain. When you have got plenty of that, you can raise disputes and strive to get another's goods.

...

For now truly is a race of iron, and men never rest from labour and sorrow by day, and from perishing by night; and the gods shall lay sore trouble upon them.

...

Both gods and men are angry with a man who lives idle, for in nature he is like the stingless drones who waste the labour of the bees, eating without working; and let it be your care to order your work properly, that in the right season your barns may be full of victual. Through work men grow rich in flocks and substance, and working they are much better loved by the immortals. Work is no disgrace: it is idleness which is a disgrace. ...

Wealth should not be seized: god-given wealth is much better; for if a man take great wealth violently and perforce, or if he steal it through his tongue, as often happens when gain deceives men's sense and dishonour tramples down honour, the gods soon blot him out and make that man's house low, and wealth attends him only for a little while.

First of all, get a house, and a woman and an ox for the plough—a slave woman and not a wife, to follow the oxen as well—and make everything ready at home, so that you may not have to ask of another.

...

Set your slaves to winnow Demeter's holy grain, when strong Orion [July] first appears, on a smooth threshing-floor in an airy place. Then measure it and store it in jars. And as soon as you have safely stored all your stuff indooors, I bid you put your bondman out of doors and look out a servant-girl with no children;—for a servant with a child to nurse is troublesome.

...

But if desire for uncomfortable sea-faring seize you; when the Pleiades plunge into the misty sea to escape Orion's rude strength, then truly gales of all kinds rage. Then keep ships no longer on the sparkling sea, but bethink you to till the land as I bid you. ... You yourself wait until the season for sailing is come, and then haul your swift ship down to the sea and stow a convenient cargo in it, so that you may bring home profit, even as your father and mine, foolish Perses, used to sail on shipboard because he lacked sufficient livelihood. (5, 15, 25, 27, 33, 47, 49)

THE WORKFORCE AND PIRACY

The following excerpt from Michael Wood's search for evidence of a Trojan War in both Greece and Anatolia explains the relationship between the workforce and piracy in Greece. Using the Linear B documents translated by Michael Ventris, the decorated pottery, and the sites of palaces unearthed, Wood relates some of the details regarding slaves in Myceneae, posits reasons why so many military expeditions were launched to bring home enslaved captives, and relates the widespread Greek piracy in Anatolia to the story of the Trojan War.

FROM MICHAEL WOOD, *IN SEARCH OF THE TROJAN WAR*

(New York: Facts on File, 1985)

In the Linear B tablets there is one remarkable body of evidence which has not been exploited in the search for the Trojan War. At Pylos in particular groups of women are recorded doing menial tasks such as grinding corn, preparing flax and spinning. Their ration quotas suggest that they are to be numbered in hundreds. Many are distinguished by ethnic adjectives, presumably denoting the places they came from, and though some of these are still not understood, several of the women come from eastern Aegean [Troy and settlements south of Troy]. ... The Pylos tablets name 700 women, with their 400 girls and 300 boys, and another 300 men and boys who "belong to them." ...

These tablets are vivid evidence for the predatory nature of Mycenaean expansion in the eastern Aegean. The women must either have been captured on pirate raids, or bought from slave dealers in entrepots such as Miletus. The fact that they are usually mentioned with their children but not with men implies the familiar raiding pattern of the sackers of cities, where the men are killed and the women carried off. The *Iliad* and the tablets complement each other here in a remarkable way, and it must be assumed that Homer is here again preserving a genuine Bronze-Age memory. ...

We must not forget the women (after all, the legend insists that the seizure of a woman was the cause of the Trojan War). Time and again Homer tells of the fight for "the city and its women." When Achilles tells Odysseus of the twenty-three cities he has sacked he mentions only "treasure and women" as his gain. This is what makes him proud, and gives him fame after his death. And the more beautiful the women, the better. ... This was what ensured the victorious king a large following, and it guaranteed their loyalty. (159–161)

ARISTOTLE'S *POLITICS* ON SLAVERY

The Greek philosopher Aristotle, born in 384 B.C. and often cited as the greatest thinker in the history of the world, revolutionized science and wrote profoundly influential texts in almost every area of human endeavor: not only science but also theology, literature, philosophy, and political thought.

His *Politics*, from which the following excerpts are taken, proposes an ideal society whose government will promote the best and happiest conditions for its citizens and the state. The excerpts, however, suggest that the citizens whose well-being the state promotes, and whom Aristotle sees as existing for the good of the state, do not include a large population of human beings who are enslaved and who exist to make life easier for others.

Thus, we see that even in the so-called enlightened period of Greek history, some four hundred years after Homer, the slavery that had flourished with the piracy of the Mycenaean kings like Agamemnon and Odysseus was still very much in existence, and was even being justified by the great ethicist Aristotle.

FROM ARISTOTLE, *POLITICS*, TRANSLATED BY HARRIS RACKHAM

(Cambridge, MA: Harvard University Press, 1944)

4

Now property is part of a household and the acquisition of property part of the economics of a household; for neither life itself nor the good life is possible without a certain minimum standard of wealth. ... So any piece of property can be regarded as a tool enabling a man to live; and his property is an assemblage of such tools, including his slaves; and a slave, being a living creature like any other servant, is a tool worth many tools.

...

A piece of property is sometimes spoken of as a part; for a part is not only part of something but wholly belongs to it, as does a piece of property. So a slave is not only his master's slave but wholly his master's property, while the master is his slave's master but does not belong to him. These considerations will have shown what are the nature and functions of the slave: any human being that by nature belongs not to himself but to another is by nature a slave; and a human being belongs to another whenever he is a piece of human property, that is a tool or instrument having a separate existence and useful for the purposes of living.

5

But whether anyone does in fact by nature answer to this description, and whether or not it is a good and a right thing for one to be a slave to another, and whether we should not regard all slavery as contrary to nature—these are questions which must next be considered.

Neither theoretical discussion nor empirical observation presents any difficulty. There can be no objection in principle to the mere fact that one should command and another obey; that is both necessary and expedient. Indeed some things are so divided right from birth, some to rule, some to be ruled. There are many different forms of this ruler-ruled relationship and they are to be found everywhere.

...

We may therefore say that wherever there is the same wide discrepancy between two sets of human beings as there is between mind and body or between man and beast, then the inferior of the two sets, those whose condition is such that their function is the use of their bodies and nothing better can be expected of them, those, I say, are slaves by nature. It is better for them, just as in the analogous cases mentioned, to be thus ruled and subject.

The "slave by nature" then is he that can and therefore does belong to another, and he that participates in the reasoning faculty so far as to understand but not so as to possess it. For the other animals serve their owner not by exercise of reason but passively. The use, too, of slaves hardly differs at all from that of domestic animals; from both we derive that which is essential for our bodily needs. It is then part of nature's intention to make the bodies of free men to differ from those of slaves, the latter strong enough for the necessary menial tasks, the former erect and useless for that kind of work, but well suited for the life of a citizen of a state, a life divided between war and peace. . . . It is clear then that by nature some are free, others slaves, and that for these it is both right and expedient that they should serve as slaves.

8

Let us then, since the slave is part of the property, go on to consider the acquisition of property and moneymaking in general, still following our usual analytical method. . . . If then we are right in believing that nature makes nothing without some end in view, nothing to no purpose, it must be that nature has made all things specifically for the sake of man. This means that it is part of nature's plan that the art of war, of which hunting is a part, should be a way of acquiring property; and that it must be used both against wild beasts and against such men as are by nature intended to be ruled over but refuse; for that is the kind of warfare which is by nature right. (31, 32, 33, 34, 40)

PROJECTS AND QUESTIONS FOR ORAL AND WRITTEN CONSIDERATION

1. Assume you are a man who went to the Trojan War with Odysseus. Write a diary of your complaints about your leader.

2. For what reason may Homer have had Odysseus assume the identity of a son of a slave?

3. Homer, like the singers mentioned in *The Odyssey*, depended on the nobility of the region for his livelihood. Write an essay analyzing his point of view as a direct result of this necessity. Are there any hints that Homer may not have shared the views of the aristocracy for which he wrote?

4. Write an essay analyzing the assumptions on which Aristotle bases his defense of slavery. Then write a logical response to his argument.

5. Reread Euripides' *The Trojan Women*. Write an essay comparing Homer's point of view with that of Euripides.

SUGGESTIONS FOR FURTHER READING

Austin, M.M., and P. Vidal-Naquet. *Economic and Social History of Ancient Greece.* Berkeley: University of California Press, 1977.

Chadwick, John. *The Mycenaean World.* Cambridge: Cambridge University Press, 1976.

De Saint Croix, Geoffrey E.M. *The Class Struggle in the Ancient Greek World.* Ithaca, NY: Cornell University Press, 1981.

Finley, M.I. *The World of Odysseus.* Rev. ed. New York: Viking Press, 1965.

Garland, Robert. *Daily Life of the Ancient Greeks.* Westport, CT: Greenwood, 1998.

Garland, Yvon. *Slavery in Ancient Greece.* Ithaca, NY: Cornell University Press, 1988.

Glotz, Gustave. *The Ancient Greek World at Work.* New York: Alfred A. Knopf, 1926.

Grant, Michael. *A Social History of Greece and Rome.* New York: Scribner's, 1992.

Hooker, J.T. *Mycenaean Greece.* London: Routledge and Kegan Paul, 1976.

Lacey, W.K. *The Family in Classical Greece.* London: Thames and Hudson, 1968.

Snodgrass, Anthony. *The Dark Age of Greece.* Edinburgh: Edinburgh University Press, 1971.

Thalmann, William G. *The Swineherd and the Bow.* Ithaca, NY: Cornell University Press, 1998.

Wace, A.J.B. *Mycenae: An Archaeological History and Guide.* Princeton, NJ: Princeton University Press, 1949.

8

Modern Applications: The Problem of Revenge

A theme of revenge or retribution runs through *The Odyssey* like an endless row of falling dominos, one action leading to another ad infinitum. Revenge and counterrevenge, along with the endless violence that it inevitably entails, pervades all the myths and the histories of ancient Greece, and even of the modern world.

Revenge would seem to be endemic to life itself, on its lowest level an animalic impulse connected to self-defense. To this the human animal added premeditation and the desire to seek vengeance for wrongs done, not only to one's self but also to those to whom one is intimately connected—the family and the clan. Revenge came to be regarded, by Homer's time, not as the low response of the brute but as a sacred duty owed one's kin and friends, and as proof of personal honor. In the days of Odysseus, it was the duty of the male members of the family to exact retribution. It was regarded as despicable and cowardly to shirk that obligation. The "justice" exacted through retribution was largely a private affair—for example, if someone had killed a member of your family group or had invaded your home with the clear intent of taking it over and killing you.

There is, in *The Odyssey*, no written law, no policeman on the corner, and no system of justice to handle retribution. Justice is personal, tribal, and has the effect of divine law.

In Homer's epics, the heroes learn from the gods to exact vengeance—divine retribution—to defend their honor. Thus Athena sides with the Greeks in the Trojan War purely for revenge against Paris because he had not awarded her the golden apple in the beauty contest; and Poseidon, seeking vengeance against Odysseus for blinding his son Polyphemos, throws up every possible obstacle to Odysseus in his long attempt to reach home.

The most pronounced acts of vengeance, however, are played out in blood, in the story of Agamemnon and in the story of Odysseus and Penelope's suitors. Agamemnon's story and the revenge of Orestes, referred to repeatedly in *The Odyssey* as a warning to Odysseus and as an example for Telemachos to emulate, is the archtypal example of the endless horror generated by vengeance. One can see clearly how one vengeful act leads fatally to another:

1. Pelops, son of Tantalus, kills Myrtilus, whom he had had bribed in order to win a contest and a wife.
2. This brings about the vengeance of Hermes, Myrtilus' father, who damns Pelops' family by setting two of his sons against each other.
3. Thyestes, feeling that he has been wronged (see the myth of the House of Atreus), arrogantly wrenches control of the throne from his brother Atreus.
4. Atreus overcomes and banishes Thyestes; later, seeking vengeance for his attempt at the throne and the seduction of his wife, he lures his brother back with false promises, then secretly kills Thyestes' children and feeds them to their father in a stew. Vengeance against Atreus is ensured when he gloats over the deed that he has perpetrated.
5. Aegisthus, Thyestes' remaining son, achieves his own revenge. While the son of Atreus, Agamemnon, is away fighting the Trojan War, Aegisthus seduces Agamemnon's wife, Clytemnestra (who has her own pattern of deep revenge to enact), jointly assumes control of the throne of Mycenae with her, and finally, upon Agamemnon's return, murders him in a bathtub.
6. Clytemnestra has reason of her own to seek revenge because her husband, the great warrior Agamemnon, had murdered her first husband and her infant son, and then had sacrificed their daughter Iphigenia at Aulis to achieve favorable winds from an offended goddess, who was herself thus seeking revenge. (In *The Odyssey*, however, it is clearly Aegisthus alone who murders Agamemnon.)
7. Then Orestes, the son of Agamemnon and Clytemnestra, avenges his father's murder by killing both Aegisthus and Clytemnestra.

From the first book of *The Odyssey*, Telemachos anticipates with great hope his father's return, even after twenty years, for he hates what the ravaging suitors have done and he wants his own revenge. The last twelve books of the epic concern Odysseus' single-minded efforts to reach home, plan and execute vengeance upon the suitors who have, as he has been learning from the goddess Athena, harassed Penelope, humiliated Telemachos, and corrupted his servants, and are presently consuming his fortune. The story of Agamemnon spurs Odysseus onward to a personal, merciless revenge against the suitors and their collaborators who now lie in wait to murder him—if he should be so foolish as to return unarmed and innocently expecting the world that he had left twenty years before to have stood still while he was away. He eventually learns that in this community, he is regarded by many as one who brought them nothing but death and heartache, as the playwright Aeschylus puts it in *Agamemnon*, in a war to regain another man's runaway wife.

For Odysseus and Telemachus, Orestes stands as an example of honorable revenge privately executed (as was expected by the values of the time) and honorably received by his compatriots, a feat for which Orestes becomes a hero. In this he is urged on by Athena, the warlike goddess of wisdom. In short, all the values of the time spur Odysseus onward: the gods, the customs of the time, his personal desire for vengeance, and his hopeless love of physical engagement.

Events of the sixth century B.C., when the city-state of Athens came close to disaster, would lead to a revolutionary change in the concept of vengeance. The oligarchs, who had replaced kings, favored government by the few in a society rigidly, deeply divided into a hierarchy without the semblance of justice, a society in which the rich became fewer, more powerful, and more repressive, and the poor became more numerous, oppressed, and rebellious.

Into this situation stepped an Athenian statesman, Draco, who was commissioned (ca. 620 B.C.) to restore order. His chief contribution was to codify the laws; to institute for the first time a series of written laws. His written laws attempted to take retribution out of the hands of individual family members and made it a responsibility of the city-state. Homicide, even for revenge, became illegal. Though he enacted needed reforms, his punishments were so harsh and cruel that he added his name to history in the form of a word—"draconian"—meaning impossibly brutal. As the ancient historian Plutarch wrote, stealing an apple or a cabbage was punishable by death, as was murder.

Draco was followed (ca. 638–558 B.C.) by Solon, a man whose reforms somewhat ameliorated Draco's harshness, and were so effective that his name has come to mean "a wise lawgiver."

ORESTES AND AESCHYLUS

The dramatization of the Agamemnon/Orestes story by Aeschylus (525–456 B.C.), one of Greece's leading playwrights, explores the evolution of the idea of revenge in classical Greece. By the time Aeschylus arose, Solon's Athenian law was already instituted. And his trilogy titled *The Oresteia*, meaning the story of Orestes, was written in praise of that law and assumed a system of justice in which private revenge was no longer publicly approved.

The first play, *Agamemnon*, deals with the great king's homecoming after the victory over Troy and his murder by Clytemnestra and her lover, Aegisthus. In *Choephoroi* (The Libation Bearers), Orestes returns to exact his own revenge: he must kill the murderer of his father. In this case, however, the killer is his mother, so Orestes faces a dilemma: according to accepted custom, he *must* avenge his father's death; but at the same time, by the same unbreakable code, he *cannot* shed the blood of a parent. Orestes gets his revenge, as commanded by Apollo, and is thereafter haunted by the Furies for his unforgivable crime of matricide. They will haunt him forever and drive him mad. *Eumenides* shows Orestes having retreated to Athens to appeal to Athena, the patron goddess of the city, to ease his constant pain. This third play of the trilogy takes the form of a court trial, with the Furies as the prosecution, advocating continued punishment; Apollo as the defense attorney, noting that Orestes acted justly in avenging his father's murder; and Athena as the judge. The jury (twelve people of Athens) renders a split decision—six for and six against—allowing Athena the deciding vote in favor Orestes. His punishment is eased and the Furies are given a new title, Eumenides, which means "the kindly ones."

The trilogy is actually a panegyric to Athenian law. It shows the evolution of justice, both among the gods on Olympus and among mortals on earth. In the former, the reign of Cronos had led ultimately to that of Zeus, who for Aeschylus stands for justice.

THE JUDEO-CHRISTIAN TRADITION

The subject of vengeance is repeatedly raised in Judeo-Christian scriptures. While a vengeful God rules the universe and himself takes vengeance, He attempts theoretically to take revenge out of the hands of the individual. Thus Deuteronomy 32:35, of the King James version of the Bible, states, "To me belongeth vengeance, and recompence." The same sentiments are expressed in other Old Testament books, including Psalm 94:1, and Jeremiah 51:6. If vengeance was to be exacted, it was to be undertaken by God, not man, a concept that is carried through in the New Testament. In Romans 12:19, the apostle Paul writes, "Dearly beloved, avenge not yourselves, but rather give place unto wrath: for it is written, Vengeance is mine: I will repay, saith the Lord." Part of the teaching of Jesus of Nazareth was to counter the endless pattern of revenge with forgiveness. Instead of hatred and so-called heroic slaughter, as one finds in *The Odyssey*, he preached peace, love, and nonviolence. The following lines are verses 38, 39, 43, and 44 from the fifth chapter of Matthew:

Ye have heard that it hath been said, An eye for an eye, and a tooth for a tooth: But I say unto you, That ye resist not evil: but whosoever shall smite thee on thy right cheek, turn to him the other also.

...

Ye have heard that it hath been said, Thou shalt love thy neighbor and hate thine enemy.
  But I say unto you, Love your enemies, bless them that curse you, and do good to them that hate you, and pray for them which despitefully use you, and persecute you.

PROBLEMS WITH THE LAW OF THE STATE

Yet even as the law of the state intervened to halt a destructive cycle of vindictive slaughter, serious problems remained.

For one thing, the state's laws were concerned above all with keeping order to preserve the state, not necessarily and not primarily with achieving justice for all. So while the laws claim the right to mediate and punish, they may not necessarily satisfy the personal need for retribution or justice.

Moreover, the law of the state, which is charged with retribution, is often polluted with the old patterns of class distinctions. In the first place, peasants usually did not have access to the courts to settle grievances against their superiors. In rare cases, when the poor could enter a court case against a rich person, justice was not meted out impartially.

Even when, as is stated in the U.S. Declaration of Independence, a nation was formed on the stated belief that "all men are created equal" and in theory have equal access to the law and retribution by the courts, the question of inherent rights continued to be a problem. The U.S. founding fathers intended "men" to mean men of property, not just anybody. And certain "inalienable rights"—like the rights to vote, to hold public office, to serve on juries, to own property—were often denied to at least half the human race, namely women. Nor did "men" include members of races other than Caucasian.

When the state is corrupt, its courts are corrupt. And the inability to find justice through retribution in the courts leads to the creation of the heroic and popular outlaw who seeks justice outside the system. Sometimes it leads to a complete social disruption or revolution.

Further problems are created when powerful groups outside the law, whether or not their grievances are defensible, like the Irish Republican Army or the Muslim fanatics in the Middle East, take retribution into their own hands.

Often even small subcultures, like the Mafia or youth gangs, operate like nations unto themselves, with their own laws and patterns of retribution that lie totally outside the national or state system of justice.

Nations, as a whole, have avenues of arbitration available to them through, for example, the United Nations. But when they consider international organizations to be ineffective or biased, they refuse to submit to extranational laws and arbitration. Then nations take retribution into their own hands.

A HISTORY OF VENGEANCE AND THE LAW IN THE UNITED STATES

Many eighteenth-century settlers in the United States traced their lineage to members of the Scottish clans who were notorious for their wars based on revenge, so ancient and entrenched that no one could remember what act had set the whole string of events in motion. Their descendants settled in the mountains of Kentucky, Tennessee, and North Carolina and continued the tradition well into the early years of the twentieth century. Most readers are familiar with the Hatfields and the McCoys, who fought and murdered one another for generations. Mark Twain uses the story of these Scottish clans in the New World in his *Adventures of Huckleberry Finn*, when Huck tries to find out from his friend Buck why the Shepherdsons and Grangerfords have been trying to kill each other for at least one hundred years:

> "Well," says Buck, "a feud is this way: A man has a quarrel with another man, and kills him; then that other man's brother kills *him*; then the other brothers on both sides goes for one another; then the *cousins* chip in—and by and by everybody's killed off and there ain't no more feud."
>
> . . .
>
> "What was the trouble about, Buck?—land?"
> "I reckon maybe—I don't know."
> "Well, who done the shooting? Was it a Grangerford or a Shepherdson?"
> "Laws, how do *I* know? It was so long ago."
> "Don't anybody know?"
> "Oh, yes, pa knows, I reckon, and some of the other old people; but they don't know now what the row was about in the first place." (*The Portable Mark Twain*. New York: Penguin, 1946, 330–331)

In the Old West of the New World, where there was a common saying that there was no law and no God west of the Pecos, and settlers were on their own to live or die, the days of ancient Greece were reenacted. When local laws *were* formulated, they were often the creation of bands of unscrupulous, greedy men who used violence to get power and enforce their own codes. A notorious example of decades of one vengeful act following on another in a history of bloodshed occurred in New Mexico, a territory controlled by a band of entrenched criminals who made and imposed laws. When these men ambushed and murdered a rancher in Lincoln County, a young cowhand taken in by the rancher vowed revenge. This was the beginning of the career of one of America's most famous outlaws—William Bonney, better known as Billy the Kid.

RETRIBUTION IN THE WORLD TODAY

Since the seventeenth century, violence between the Irish (primarily Roman Catholic) and their English rulers (primarily Protestant) has ripped Ireland apart. After full Irish independence, the violence, especially since the 1970s, has raged on especially in Northern Ireland, where matters of governance have never been resolved to the satisfaction of the Catholics and the large Protestant population who live there. Despite attempts by mediating councils inside and outside Northern Ireland to put an end to the cycle of violence, extremists within these groups insist on settling their own scores, and refuse to acquiesce to outside arbitration. Killings by Catholics provoke vengeful killings by Protestants, which provoke vengeful killings by Catholics, ad infinitum.

In the Middle East, retribution has been state sanctioned, even state planned, for many years as Israelis battle Arabs over the issue of the Palestinians displaced when the state of Israel was created after World War II. In fall and winter of 2001–2002, violence escalated to the edge of war as Palestinian suicide bombers killed Israeli civilians, and Israelis retaliated each time with attacks on Palestinian strongholds, which, in turn, provoked more attacks from Palestinians.

THE CONCEPT OR REVENGE CREATED BY SEPTEMBER 11

On September 11, 2001, fanatics flew planes into the World Trade Center and the Pentagon, and were brought down before attacking the White House, thereby killing in peacetime thousands of innocent people, only a few of whom had the remotest military connection. The death toll at the World Trade Center alone was verified at around 2,830 people. The attacks were soon discovered to be acts of revenge against the United States for its support of the state of Israel. The quandary over the idea of revenge soon arose in the mind of a public that associated revenge with savagery. The immediate response of many, including President George W. Bush, was to urge retribution for what had occurred. Even writers with reputations for measured actions taken within the law seemed overcome with the impulse to seek retribution in the name of the thousands who had died in the attacks and the many more who were left widowed or orphaned, or were injured in the attacks.

But a counter to the call for vengeance soon arose even among those who supported a military response as absolutely necessary for self-defense. Perhaps it was only a matter of semantics, but signs soon appeared pleading for "Justice, Not Vengeance." In any case, as imperfectly as the civilized world has controlled the savagery and destructive pattern of retribution, whether on the part of gangs or the national government, our discomfort with the concept of vengeance is a far cry from the days of the ancient Greeks, when retribution was the unquestionable duty of the oldest male in the family, and failure to obtain it would leave him disgraced and dishonored.

JUSTICE IN *THE EUMENIDES*

In the history of drama, Aeschylus (ca. 525–456 B.C.) stands as a giant. The grandeur of his plays, dealing characteristically with religious and philosophical themes in superb and elegant verse, has seldom if ever been equaled. Born into a good family, he produced his first play in 499. In 490, at age thirty-five, he and two of his brothers fought in the battle of Marathon; one brother died, and all three fought with such distinction that Athens had a painting made in their honor. Ten years later (480), at forty-five, he fought at the battle of Salamis; and one year after that (479) at Plataea. He dominated drama for an entire generation in Athens. In 458, two years before his death, he won his last victory at the annual greater Dionysian festival with the presentation of *The Oresteia*.

When he died, the epitaph, according to legend of his own devising, made no mention of his literary merits, but said only that the groves at Marathon could speak of his prowess in battle and that the long-haired Persians knew it well. While he showed no love of extreme democracy, he clearly understood the miseries of battle, and he demonstrated sincere admiration for constitutional government and the laws of Athens. *The Oresteia* commemorates both. Philosophically, it represents a quest for justice, for an end to the bloodbath of personal revenge and the arrival of Law to take its place.

In the selections given below, from *The Eumenides*, Athena ends the old pattern of private justice and notes that henceforth all cases of homicide will be tried at the court in Athens. The Chorus (the Furies) objects because Athena has taken away their historic duty to persecute people who, like Orestes, commit such brutal crimes, and has relieved them of their prerogative to demand that personal vengeance be exacted outside the law. Athena appeases them by offering them a permanent home in Athens, as the "kindly ones."

FROM AESCHYLUS, *THE EUMENIDES*, TRANS. PHILIP VELLACOTT

(New York: Penguin Books, 1956)

Athene: Citizens of Athens! As you now try this first case
of bloodshed, hear the constitution of your court.
From this day forward this judicial council shall
For Aegeus' race hear every trial of homicide.
Here shall be their perpetual seat, on Ares' Hill.

...

Here, day and night,
Shall Awe, and Fear, Awe's brother, check my citizens
From all misdoing, while they keep my laws unchanged.

...

Chorus: The old is trampled by the new!
Curse on you younger gods who override
The ancient laws and rob me of my due!
Now to appease the honour you reviled
Vengeance shall fester till my full heart pours
Over this land on every side.
Anger for insult, poison for my pain—

...

Daughters of Night and Sorrow, come with me,
Feed on dishonour, on revenge to be!

...

Athene: ... [D]o not cast upon my fields
Whetstones of murder, to corrupt our young men's hearts
And make them mad with passions not infused by wine;
Nor plant in them the temper of the mutinous cock,
To set within my city's walls man against man
With self-destructive boldness, kin defying kin.
Let war be with the stranger, at the stranger's gate;
There let men fall in love with glory; but at home
Let no cocks fight.
Then, goddesses, I offer you
A home in Athens, where the gods most love to live,
Where gifts and honours shall deserve your kind good-will. (170, 173–74, 176)

IRELAND AND VENGEANCE

On almost any date in the last two hundred years, one could pick up a newspaper and find some act of retribution carried out by Catholics against Protestants or Protestants against Catholics in Ireland, especially Northern Ireland, but sometimes in British cities as well.

The illustration below of the brutal vengeance on both sides that in the process makes innocent people, especially children, the victims, occurred in 1998. The first excerpt is from an article from the *New York Times*, published on July 3, reporting that fanatical Protestants had set fire to ten Roman Catholic churches throughout Northern Ireland, with the purpose of halting the peace negotiations between Catholics and Protestants. The second, from a *New York Times* article published on July 12, indicates that violence was rising from the insistence of fanatical Protestants to march with full military bravura through a Catholic neighborhood to celebrate the Protestant victory over Catholics in seventeenth-century Ireland. The third excerpt reports on events of July 13, when Protestant extremists torched the house of a Catholic family living in a Protestant neighborhood, killing three boys, aged seven, nine and ten.

In early August 1998 the radical wing of the Irish Republican Army (IRA) set off a bomb in County Down, Ireland, and on August 16, the Guardian Newspapers Unlimited reported Catholic retaliation in one of the worst acts of violence in Ireland, a bombing carried out by the "Real IRA," a militant Catholic group, that killed 27 Catholics and Protestants and injured 190 people, the worst attack in over a decade. This was in retaliation for Protestant attacks and was designed to damage any peace process.

FROM JAMES F. CLARITY, "ARSONISTS BURN 10 CATHOLIC CHURCHES IN ULSTER"

(*New York Times*, July 3, 1998)

Arsonists believed to be members of a dissident Protestant group set fire to 10 Roman Catholic churches in Northern Ireland causing fears that wider sectarian violence could return to the British province.

The police said the fires were probably the work of the Loyalist Volunteer Force, a Protestant group opposed to the peace effort, which has produced cooperation between Protestants and Catholics in a new provincial assembly. Three churches were completely destroyed.

...

The arsonists were apparently retaliating against Catholics for a British Government decision on Monday forbidding Protestant marchers next Sunday to pass through a Catholic area.

The dispute threatens more violence, possibly retaliation by Catholics against Protestant churches and against meeting halls of the Orange Order, which runs some 3,000 parades in the province.

Both Catholics and Protestants fear Sunday's parade in the Drumcree district of Portadown, west of Belfast, could cause violence across the province, as it has for the last three years.

The officials are trying to arrange a compromise that would provide for a quiet, token march by the Orangemen through the Catholic enclave, without the traditional martial airs, loud drums, bugles and fifes. That way, the Government ban could be rescinded and both Orange and Catholic militants could save face.... Many Catholics resent the marches as triumphalist: they celebrate the decisive victory of William of Orange over his father-in-law, King James II, in 1690. (1, 4)

FROM JAMES F. CLARITY, "ULSTER FOES SUSPEND A LAST-DITCH EFFORT TO AVOID A CLASH AFTER SLIGHT PROGRESS"

(*New York Times*, July 12, 1998)

The Catholics insisted that there be "no Orange feet on the Garvaghy Road," that the Government ban on the march must be enforced. Their leader, Breandan MacClonnaith, also insisted that the Orangemen meet him face to face if they wanted to compromise. They rejected his offer to allow a modest parade to pass down the road next year, but not this year.

The Orangemen object to meeting Mr. MacClonnaith because they consider him a terrorist. He served three years in a British prison for his role in the bombing of a Protestant meeting hall in Portadown in 1981. He is not a member of Sinn Fein, the political wing of the Irish Republican Army, but Sinn Fein helps him to be elected a local councilor by not running its own candidates.

Politicians and security officials fear that if there is no resolution to the dispute by tonight, tens of thousands of Protestants from all over the province will march on Drumcree and clash with the security forces blocking the roads connecting the Protestant and Catholic areas.

...

Since Sunday, the day the march was blocked, Protestant protesters have attacked the police with more than 500 gasoline bombs, hijacked and burned dozens of cars, and blocked major roads.

In recent days, protesters have broken through the first line of three barbed-wire coils forming the defensive cordon, and they seriously injured three policemen with homemade pipe bombs. Other protesters shot large ball bearings from slingshots. The police responded by firing plastic bullets. (8)

FROM JAMES F. CLARITY, "THREE CATHOLIC BROTHERS KILLED IN FIRE, STUNNING ULSTER AND RAISING FEARS"

(*New York Times*, July 13, 1998)

Three young Roman Catholic boys were burned to death in their home early this morning in an arson attack that the police said was the work of Protestants.

Political and religious leaders, both Protestant and Catholic, throughout the British province denounced the killings, which followed more than a week of Protestant violence linked to the banning of a Protestant march through a Catholic area and heightened fears of a breakdown in the Northern Ireland peace agreement reached this spring.

...

The boys' mother, Christine Quinn, 29; her Protestant boyfriend, Raymond Craig, 31; and a woman friend who was in the house were unable to reach the children before they escaped themselves.

...

"They were just typical boys—just ran about and played football, sat about watching video," said Shirley Patton, Mrs. Quinn's cousin and a Protestant.

She said that although Mrs. Quinn is a Catholic, she sent her sons to a local public school.

"All but a few families in the area are Protestant," Mrs. Patton said, standing in her doorway; a British Union Jack fluttering from the side of her house.

...

He [another neighbor], like many others, linked the boys' deaths to the outbreaks of violence by Protestants that have accompanied a standoff between British security forces and members of the Protestant Orange Order protesting a ban on parading through a Catholic neighborhood in Portadown, south of here.

...

At Drumcree, where the Orangemen have been attacking policemen blocking the roads to the Catholic area, a few Orange Protestants said today that the boys' deaths might decrease the number of protesters, particularly on Monday, when about 500 Orange parades are to take place around the province to celebrate the 17th-century Protestant victory over Catholics.

...

But the prevalent view seemed to be that of a 41-year-old civil servant, who declined to give his name for fear of reprisals. He said the protests must continue at Drumcree. "It's a matter of our freedom, our right to walk on the Queen's highway," he said. (1, 9)

VENGEANCE IN THE NEAR EAST

Few areas in the world have been so devastated by a pattern of continual vengeance as has the Near East. The history of the prevailing conflict began in May 1948 with the expiration of the British colonial mandate over Palestine and the establishment of the state of Israel. Tensions between Arabs and Israelis mounted over the years over many issues: the establishment of the state of Israel, the plight of Palestinians who felt displaced, access to the Suez Canal, diversions of water from the Jordan River, disputes over so-called neutral territories between Israel and Syria (the Golan Heights), between Israel and Jordan (the West Bank), and the Gaza Strip.

In 1967, Egypt mobilized forces and Israel launched an attack, leading to the Six-Day War, during which Israel seized control of the Gaza Strip, the Sinai Peninsula, East Jerusalem, the Golan Heights, and the West Bank, placing Arabs in these areas under military occupation and opening some of the territory to Israeli settlement. The Yom Kippur War in 1973 began when Egypt attacked Israel, and it ended with Israel winning Syrian territory. Palestine Liberation Organization (PLO) raids from Lebanon into Israel caused war between those two countries in 1982, and the PLO was forced to withdraw. In 1987, an Arab holy war (*intifada*) began over Israeli occupation of the West Bank and the Gaza Strip. Despite negotiations for peace and Israel's plans to withdraw from most of the Gaza Strip, Jericho, the West Bank, and Hebron, and to discuss the status of Jerusalem, attacks and counterattacks continued, with the fanatical arm of the PLO, Hamas, encouraging suicide bombing.

Violence erupted again in the area after the September 11, 2001, Muslim attacks on the World Trade Center and the Pentagon in the United States. Many sympathetic to Muslim extremists claimed that the attacks were largely provoked by U.S. sympathy for Israel. The subsequent war that the United States waged against the Taliban in Muslim Afghanistan provoked escalating Palestinian attacks on Israelis and counterattacks by Israelis on Palestinians.

The first excerpt included here is from a March 7, 2002, news story detailing Israeli attacks on Palestinian camps in the Gaza Strip, where leaders of Hamas were presumed to plan suicide bombing of Israel, after rockets were fired into an Israeli town. The second story, filed the same day from the West Bank, includes an interview with a Palestinian leader and shows little hope that the retribution will come to an end, even if peace talks begin. On March 13, 2001, a typical headline from the *Los Angeles Times* underscored the mounting violence in the Middle East as a matter of retribution and counter-retribution: "In Retaliation for Palestinian Attacks, the Army Moves In." By mid-April, after several devasting Palestinian suicide bombings in Israel, including one during Passover, the Israeli army invaded the West Bank, determined to wipe out Palestinian terrorists.

FROM SERGE SCHMEMANN, "ISRAEL STRIKES HARD AT GAZA STRIP"

(*New York Times*, March 7, 2002)

Israeli forces struck hard today by land, sea, and air at the teeming Gaza Strip, where Palestinians breached another red line on Tuesday when they fired rockets into an Israeli town. With the mounting carnage, which added 10 Palestinians and two Israeli dead to the toll, the government of Ariel Sharon received an usual rebuke from Secretary of State Colin L. Powell.

...

Palestinians also reported that Israeli naval vessels approached the Gaza shore and fired missiles at the Palestinian naval police, killing four.

The Israeli commander for Gaza, Brig. Gen. Yisrael Ziv, called the operations successful and said they would continue. "This is part of an ongoing operation, and our success will be measured by our perseverance, results, and patience," he said.

The army ordered the raids into Gaza after two crude Qassam rockets, which the Israelis say are manufactured by the militant movement Hamas, were launched into the town of Sderot on Tuesday. One struck a building and injured a child. Israel had warned that firing rockets into urban areas would have serious consequences. But with the carnage at record levels, there was little to distinguish retaliation from escalation. (A1, A8)

FROM JAMES BENNET, "FOR FATAH, ONLY A WAR CAN BRING PEACE TO THE MIDEAST"

(*New York Times*, March 7, 2002)

Since the beginning of the year, it has been Palestinian militants tied to Yasir Arafat's Fatah faction who have carried out most of the attacks against Israelis—and the most lethal attacks, Israeli and Palestinian officials say.

Israel's leaders see this as supporting their case that Mr. Arafat and his top Fatah lieutenant in the West Bank, Marwan Barghouti, are terrorists.

...

A wry and subtle man with credentials as a peacemaker as well as a fighter, Mr. Barghouti has become one of the most popular Palestinian leaders, partly by advocating violence. On Tuesday, declaring that the conflict had reached a "point of no return," he exhorted Palestinians to strike every Israeli checkpoint in the West Bank.

. . .

[Israeli Prime Minister] Sharon made a similar argument this week in support of Israel's actions, insisting that only after the Palestinians had been "battered" would Israel be able to conduct peace talks. (Mr. Sharon did not suggest that such violence would also enhance his party's standing.)

Mr. Sharon insists that seven days of absolute calm must precede even preliminary steps toward negotiations. Mr. Barghouti says Palestinian violence must continue even should negotiations begin.

. . .

Mr. Barghouti said in the interview that Fatah members stepped up their attacks on Israelis after Jan. 14, when Israel killed a Tanzim leader, Raed al-Karmi, with a hidden explosive. Many Palestinians and some Israelis now regard that event, after a period of relative calm, as a turning point.

The Israeli military official acknowledged that "maybe there is a link" between the killing of Mr. Karmi and the increased violence. But he said the violence would have erupted eventually anyway.

After Mr. Karmi's killing, Mr. Barghouti said, Fatah activists began attacking Israelis across the 1967 boundary, even conducting suicide bombings. He says he still argues internally against such attacks, "not only for humanitarian reasons, but for practical reasons." Such attacks can undermine the Palestinian cause, he says.

But he was clearly delighted by recent attacks on Israeli soldiers in the West Bank. (A8)

. . .

THE DEBATE ABOUT VENGEANCE FOLLOWING THE FANATICAL MUSLIM ATTACKS ON THE UNITED STATES

On September 11, 2001, fanatical Muslims, members of the Taliban Al-Qaeda, attacked the United States, in part as retaliation for U.S. support of Israel. The immediate reaction of a traumatized nation was grief over the dead, as well as alarm and recognition of an urgent need to plan and forestall any further attacks. Anger also surfaced, along with the desire for retribution. The first official response from the Bush administration spoke of "retaliation," many angry citizens made no secret of wanting revenge on those who had launched the attacks, and many U.S. soldiers later saw their mission as "paying back" the Taliban for the attacks on the Pentagon and the World Trade Center.

At the same time, the morality and practical wisdom of taking revenge also came into the conversation. Even many people who supported some kind of armed conflict with the Taliban and with countries supporting the Al-Qaeda, tried to draw a distinction between military force for the purpose of self-defense and for the purpose of retribution. Along with the American flag, signs appeared, urging "Justice not Vengeance."

The following excerpts show something of the range of this debate. On September 11, President George W. Bush addressed a nation that had just been attacked by fanatics. The *New York Times* headline of a page 1 article on September 12, by Serge Schmemann, summed up his sentiment: "President Vows to Exact Punishment for 'Evil.'" There is an excerpt from an editorial in the same issue of the *Times* that brings up the complexity of the concept of retribution. There are also excerpts from a news story in the *Times* on September 13 and from a news story on public sentiment throughout the United States on September 14.

FROM "THE WAR AGAINST AMERICA. AN UNFATHOMABLE ATTACK"

(New York Times, September 12, 2001)

...

What we live with now, beyond shock and beyond the courage witnessed on the streets in New York and Washington yesterday, is an urge for reprisal. But this is an age when even revenge is complicated, when it is hard to match the desire for retribution with the need for certainty. We suffer from an act of war without any enemy nation with which to do battle. The same media that brought us the pictures of a collapsing World Trade Center show us the civilians who live in the same places that terrorists may dwell, whose lives are just as ordinary and just as precious as the ones that we have lost. That leaves us all, for now, with fully burdened emotions, undiminished by anything but the passage of the few hours that have elapsed since midmorning yesterday. There is a world of consoling to be done.

FROM ERIC SCHMITT AND THOM SHANKER, "ADMINISTRATION CONSIDERS BROADER, MORE POWERFUL OPTIONS FOR POTENTIAL RETALIATION"

(*New York Times*, September 13, 2001)

The stunning loss of life in Tuesday's terrorist attacks and the sense, expressed by President Bush, that these were "acts of war," have freed the administration to broaden potential retaliation beyond the low-risk, unmanned cruise missile strikes of the past, military and civilian officials said today.

Instead, the options under consideration include more powerful, sustained attacks that accept greater risk to American forces, and may include bombing attacks by manned aircraft and landing special forces troops on the ground.

"The constraints have been lifted," said one military officer.

No decisions on retaliation have been made as American intelligence officials try to determine who is to blame for the assaults on the World Trade Center towers and the Pentagon. Nor is there a timetable yet for any action, officials said.

...

Placing troops in harm's way to retaliate against those responsible for the attacks, and to prevent further terrorist action, "now seems completely justified," one military officer said. "Our senior leaders are describing this as war, so those in uniform are willing to accept the risk. And we know the public will support us."

...

During a Pentagon news briefing today, Mr. Rumsfeld hinted at the broader approach to potential retaliation, while noting the difficulty of combating terrorism.

...

Any military action carries political consequences as well as risks to the fighting forces, and there is never a guarantee of success, as the United States found out when it tried to retaliate against the Saudi dissident Osama Bin Laden for the bombing of two United States embassies in Kenya and Tanzania in 1998. (A15)

FROM BLAINE HARDEN, "FOR MANY, SORROW TURNS TO ANGER AND TALK OF VENGEANCE"

(*New York Times*, September 14, 2001)

Having donated more blood than victims needed, having wallpapered their towns with flags, and with little choice but to stew over television reruns of terror in their homeland, more than a few Americans are beginning to obsess about how to get even.

Phil Beckwith, a retired truck driver, announced his modest proposal for avenging the attacks on New York and Washington in the editorial offices of The Ranger, a newspaper that serves Fremont County, Wyo., one of the largest and emptiest counties in the nation. He had gone to the paper to buy a classified advertisement.

"I know just what to do with these Arab people," Mr. Beckwith proclaimed on Wednesday to the newspaper staff. "We have to find them, kill them, wrap them in a pigskin and bury them. That way they will never go to heaven."

. . .

"I don't like the word, revenge," said Jim Willhoit, 58, pastor of the First Church of Christ in Highland, Ind. "The word, retaliate means much the same thing. But I believe there needs to be some retaliation. But I also believe we need to retaliate to the person who did it."

. . .

In Ogden, Ill., population 500, similar sentiments were expressed. "If I could get my hands on bin Laden, I'd skin him alive and pour salt on him," said Bruce Cristina, 45, a worker at Ogden Metalworking. "Nothing would be cruel enough."

. . .

At an enlistment center in the Aurora Mall in the Denver suburbs, Jason Stuart, 24, was one of the few young people to respond to recent events by trying to join the Army. . . .

"I thought, 'Somebody's got to pay for this,'" he said, after enlisting. (A15)

QUESTIONS FOR WRITTEN AND ORAL EXPLORATION

1. *The Odyssey* is an excellent example of how an author arranges material so as to make the reader sympathize with Odysseus, the avenger. In an essay, point out concrete details that help Homer achieve this purpose.
2. Write a first-person narrative from the point of view of Aegisthus or Clytemnestra, who murder Agamemnon.
3. From your own experience or reading, write an analysis of an actual instance, not necessarily murder, of personal revenge.
4. Conduct some newspaper and library research on youth gang codes of revenge and killings. Write an essay on your findings.
5. Read Edgar Allan Poe's "The Cask of Amontillado." What, according to the narrator, constitutes perfect revenge? Does the narrator achieve that? Have a class discussion on the topic.
6. Write your own short story titled "Perfect Revenge."
7. Conduct research on the topic of a particular instance of revenge in the Old West. The Lincoln County War in New Mexico, the Johnson Country War in Montana, or the Mountain Meadows Massacre might be a starting place.
8. Read Henry David Thoreau's "Civil Disobedience" and conduct a class debate on the wisdom of his ideas.
9. Research and write a report on Mohandus Gandhi's and Martin Luther King's views on nonviolence. Include in your report your own response to what they say.
10. Interview someone in the peace movement about the U.S. war in Afghanistan. Find out what alternatives he or she suggests to armed intervention, and write your reaction to his or her arguments.
11. Have a debate on this proposition, drawing on current events: Revenge is never a civilized response to any grievance.

FURTHER READING

Alexander, Yonah. *Osama bin Laden's al-Qaida.* Ardsley, NY: Transnational Publications, 2001

Bailey, Sydney. *Four Arab-Israeli Wars.* New York: St. Martin's Press, 1990.

Beilin, Possi. *Israel: A Concise Political History.* New York: St. Martin's Press, 1993.

Bew, Paul. *Northern Ireland.* Lanham, MD: Scarecrow Press, 1999.

Biel, A. James, and Carl Leiden. *Politics in the Middle East.* New York: HarperCollins, 1994.

Brotherhood. Text by Tony Hendra. New York: American Express, 2001.

Bruce, Steve. *God Save Ulster: The Religion and Politics of Paisleyism.* Oxford: Oxford University Press, 1989.
De Breadun, Deaglan. *The Far Side of Revenge.* Wilton, Ireland: Collins, 2001.
Doumitt, Donald. *Voices of Ulster.* Huntington, NY: Kroshka Books, 2000.
Duncan, Andrew. *War in the Holy Land.* Stroud, UK: Sutton Publications, 1998.
Haski, Pierre. *Israel.* Milan: Toulouse, 1997.
Kedowie, Elie. *Politics in the Middle East.* Oxford: Oxford University Press, 1992.
Klein, Misha, and Adrian McIntyre. *September 11, Contexts and Consequences: An Anthology.* Berkeley, CA: Copy Central, 2001.
Kurgan, Laura. *Around Ground Zero.* New York: Laura Kurgan, 2001.
MacDonald, Michael. *Children of Wrath.* New York: Blackwell, 1986.
Paul, Arthur. *Northern Ireland Since 1968.* Oxford: Blackwell, 1996.
President Bush's Address to Congress. ABC News, 2001. Videorecording.
Target America. Produced by Michael Kirk and Martin Smith. BBC, 2001. Videorecording.

9

Contemporary Applications: The Athlete and Athletics

THE HOMERIC ATHLETE HERO

The familiar fascination of the Greeks with the athlete and athletic games, which culminated in the official organization around 776 B.C. of the Olympic Games, has a parallel in contemporary culture, which also often takes its heroes from the ranks of famous athletes.

In Greece, athlete heroes are traceable back to the mythology of ancient history and to the epics of Homer. Some of the famous mythic athletic contests include a wrestling match between Zeus and his father, Cronos, to determine who would rule the world. Zeus' victory was often celebrated in festival games. In a number of instances in mythology, athletic contests determined which man would have a particularly desirable woman for a wife. King Oenomaos, for instance, held chariot races with men who wanted to marry his daughter Hippodaemia. Oenomaus always overcame the contender, and slaughtered him, until a suitor named Pelops came along and bribed Oenomaus' charioteer to throw the race. Another example is Atalanta, who had a foot race with suitors for her hand in marriage. In this case, as in the case of Hippodaemia, the suitor is able to be the victor only by devious means, not by superior athletic ability. Hippomenes distracts Atalanta by throwing golden apples in her path. Stopping to pick them up, she slows down, which enables Hippomenes to reach the finish line first. Another legend has it that Odysseus won the hand of Penelope by winning a foot race set up by her father, Icarios. (Also note below the bow-stringing contest Penelope contrives to determine which man she will marry.) Paris Alexander, who in essence

Foot race

Warriors running

The depiction of a long-distance foot race on fourth-century B.C. Greek vases now in the British Museum. *Source:* Hill, G.F. *Illustrations of School Classics.* London: Macmillan, 1903, 317.

causes the Trojan War, rises from obscurity as a shepherd boy when he goes to Troy and distinguishes himself in the athletic games, ironically set up as funeral games for the child the king thought had been killed at his command many years before.

Funeral games also have importance in *The Iliad* when Achilles arranges an elaborate event in honor of his childhood friend Patroclus, who has been killed in battle. Funerals were not the only occasions for athletic contests. Many were held on a regular basis during festivals to the gods. Both funeral and festival games, as well as the Olympic Games, had strong religious overtones.

Athletic events are in evidence in the oldest Greek cultures recorded. Crete was famous not only for its boxers and wrestlers, but especially for its acrobats and tumblers, who grabbed the horns of a raging bull, did a somersault onto the bull's back, and leaped off behind the animal. Different sports developed in Mycenaean Greece during Odysseus' day, although athletes continued to participate in individual rather than team sports. These were the same ones that became part of the first Olympic Games: wrestling, boxing, jumping while holding weights, foot racing, discus and spear throwing, and, later, chariot and horse racing. The Olympic contests were offered in homage to the gods, and only pure Hellenes and those who had not angered or dishonored the gods could take part.

Unlike funeral, festival, and Olympic Games, the athletic contests in *The Odyssey* lack religious significance. There is even something frivolous and irresponsible in the games Penelope's suitors invariably play before going in to consume Odysseus' food and drink and to corrupt his household. In books IV and XVII, they are described as amusing themselves with throwing the discus and javelin in contests. On two occasions athletic displays are intended to be entertainment for spectator guests. Two tumblers in Menelaos' palace whirl about for the amusement of Telemachos. Acrobatic dancers also entertain the court of King Alcinoos in book VIII.

Athletic ability often takes a far more serious turn when Odysseus participates. Even if such participation still has little direct religious meaning, it has to do with personal honor and greatness of heart. The reader has foreknowledge of the athletic superiority of legends and heroes when, at the court of Menelaos, mention is made of the fighting and running skill of Antilochos and of the wrestling skill of Odysseus. Odysseus' particular strength—as will be demonstrated in his sea journey to Phaeacia, his answer to a challenge there, and his activities in Ithaca—is in his huge shoulders and massive thighs. Thus, he excels in swimming (for nine days, floating in the sea on a piece of boat timber, he propels himself only with his arms), wrestling, discus and spear throwing, and archery. And although one tradition has it that he won Penelope in a foot race, he did not have the long legs and slim body of a runner. When he is challenged in Phaeacia, he feels confident that he can outperform others in almost any feat except running. And his ability to throw the discus much farther than any challenger on this occasion cools the ardor of the young Phaeacians to enter further contests with him.

On Ithaca, even though the surly Iros challenges Odysseus to a fight, the beggar tries to run away when he actually gets a good look at the size of Odysseus' thighs; he has to be carried to the fight by the suitors. Odysseus breaks his neck with a single blow.

Penelope sets up the third major contest to see who can best string Odysseus' bow and shoot through twelve axes. We are often reminded in the epics that the abilities of the athlete and the warrior are one. The outcome of the bow-stringing contest, like that of the earlier wrestling match, again reveals the athlete as a killer.

Odysseus' athletic ability seems to attest to his superior rank, his superhuman strength, and his courage, as well as his superior training and knowledge of a variety of sports. From the time of ancient myth to the Olympic Games, the athlete hero like Odysseus was considered almost superhuman. Cities idolized local men who won the Olympic Games, often turning them into minor deities. At their homecomings, they were invited to symbolically tear down a piece of the city wall, as a sign that the city which was the home of such an idol would be invulnerable to attack, just as today a local athlete who meets with success brings honor to his or her town, race, or the nation.

THE ATHLETE HERO IN THE TWENTIETH AND TWENTY-FIRST CENTURIES

To a great extent the status of athletes in the modern world is similar to that held by athletes in *The Odyssey*. One assertion can be made with confidence: as in Homeric Greece, so in contemporary culture, athletics occupies a place of extraordinary importance. A comparison of the position of athletes in the two eras sheds light on both cultures. The Olympic Games begun in ancient Greece continue in the twenty-first century, involving, of course, not just one country but virtually all the countries of the world. But the Olympics have never been free of national and international politics. One example of this occurred in 1964, when South Africa was barred from Olympic participation in Japan. By 1968, the barring of South Africa had become a hot issue and various nations put pressure on members of the Olympic committee either to maintain the ban or lift it. At the 1964 Olympics in Mexico City, two African-American athletes who were receiving the gold and bronze medals raised their fists in a gesture of black power as the national anthem was being played. A noteworthy threat to boycott the Olympics planned for Moscow occurred in 1980. As a response to the Soviet invasion of Afghanistan, President Jimmy Carter ordered a U.S. boycott of the games. As in ancient Greece, the athlete, almost as much as the political leader, represents his or her homeland, and those who excel in the Olympics bring great honor to their countries. The competition can become fierce as countries vie for gold medals in key events. For example, in the 2002 Winter Olympics in Salt Lake City, Utah, a French judge of the figure skating event was dismissed from the panel when she admitted yielding to pressure to award the gold medal to Russian rather than Canadian skaters (though the latter presumably had the superior performance). The intensity of national pride and competition was displayed when, at one point, the Russian Olympic team threatened to withdraw all its athletes.

The importance of athletics, and especially the Olympics, can be seen when extremism and violence enter the Olympic arena. On many occasions factions attempt to use athletes or the occasion of the games for political purposes. In 1936 Nazi leader Adolf Hitler became enraged when Jesse Owens, an African American, won gold medals in track events. By training Germans to win these events, Hitler had planned on proving to the world the superiority of the blond "Aryan" race. Even though Germany was the host country for the Olympics, Hitler snubbed Owens and made his disgust and anger plain for all to see.

In 1972, again in Germany, tragedy struck when Palestinian terrorists took the occasion of the Munich Olympics to kidnap and murder eleven Israeli athletes. And a bomb was planted in Atlanta during the 1996 Olympics, killing two people.

Many athletes are important not only as representatives of their countries, but also as inspirations to members of their race, as Jesse Owens was in 1936; as Jackie Robinson was in breaking the barrier of racial segregation in professional baseball; as Joe Louis was in boxing; as Althea Gibson was in women's tennis and golf; as Wilt Chamberlain was in professional basketball; as Arthur Ashe was in men's tennis; and as Tiger Woods was in the gentleman's game of golf.

While personal and national pride is often as apparent in—even endemic to—competitive athletics today as it was in King Alcinoos' court when Odysseus was taunted, the character of athletics today is in sharp contrast to that of Homer's Greece. One of the biggest differences is the importance of team sports and the emergence of superstar athletes, especially in professional football, baseball, and basketball. Many athletes who have achieved legendary, even heroic, status played team sports: Red Grange, Bronko Nagurski, Johnny Unitas, Tom Harmon, Joe Namath, and Joe Montana in football; Dizzy Dean, Hank Greenberg, Jackie Robinson, Babe Ruth, Lou Gehrig, Ted Williams, and Joe DiMaggio in baseball; Wilt Chamberlain, Kareem Abdul-Jabbar, and Larry Bird in basketball. Boston even named a major city tunnel for baseball great Ted Williams.

Because tremendous profits are realized from ticket sales and related businesses, many of these athletes are among the highest paid individuals in our culture. For example, *Parade* Sunday magazine of March 3, 2002, listed baseball player Mike Piazza's yearly salary as $15 million, basketball player Shaquille O'Neal's salary as $24 million, and pro football player Adrian Ross' salary as $920,000. Admittedly, the working life of such athletes is not very long, yet a comparison of these salaries with others in our society is revealing of our priorities. These high salaries are in stark contrast to a public school teacher's annual salary of $34,000, a child-care supervisor's salary of $25,000, a corrections officer's salary of $25,000, a firefighter's salary of $50,000, a college professor's salary at $71,000 or even the above-average salaries of a U.S. congressman ($150,000), a pediatrician ($103,000), or the president of a major university ($335,000).

The million-dollar salaries of athletes on professional ball teams, as well as those in such fields as boxing (Mike Tyson made $48 million in 2001) and professional tennis (Anna Kournikova made $10 million in 2001) are a far cry from the accomplished athletes in ancient Greece, who were awarded only olive wreaths.

American society at the turn of the twenty-first century continues to name its heroes from team sports: Barry Bonds, of the San Francisco Giants, who holds the single-season home-run record in baseball; Sammy Sosa, of the Chicago Cubs and Mark McGwire of the St. Louis Cardinals, who both surpassed the home run records of Babe Ruth and Roger Maris in 1998. Basketball heroes included Michael Jordan of Chicago Bulls and the Washington Wizards, Larry Bird of the Boston Celtics, and Shaquille O'Neal and Kobe Bryant of the Los Angeles Lakers. Football had, among others, Peyton Manning, quarterback for the Indianapolis Colts; Kurt Warner, quarterback for the St. Louis Rams; and Jerry Rice, wide receiver for the San Francisco 49ers and the Oakland Raiders. At the turn of the twenty-first century, nonteam sports also had their superstars, including Tiger Woods in golf and Venus and Serena Williams in tennis.

The contemporary athlete also differs from the athlete of ancient Greece in typically being far more specialized than was, say, Odysseus, a wrestler, swimmer, archer, and spear and discus thrower. Great athletes today tend to excel in one or two sports only.

Another stark difference is that while the hero athletes of *The Odyssey* are members of the nobility (Achilles is the son of a sea nymph, Odysseus is a king, and the athletes in Phaeacia are young aristocrats), most of the outstanding athletes of the twentieth and twenty-first centuries come from the ranks of the poor and working classes. Many of them are African Americans, and some of them are women. Many of them are men of modest education. The exceptions include Bill Bradley, a Rhodes scholar, Princeton graduate, and later U.S. senator, who played professional basketball, and Byron "Whizzer" White, also a Rhodes scholar, Yale Law School graduate, and a U.S. Supreme Court justice, who made a reputation for himself as a college football player. Curiously enough, great athletes in the twentieth and twenty-first centuries have rarely been, as in *The Odyssey*, great warriors. On the contrary, boxer Muhammad Ali, one of the greatest athlete heroes of the twentieth century, was a conscientious objector on religious grounds during the Vietnam War.

It is the young who primarily perceive outstanding athletes as heroes, possibly because they are seen as hopeful evidence that one can rise above poverty, sometimes rise above racial inequality. The primary reasons why many young people name athletes as heroes are not so different from the reasons ancient Greeks admired athletes: for their skill, courage, drive, success, competitiveness, professionalism, discipline, and physical attractiveness. But to these qualities, many young people added charity, social responsibility, and moral leadership.

One of the documents that follows is a biographical sketch of the person chosen as the greatest athlete of the first half of the twentieth century—Jim Thorpe—a man who excelled in multiple Olympic events and played both professional football and baseball. Thorpe, a Native American with the rare ability to excel, like Odysseus, in numerous athletic endeavors, nevertheless stands in sharp contrast to the Greek king. Thorpe was a man doomed to poverty and badly treated by the country to which he had brought great glory in the Olympic Games.

The second document is pertinent to another Olympic winner, Jesse Owens, who was briefly lauded as a returning hero but not accorded recognition by his country until eight years after he died, when he was awarded the Congressional Gold Medal.

The third document consists of two tables. The first shows the number of athlete heroes among all heroes in a poll of schoolchildren. The second displays the rank order of "the most frequently selected praiseworthy athletes" in three polls. It illustrates the preponderance of players of team sports among athlete heroes.

JIM THORPE

Jim Thorpe, often called the greatest American athlete of all time, occupies a major place in the history of the Olympics written by Richard Schaap, a well-known sportswriter and broadcaster.

Thorpe had an impressive range of athletic ability in both individual and team sports. He was a natural athlete who, Schaap says, trained for his role in the 1912 Stockholm Olympics by sleeping while his teammates and competitors practiced their running and jumping. He was an all-American football player in college, and in 1912 scored twenty-five touchdowns. He was voted into the National Football Hall of Fame in 1963. He also played baseball for the New York Giants and the Boston Braves.

His fame in Stockholm was such that the king of Sweden presented him with bronze and silver presents and the 1912 Olympics was commonly referred to "the Jim Thorpe Olympics." A little town in Pennsylvania near the Carlisle Indian School he had attended was renamed "Jim Thorpe," and continues to this day. His birthplace in Oklahoma maintains a museum and hosts annual celebrations in his honor.

Stockholm was Thorpe's battlefield, as Troy was Odysseus', and awaiting the returning hero was a tragedy of epic proportions. As Schaap points out, when the Olympic Committee discovered in 1913 that Thorpe had played in a minor semiprofessional baseball league for a few bucks in 1910, he was stripped of his medals. He died in 1953, a victim of loneliness, poverty, and alcoholism.

Several significant events concerning Jim Thorpe occurred after the publication of Schaap's history. In 1982, the Olympic Committee restored his gold medals to his family after repeated appeals. And at the end of the twentieth century, as various groups were identifying the best men and women of the century in various endeavors, the U.S. Senate recognized Jim Thorpe as the American athlete of the century.

FROM RICHARD SCHAAP, *AN ILLUSTRATED HISTORY OF THE OLYMPICS*

(New York: Alfred A. Knopf, 1963)

Jim Thorpe, born in Prague, Oklahoma, on May 28, 1888, a member of the Sac and Fox Indian tribe, six feet tall and 190 pounds in his prime, was the finest athlete the United States has ever produced. In 1950, the Associated Press conducted a poll of American sportswriters to select the greatest male athlete of the half-century, 1900–49. Thorpe received 252 first-place votes; all his rivals combined polled only 141.

Jim Thorpe. *Source:* Associated Press archives of Wide World Photos.

Thorpe could excel in any sport, but the three he played best were football, baseball, and track and field.

...

In the 1912 version of the pentathlon, a strenuous test of versatility combining five separate events, Thorpe defeated all challengers in the broad jump, discus throw, 200-meter dash, and 1,500-meter run. He proved he was human by placing only third in the javelin throw. Thorpe won the pentathlon gold medal by a mile.

...

In the decathlon, a blend of ten events, Thorpe defeated all rivals in the high jump, high hurdles, shotput, and 1,500 meter-run.

...

The 1912 Olympic Games provided Jim Thorpe with his greatest glory. They also provided him, as matters developed, with his most bitter setback. In 1913, a year after the games ended, the International Olympic Committee discovered that Thorpe had earlier played baseball for money, declared him a professional, stripped him of his medals, and erased his records from the official Olympic history. (126, 127–128, 128, 135)

CONGRESSIONAL GOLD MEDAL FOR JESSE OWENS

Jesse Owens is another versatile athlete, but chiefly a runner and broad jumper, whose return home from victory can be compared and contrasted with Odysseus'. Owens, not a king like Odysseus, but the grandson of a slave and the son of a black sharecropper, won four gold medals at the 1936 Berlin Olympics and set records that remained unbroken in the twentieth century. With Adolf Hitler rising to power and eager to prove his racial theories, this became one of the most politicized Olympics up to that time. While the German athletes were cordial to Owens, Hitler and his henchmen insulted both Jewish and African-American athletes. One high official in the German Foreign Ministry told the daughter of the U.S. ambassador to Germany that the United States should be ashamed for allowing "non-humans, like Owens and other Negro athletes" to participate.

But in this historical moment before the outbreak of World War II, Owens stood as the grand embodiment of the vigor and hope of the United States. Like the athlete returning to his home in glory in ancient Greece, Owens was celebrated with parades and ceremonies in his home state of Ohio and in New York City. In the year following the Olympics, he was able to cash in on his fame with contests and endorsements. But after that one year of financial success, the returned hero faced continual obstacles. He was never able to compete in the Olympics again after he impulsively signed a contract that would have given him professional status. Although the terms of the contract were never carried out and Owens never received the pay that the contract promised, word of the contract reached the Amateur Athletics Union, and his amateur status was taken from him.

For a time Owens participated in exhibitions where he raced against horses, an activity from which he benefited financially but which he found to be personally demeaning. Thereafter, however, he had a constant struggle to make a living, became heavily in debt, and often found himself on a collision course with both the white establishment and younger black activists. Owens died in 1980. In 1988, a committee of the U.S. House of Representatives heard testimony to support the awarding of a Congressional Gold Medal to Jesse Owens, to be given to his widow. The record of the committee's hearings attests to Jesse Owens' status as a heroic athlete.

FROM "GOLD MEDAL FOR JESSE OWENS," HEARINGS BEFORE THE SUBCOMMITTEE ON CONSUMER AFFAIRS AND COINAGE, 100TH CONGRESS, JULY 12, 1988

(Washington, D.C.: U.S. Government Printing Office, 1988)
Tuesday, July 12, 1988

House of Representatives, Subcommittee on Consumer Affairs and Coinage, Committee on Banking, Finance and Urban Affairs,

Washington, D.C.

The subcommittee met, pursuant to call, at 10 a.m., in room 2128, Rayburn House Office Building, Hon. Frank Annunzio [chairman of the subcommittee] presiding.

Present: Chairman Annunzio, Representatives Pelosi and Hiler.

Chairman Annunzio. The meeting of the subcommittee will be in order.

The subcommittee will now hear testimony on H.R. 1270, legislation authorizing the President to present, on behalf of the Congress, a gold medal to Mrs. Jesse Owens in recognition of the late Jesse Owens' athletic achievements and humanitarian contributions to public service, civil rights and international goodwill.

[Text of H.R. 1270 can be found in the appendix.]

Chairman Annunzio. I want to congratulate our distinguished colleague from Ohio, Mr. Stokes, for introducing this legislation and obtaining 228 cosponsors. This is more than the majority of House Members required under the rules of the Banking Committee for consideration of gold medal legislation. I am proud to be one of the cosponsors of this bill.

Jesse Owens is best known for his performance at the 1936 Olympics at which he became the first athlete ever to win four gold medals in a single Olympics. Not only did he win the gold medals, but he did it in front of Adolph [*sic*] Hitler, making a mockery of his Arian [*sic*] "master race" philosophy.

Owens was a great athlete. His Olympic times would have won medals through 1964, and his broad jump performance through 1968. In 1935 he turned in what may have been the greatest single performance in the history of track and field. On May 25, 1935, in a 45-minute period, he broke three world records and tied a fourth.

But it is not just for his athletic achievements that we honor Jesse Owens. He was a man about whom President Carter said, "Perhaps no athlete better symbolized the human struggle against tyranny, poverty and racial bigotry."

The grandson of slaves, he worked as a night elevator operator to pay his way through Ohio State University. Scorned by the Nazis as a member of "America's black auxiliaries" at the Olympics, he lifted American spirits through his achievements, but was forced to ride in the back of the bus upon his return to his native land.

Jesse Owens never lost his dignity. Throughout his life he never gave in to setbacks. He became an inspiration both through the speeches he gave and the example he set. His speeches reflected his creed. "We all have dreams," he said, "but in order to make dreams into reality, it takes an awful lot of determination, dedication, self-discipline and effort. These things apply to everyday life."

Jesse Owens lived by what he said. We honor him today with Congress' highest honor. It is woefully inadequate and at least 8 years too late. Jesse Owens died in 1980, but his example and his triumph are timeless. The congressional gold medal is a belated recognition of his great contributions to the world of sports and the American spirit.

Ms. Pelosi has a statement.

Ms. PELOSI. Thank you, Mr. Chairman.

I want to commend you for holding this hearing today on this happy occasion.

Today's hearing on legislation to award the gold medal to Jesse Owens gives us an opportunity to recognize the achievement of a person who made a major contribution to American society. Jesse Owens' contribution to America goes far beyond his unparalleled Olympic achievements. He could easily and comfortably have rested on the laurels of his athletic accomplishments. He did not, however, and his humanitarian contributions to public service, civil rights and international goodwill made him a leader not only in the United States but in the larger world community. Awarding Jesse Owens a gold medal is an action long overdue.

. . .

STATEMENT OF HON. LOUIS STOKES, A REPRESENTATIVE IN CONGRESS FROM THE STATE OF OHIO

. . .

Mr. STOKES. Mr. Chairman, I want to thank you for the opportunity to speak in support of legislation which I introduced, H.R. 1270, to award a congressional gold medal to Mrs. Ruth Owens in honor of Jesse Owens. I am proud to serve as the author of this important legislation, to recognize the achievements of a great American and the greatest Olympic hero in our history, Jesse Owens.

This hearing comes at a very appropriate time, just 2 months before the 1988 Olympic games. As we send our athletes to Seoul, Korea, it is only fitting that we remember the athletes who brought home the gold in past Olympiads.

Jesse Owens was born in Alabama, the son of a sharecropper and grandson of slaves. His family moved to Cleveland when he was nine. He ran his first race at thirteen. He excelled at East Tech High School and set records at Ohio State University.

I would like to remind the members of the committee of Jesse Owens' performance at the 1936 Olympics. We just witnessed a heart-touching rendition of that great historic event. But the fact that Owens captured four gold medals and became the first athlete to capture that many deserves remembering.

Almost 52 years ago Jesse Owens traveled to a Germany overwhelmed by Hitler's theories of white supremacy. Black members of the team were referred to as the black auxiliaries, by the Nazi hosts. It was in this face of racism that Jesse Owens captured four gold medals and the imagination of the German crowds, who rose to their feet. It was also a triumph of humanity and of the Olympic spirit over evil.

Mr. Chairman, I was eleven years old when Jesse Owens returned to the United States from the Olympics. I vividly recall sitting on an old horse-watering trough at the corner of 69th and Central Avenue in Cleveland and watching Jesse wave to the crowd from an open automobile.

In 1936 black ghetto youths such as myself had few heroes to aspire to be like. In 1936 there was only one black Member of Congress, Arthur Mitchell, a Democrat from Illinois. I can recall that almost every black family had three photographs of their heroes on the walls of their homes: Franklin Delano Roosevelt, Joe Louis and Jesse Owens. Those were the days when my friends and I would race against one another on the streets in an attempt to emulate Jesse Owens and hoping to become like him, an Olympic star.

He set high standards for all of us in Cleveland as we attempted to journey down the road of life. He was a gentleman, and carried himself with dignity. He was the consummate sports hero, gracious in victory. Throughout his life he maintained a commitment to community service and sportsmanship. He devoted and left his expertise to youth athletic programs. He traveled widely, speaking of the virtues of fair play and advocating the power of sports to bridge differences between races, classes and cultures.

Jesse Owens died in 1980, but his spirit lives on. He was more than a sports legend, more than a national figure, greater than a hero. He was the embodiment of fair play, perseverance under pressure, dignity in the face of discrimination and prejudice.

I have to say candidly, no matter how long or how difficult the race was, he rose to the occasion. His contributions to American sports, society and history are invaluable.

I am pleased that such a panel of distinguished guests has assembled today to reflect on the achievements of Jesse Owens and the importance of this legislation.

I also want to recognize the special efforts of an individual who is unable to be present today, Mr. Dave Albritton, a former United States high-jump champion and a teammate of Jesse Owens, and our distinguished former Congressman, Sam Devine. Dave was a teammate of Jesse Owens at East Technical High School and Ohio State University.

Dave contacted me in 1986 regarding the need for Congress to recognize the achievements of Jesse Owens. Due to recent surgery, Dave cannot be present today to witness the support for his good friend and teammate, but he was kind enough to submit a statement, which will be recorded in today's historical proceedings.

...

STATEMENT OF ROBERT H. HELMICK, PRESIDENT, UNITED STATES OLYMPIC COMMITTEE

Mr. HELMICK. It is a privilege for the United States Olympic Committee to testify in support of this bill.

As we prepare for our opening ceremony in South Korea and as our athletes ready themselves for competition, it gives us great comfort and a sense of security to know that, because of you and this committee, we can begin planning for the next quadrenium [*sic*] knowing we have funds from the coin bill.

The legend of Jesse Owens is more than 50 years old, but there is nothing so revered as the memory of this great athlete. His achievements for the United States in 1936 at the Berlin Olympic Games have been a source of inspiration for thousands of our finest athletes.

By any definition, Jesse Owens is among the greatest athletes of all time, one of the greatest Americans of the century and a role model for athletes and all young people.

His Olympic accomplishments are well known to most Americans: four gold medals in Berlin in 1936 while Adolph [*sic*] Hitler watched this supposedly "inferior" human being beat his own German sprinters and jumpers. And earlier in 1935 he set five world records in 1 day at the Big Ten track and field championships at the University of Michigan.

Jesse Owens should be given special recognition because he contributed his talent, his patriotism and his legend to this Nation, despite the discrimination and hardships he experienced at the hands of his fellow Americans.

Henry Kissinger tells a story about Jesse Owens and the impact he had on his life and how the accomplishments of this athlete were turned into inspiration and courage that may have changed the course of history.

As a young Jewish boy growing up in Germany in the early 1930s, Henry Kissinger gradually fell victim to the cancerous brutality that slowly crept across his fatherland. Hitler first separated and isolated the Jews from the rest of the country, then he took away all their legal rights, and finally he denied them even the right to be treated as humans.

The year was 1936 and the Olympic games were being held in Germany. Hitler was hoping to use them to prove the superiority of his so-called Arian [*sic*] race. Meantime the world was not aware of the mounting horror this man was orchestrating.

Somehow, in some way, this isolated and oppressed Jewish boy named Henry Kissinger and others like him learned of something very special that happened during those Olympic games. They heard about an American athlete, a black American athlete, who did better than all the others, who won honor and gold for his country, and they then realized that if the United States could have a black athlete as the honored leader of its winning team, then surely the USA was a country where there was hope, where there was opportunity for everyone. (1–2, 3, 4, 5, 7, 8)

ATHLETES AND THE AMERICAN HERO

Janet C. Harris, a university scholar of sports and athletics, studied athletics and the hero and in the course of her study she determined the values of the society as they are revealed in the public's choosing of sports heroes. Harris contends that "part of the reason for the prominence of spectator sports in many societies—including American society—is that they are cultural performances" (ix). And the high value that many cultures throughout history have placed on entertainers tends to make a hero of the athlete entertainer. The kinship between athletics and performance can even be seen in *The Odyssey* when exhibition dancing and sports go together in the courts of the various Greek kings.

Statistics from the first table, gathered from schoolchildren in Greensboro, North Carolina, shows the total number of heroes named by the participants and how many among that total were athletes.

The second table lists the most admired athletes named in three polls taken in three different years. The first column is from a poll taken by L. Vander Velden in *Psychology and Sociology of Sport: Current Selected Research* (New York: AMS Press, 1986), vol. 1, 205–220. The second is from H.U. Lane's "Heroes of Young America: A National Poll," in *The World Almanac and Book of Facts 1981*. (New York: Newspaper Enterprise Association, 1980), 39. The third column is from Janet Harris' Greensboro, North Carolina, poll taken in 1982.

FROM JANET C. HARRIS, *ATHLETES AND THE AMERICAN HERO DILEMMA*

(Champaign, Ill.: Human Kinetics Publishers, 1994), 29

Table 2.1
Hero Selection from Athletics and All Walks of Life

Total Frequency	
All Walks of Life, Including Athletes	791
Athletics Only	510

Table 2.2
Rank Orders of the Most Frequently Selected Praiseworthy Athletes

1978	1980	1982
Muhammad Ali	Eric Heiden	Tony Dorsett
Brooks Robinson	Sugar Ray Robinson	Reggie Jackson
Julius Erving	Kurt Thomas	Ralph Sampson
Bert Jones	Terry Bradshaw	O.J. Simpson
O.J. Simpson	Julius Erving	James Worthy
Bjorn Borg	Earl Campbell	Julius Erving
Jimmy Connors	Kareem Abdul-Jabbar	Sam Perkins
Arthur Ashe	Muhammad Ali	Danny White
John Havlicek	Willie Stargell	Muhammad Ali
Billie Jean King	Pete Rose	Kareem Abdul-Jabbar
Pete Maravich		John McEnroe
Joe Namath		Babe Ruth
Johnny Unitas		Roger Staubach
Chris Evert		

PROJECTS FOR WRITTEN AND ORAL EXPLORATION

1. What conclusions can you make about values and the criteria for choosing heroes by examining the poll excerpts above?
2. Conduct a similar poll of most admired athletes. Engage in your own class discussion to determine which of the figures named deserve to be accorded heroic status, and why. Compare your own poll with the ones included in the documents.
3. Each member of the class should write an essay on his or her conclusions about social values based on the lists collected.
4. Conduct a class debate on the validity of the following assumption: athletic competition has had a beneficial effect on current society.
5. Conduct a class debate on the validity of the following statement: it is not whether you win or lose, but how you play the game.
6. Have a separate discussion of how coaches you know regard the statement in theory and in practice. Be prepared to support your point of view with specifics.
7. On the basis of your own additional research on Jim Thorpe, debate whether he should have had his medals taken away, and whether he deserved to be called a hero.
8. Make a report on any one athletic figure you consider to be a hero.

SUGGESTIONS FOR FURTHER READING

Browne, Ray B., M. Fishwick, and M.T. Mardsen, eds. *Heroes of Popular Culture.* Bowling Green, OH: Bowling Green State University Popular Press, 1972.

Crepeau, Richard C. "Where Have You Gone, Frank Merriwell? The Decline of the Sports Hero." In *American Sport Culture.* Cranbury, NJ: Associated University Presses, 1985.

Dodd, Martha. *Through Embassy Eyes.* New York: Harcourt Brace, 1939, 212.

Harris, Janet C. *Athletes and the American Hero Dilemma.* Champaign, Ill.: Human Kinetics, 1994.

Isaac, Neil D. *Jock Culture USA.* New York: W.W. Norton, 1978.

Lipsky, Richard. *How We Play the Game: Why Sports Dominate American Life.* Boston: Beacon Press, 1981.

Nixon, Howard L. *Sport and the American Dream.* New York: Leisure Press, 1984.

Oriard, Michael V. *Dreaming of Heroes: American Sports Fiction, 1868–1980.* Chicago: Nelson-Hall, 1982.

The Olympic Games in Ancient Greece. Athens: Ekdolike Athenon, 1982.

Robinson, Rachel Sargent. *Sources for the History of Greek Athletics in English Translation.* OH: Printed by the Author, 1955.

Williams, Peter. *The Sports Immortals.* Bowling Green, OH: Bowling Green State University Popular Press, 1991.

10

Modern Applications: The Evolution of the Heroic Ideal

The age of which Homer wrote has been labeled the Heroic Age because it was shaped by the superheroes of ancient Greece. And not only was *The Odyssey* a picture of the heroic ideal as it had been passed down in oral accounts from generation to generation; it was also a work that actually shaped the heroic ideal for the entire classical world. In the first decade of the twenty-first century, after years of bloody and disastrous wars, and the likelihood of more to come, one may find heroic qualities to admire in both of Homer's heroes of long ago—Achilles and Odysseus. At the same time, however, our view of the heroic ideal has profoundly changed from the time of ancient Greece.

We find suggestions of what constituted the Greek hero in Homer's great store of descriptive phrases ("Homeric epithets") that he uses in *The Iliad* and *The Odyssey* to depict and, in minutiae, to characterize each hero, selecting phrases to fit the occasion and to satisfy the metrical or aesthetic demands of dactylic hexameter lines. The words most commonly used to describe Odysseus are "Sacker of Cities" and "wily Odysseus"—words that present the heart of the man and the concept of heroic virtue inherent in his actions. He is praised because he is the man of might and force and cunning, in combination unequaled in the ancient world, for nobody can surpass this man in his ability to destroy, to kill, to gather gold, glory, and women by utterly destroying a magnificent city like Troy. His was the deceptive device of the Trojan Horse, which depended for its success on the tendency of the Trojans to honor the gods and to drag within their walls this symbol of the Greek "retreat" and their parting "sacrifice" to the gods. Odysseus was the one to invent clever, deceptive, and

Sergeant Alvin C. York in uniform during World War I. *Source:* Associated Press archives of Wide World Photos.

convincing lies with which to make his way in an often hostile and always dangerous world.

There was no shame and no dishonor attached to Odysseus's epithet "Sacker of Cities." It was praise. It was part of the essence of his heroic personality. What one did when he sacked a city was to kill every male, including young boys, and to take the women as slaves: the young and the pretty ones to be concubines—for example, Cassandra, whom Agamemnon brings home with him to Mycenae—and other women who are assigned various duties in the household or the field. Thus we find that Odysseus's first adventure upon leaving the vanquished city of Troy was an attempt to raid and destroy a city whose people had done him no wrong whatsoever; his motive, as usual, was the acquisition of women, money, and honor.

The concept of honor also is crucial in the heroic ideal. It was not, as it usually is in the modern world, a matter of internal adherence to a noble concept of right and wrong, or of private turmoil involving conscience and community with God, despite or in contrast to what the world may think. Instead, honor in Odysseus' time was the very essence of what the world thought. The honor that defined the hero was the achievement of eternal and lasting glory in the eyes of all the people around him.

It was a system that gave overwhelming significance to results, not on motive. Achilles, for example, achieved honor for what he *did* on the field of battle and on the plains of Troy, even though to achieve this he had to slaughter people in massive numbers. Likewise, Odysseus was honored because he, too, had achieved matchless glory on the Trojan plains and because he had devised the scheme—the Trojan Horse—that, after the death of Achilles, finally brought victory to the struggling Achaeans.

While to the modern mind this may seem crude, barbaric, and cruel, in a chaotic world in which all of civilization was crumbling (as it was in the twelfth century B.C. or in the subsequent Dark Ages), the military hero, the man who can conquer all assailants in hand-to-hand battle and can drive off all casual and brutal raiders, possesses a virtue supremely to be desired. This was true in the Mycenaean Age and in the chaos resulting from the collapse of the Mycenaeans; so has it always been in a world where people take all by force: a world, that is, in which war prevails.

As a consequence, the hero in ancient Greece was the successful military leader, for to lose in battle meant not only the death of men but also the death of cities, cultures, even civilizations. This being so, since war and predatory raids began, every nation has briefly honored its military leaders.

In contrasting Achilles and Odysseus as military heroes, two different aspects of the Greek hero emerge, tailored for two different ages. Achilles, the supreme hero of *The Iliad*, who makes an appearance in the Land of the Dead in *The Odyssey*, is the hero for a stable society (the Mycenaean Age at its most powerful) and is, as a consequence, one who is straightforward and courageous in battle. Odysseus, the hero of *The Odyssey*, begins coming home in the Dark Ages, as his society is in disarray and crumbling. For such a hero, personal survival and survival of his homeland can be accomplished only by wiliness and deception.

Achilles, while possessing all the skills expected of an ideal young man, has devoted his entire existence to the achievement of glory in battle; and he is always straightforward and true: what you see is invariably what there is. He is the military hero without peer and without deception. Even in his quarrels with Agamemnon and in his withdrawal from battle, he seems incapable of deception. Achilles achieves his glory through his death on the plains of Troy, in battle.

In *The Iliad*, when Odysseus leads the delegation from Agamemnon to Achilles, accurately presenting Agamemnon's offer to restore all that he has taken from Achilles and to give him in addition great heaps of treasure and his own daughter in marriage, but withholding Agamemnon's insistence that Achilles must still bow down to him as the greater king and the greater man, Achilles, who sees through this subterfuge or at least suspects it, replies with ultimate scorn: "Him do I hate even as the gates of hell who says one thing while he hides another in his heart. Therefore I will say what I mean" (Butler, 9. p. 134.)

Odysseus, on the other hand, is the essential deceiver, the liar, the man who regards it not as dishonor but as virtue to succeed by lies and by deception if necessary, and who, in *The Odyssey*, rarely tells the truth in the wild and eternally dangerous world into which he is thrown. In *The Odyssey*, he finds himself in positions in which he first must determine who his enemies and his friends are before revealing anything of his identity or his true nature. Odysseus is the hero of an ever-changing world in which only the best can survive; he is determined to survive and, ultimately, to exact a terrible revenge on the men who have ravaged his home and harassed his wife for many years. And so he is eternally the master of disguise. He invents a tall tale (he lies) at every step of the way; and he reveals himself only when he knows without question that it is safe to do so.

Furthermore, Homer presents cases in which Odysseus is so patently confronted with villainy that only deception can enable him to triumph; thus he elicits empathy with or admiration for his chameleon hero while at the same time presenting his heroic quality. Thus, when trapped in the cave of Polyphemos, the one-eyed giant who is set upon devouring all his captives one by one, Odysseus first gives his name as Noman, and then devises a clever scheme to escape from the giant, with himself and his men hiding under the bellies of sheep. Then, when he is presumably out of reach in his ship, leaving the harbor, his sense of honor, and/or heroic pride, impels him to shout out his own name—"Say that it was Odysseus ... the waster of cities" (Butcher and Lang, 9. p. 128)—thus incurring the enmity of Poseidon.

Even among the Phaecians, who treat him as a stranger, with honor and respect, as someone who knew the great heroes of the Trojan War, Odysseus spins a false tale. When the local champion athlete taunts him for refusing to participate in games (by calling him a "merchant"), Odysseus cannot resist showing that he is indeed "noble" and "great." To prove this fact, he hurls the javelin farther than anyone else possibly could, and then challenges one and all to any kind of contest. At last, he declares with pride: "I am Odysseus, son of Laertes, who am in men's minds for all manner of wiles, and my fame reaches unto heaven" (Butcher and Lang, 9. p. 113).

Even when Odysseus arrives in Ithaca, the sole survivor of his disastrous voyage home, he is forced—out of absolute necessity—to disguise himself as a beggar; and as such he lies to everyone, until at last he exacts his terrible revenge: rising to heroic proportions of slaughter and scorning pleas for mercy, he kills all of the suitors, has the faithless serving women killed, and mercilessly tortures and mutilates the goatherd who had insulted him.

A further contrast in heroic ideals represented by Achilles and Odysseus is shown by Homer's conclusions of their stories. Achilles' story in *The Iliad* ends with at least a momentary sense of compassion as the Greek warrior faces Priam, the aged father of Hector, the man he has slain. Odysseus' story ends with one of the bloodiest homecomings ever devised; he shows no mercy whatsoever to the offending suitors and their friends. There is no suggestion here of any tradition that permits mercy for a beaten warrior who totally surrenders and throws himself at the victor's feet. There is instead pure revenge. Yet the actions of both Achilles and Odysseus were equally "heroic."

There is in *The Odyssey* more than a mere suggestion that times have changed since the "glory" days of the Trojan War. Just as the greatness of Mycenaean Greece fell in the twelfth century after the real or imagined sacking of Troy, so the concept of hero and of heroism significantly shifts from the epic battles of Achaeans and Trojans in *The Iliad* to that of adventurous survival in *The Odyssey*. If the *Iliad* may be said to represent the last flash of greatness of the Mycenaean Age, *The Odyssey* may vividly portray the uncertain fate and the shifting standards of the Greek world following the Dorian supremacy.

Homer wrote at the end of the so-called Dark Ages in Greece, describing a civilization that existed four to five hundred years before his own time; and he is said, variously, to describe both Mycenean society and the Dark Ages. Regardless of the truth or the fiction of the Trojan War and its heroes, Homer's two epics in effect symbolize the divergent concepts before and after those two disasters. Commercial trade, social stability, customs, standards of conduct, and easy acceptance of life or of a neighbor all vanished after the twelfth-century collapse of Mycenae. Odysseus is a hero for the Dark Ages with its uncertainty, violence, distrust, and determination to survive regardless of all obstacles and all foes.

At the same time, ironically, after the war is over, the heroes who are not dead face almost insurmountable troubles at home, as in the case of Odysseus. All of his men died either on the battlefield or after leaving Troy. Only Odysseus reached home alive; and even he, upon reaching it, was forced to adopt the guise of a beggar to survive his return. Nations have, more often than not, tended not to make heroes of their returning common soldiers, but to ignore them. After they have served their purpose, they are left free to wander the city streets or the roads between town and town or farm and farm, or to die from ailments or injuries achieved in the process of saving the world that ignores them. Sometimes the returning warrior has not even been free to do that, for, as in the Elizabethan world, after England's defeat of the Spanish Armada, maimed or unemployed veterans of that battle wandering the streets and the lanes became such a nuisance that special laws were passed to deny their presence, and often their lives. And so it was after the Napoleonic Wars.

In comparing Homer's heroes with those of the twentieth and twenty-first centuries, one finds that much of the quality of the hero has endured. Courage emerges as one of those supreme enduring characteristics of the hero in every age and every culture. But courage alone does not make a hero, as it often seemed to do in Homer's time. Consider the suicide bombers who killed thousands of people in the World Trade Center. There is no question that such an act required courage, but the bombers are scarcely heroic in the eyes of most of the world. And the field on which courage is played out has expanded. Even the definition of courage has changed. Those who courageously face enemy fire on the battlefield are not the only heroes in our society. Others show courage as corporate whistle-blowers, for instance, risking livelihoods, careers, and reputations to stand up for what they regard as right. The definition of courage is no longer limited, as it was in Achilles' day, to physical deeds; the contemporary world finds heroic courage at the spiritual and psychological levels: in a young widow, wrenched by grief, who pulls her family together to continue their lives; in the compassionate caregiver of a sick relative; in a paralyzed man or woman who refuses to give up.

One of the biggest differences in the concept of the hero between Odysseus' time and ours is that the heroes of the Homeric epics were invariably kings. The great Greek philosopher Aristotle indicates this in his *Poetics* when he asserts that only a king can be a tragic hero in Greek drama. But the warrior heroes of the twentieth century came not from the ranks of the generals, but from the ranks of the common soldier, as is illustrated by the fact that the most decorated heroes of our two world wars—Alvin C. York and Audie Murphy—were both of humble origins and had little education.

The changing attitude toward war has altered the idea of the hero. Admittedly, religion continues to be invoked in wars in the twenty-first century: Catholics and Protestants battle in Northern Ireland; Christians and Muslims fight each other in the Balkans; Hindus and Muslims are at war in India and Pakistan; Jews and Muslims fight in the Middle East. But many of the great religions of the world, notably Christianity, Buddhism, and Hinduism, have also contributed a religious conviction that killing is wrong and that war is to be avoided at all costs. Even a soldier like Alvin York, with a record of killing the German enemy with his rifle, was torn between his Christian religion, which forbids killing, and his country's call to go to war. So great was the pacifism of his religious background that his minister appealed on York's behalf to exempt him from military service.

While results are still often accomplished in war without regard to means—in slaughtering civilians to achieve victory—and while massacres and looting in the mold of Achilles and Odysseus still occur, mainstream twentieth- and twenty-first-century society no longer admires such behavior as heroic or condones it. The Allies prosecuted Nazi war criminals after World War II, prosecutions followed the My Lai massacre in Vietnam, and in 2001 there was the trial of the former president of Yugoslavia, Slobodan Milosevic, for crimes against humanity during the war in the Balkans.

Perhaps the biggest difference between heroes of Homer's Heroic Age and the hero, even the war hero, in the twentieth and twenty-first centuries is their motivation. Odysseus always acts out of his own self-interest in leading his men into peril and looting cities, and Achilles does so while insisting on being pampered and glorified above all else. But the contemporary hero is the person who acts courageously by placing himself or herself in danger to save other people, as the documents included here make clear.

Also, in the tradition of the great religions of the Western world and the great social revolutions of the eighteenth and nineteenth centuries, heroes in the twentieth and twenty-first centuries have come more often to be regarded not as defenders of the dominant culture (like Odysseus) but as challengers of the power structure and status quo, like Mohandas Gandhi, Martin Luther King, and Cesar Chavez.

Heroes like Audie Murphy emerged in World War II in part because of the perception that this was a "necessary war," waged to save the world, not only the country, from the fascist Axis powers, led by Germany and Japan, that had already forcibly enslaved other countries and carried out massive genocide. The emerging stories of atrocities like the rape of Nanking in China, as well as the liberation of concentration camps in Europe, confirmed the necessity of having had to take up arms. Those who did so courageously became the country's heroes.

Twenty years afterward, however, pacifism and suspicion of government and the military grew stronger. At the same time, the United States escalated its military involvement in Vietnam. The public and soldiers who went there in greater and greater numbers were told that democracy was at stake. The antiwar movement grew stronger as the war escalated, and returning soldiers felt either that they had been sacrificed in a futile and wrongheaded mission, or that the public, far from seeing them as heroes, disparaged them. For whatever reason, during the war and after, no specific soldier superheroes surfaced in the public mind. The unquestionable emotional response elicited by the

Vietnam Memorial arises because individual men and women listed there are viewed not as superheroes, but rather as victims of a senseless engagement.

After decades of regarding the government with suspicion and refusing to elevate any one person—especially a member of any governmental organization—to the status of hero, a cataclysmic change occurred in the public view of heroes on September 11, 2001. On that morning, airplanes hijacked by Muslim extremists crashed into New York City's World Trade Center, the Pentagon, and a field in Pennsylvania, killing thousands of people. Hundreds of firefighters and police officers lost their lives in the rescue efforts. In those hours, the idea of the hero strongly reemerged in the public consciousness. Although no single proper name of a hero became a household word, the dead firefighters as a group of heroes gripped the world's emotions as few heroes had ever done before.

Despite a degree of pacifist sentiment, what also changed was the general public's commitment to waging a military operation in the name of preserving the home culture of freedom and democracy, and in defense of its citizens. Soldiers willingly went to war with a moral confidence that neither Odysseus nor Achilles nor Sergeant York experienced when called up. And there seemed to be a public eagerness to pay homage to every single fallen soldier as a hero, in contrast to the general attitude in the Vietnam War.

Whether one looks to ancient or contemporary concepts of heroism, however, one thing becomes clear: the hero's return to the ordinary world is exceedingly difficult. Sergeant York, after World War I, struggled with little success in the Tennessee mountains to bring his people out of isolation, ignorance, and poverty, and into the larger world he had discovered during the war. Audie Murphy, celebrated as a movie star by day, suffered horrifying nightmares by night, part of post-traumatic stress syndrome, which also devastated massive numbers of Vietnam veterans upon return home.

The following documents, which tell the stories of modern-day heroes, include excerpts from the World War I diary of Sergeant York; the citation for bravery that Audie Murphy received after World War II; the testimony of Hugh Thompson after the Vietnam War and the citation he received twenty-eight years later; and excerpts about the heroic firefighters and police officers on September 11, 2001.

WORLD WAR I: SERGEANT ALVIN YORK

Alvin C. York, the most acclaimed hero of World War I, was not a West Point graduate schooled in the history and strategy of warfare; he was not a general, not even an officer; nor was he a career soldier. He was an uneducated, deeply religious man born in the isolated Tennessee mountains to a poor farmer who augmented the family's meager diet by hunting. To paraphrase Herman Melville, York's Harvard and his Yale College were the hills of the Great Smoky Mountains, where he learned to shoot game with a rifle without wasting a single shell.

When U.S. involvement in World War I began, York answered the draft call with great trepidation, for his religion had taught him that war and killing other human beings was a sin. Yet he also was profoundly patriotic, and thought his country had a legitimate need of soldiers to fight the Germans. His conflict was reluctantly resolved in favor of taking up arms, not for sport or for food, but to kill the enemy.

In his most heroic mission, under heavy fire during the battle of the Argonne in France, York killed twenty-five men and captured 132 prisoners. After the war he remained in France for seven months before returning to the United States. In February 1919, he was awarded the Distinguished Service Cross in France; in April, the French Croix de Guerre and the Medal of Honor. Although he was quickly regarded as a hero in France, few people in the United States, including those in his home state of Tennessee, were aware of his exploits, largely because of the failure of the army's top brass to recognize his heroism. It took the investigative reporting of the *Saturday Evening Post* to discover what York had done and reveal it to the public in an article.

Before going home to Tennessee, York and other soldiers of World War I were honored in a ticker-tape parade in New York City. York was also invited to Washington to meet with Congress and the secretary of war.

York refused to capitalize on his fame or accept publicity when he returned. Not until many years later, as World War II loomed, did he approve the famous movie about him, starring Gary Cooper. York contributed the money he was given for the movie to the people of his region. He spent the rest of his life in service to his mountain people, lobbying for better roads and establishing foundations for education.

The following excerpts are from York's diary, which he began keeping on the day he got his draft notice and which he kept throughout the war until he came home in May 1919.

The values and outlook of this early twentieth-century hero serve as an interesting contrast to the ideals of ancient Greece. York's diary is a story of war and return, just as *The Iliad* and *The Odyssey* are stories of Odysseus' war and return home. Curiously, we find that both men went to war reluctantly, their quandaries and hesitations forming major episodes in their lives—an ironic situation, in light of their later courage and skills on the battlefield. The ultimate goal of both men was to come back home, but like Odysseus, York took his own sweet time in returning, traveling for several months after the war around France, a land that was likely as strange and fascinating to him as Circe's island was to Odysseus. And both men became legends in their own time.

But the differences between the two heroes are greater than the similarities, revealing the ever-changing nature of heroism. Odysseus actively sought personal glory, honor, riches, and revenge. By contrast, York was a humble man, motivated by none of these pursuits. And his refusal to capitalize financially from his war experiences and his failure to feel hatred for the Germans were as much responsible for the public's elevation of York to hero as was his valor in battle. There is, moreover, an abiding sense of ethical behavior and religious faith that permeates York's story—elements entirely lacking in *The Odyssey*.

FROM *SERGEANT YORK: HIS OWN LIFE STORY AND WAR DIARY*, ED. TOM SKEYHILL

(Garden City, NY: Doubleday, Doran, 1928)

николаем *NOVEMBER 14, 1917*

Jamestown, Tennessee: So later I sure received a card that said report to your local board. So I went to Jamestown and reported to the local board, and I stayed all night that night at Dr. Alexander's. I knew now I was in it. I was bothered a plenty as to whether it was right or wrong. I knew that if it was right, everything would be all right. And I also knew that if it was wrong and we were only fighting for a bunch of foreigners, it would be all wrong. And I prayed and prayed. I prayed two whole days and a night out on the mountainside. And I received my assurance that it was all right, that I should go, and that I would come back without a scratch. I received this assurance direct from God. And I have always been led to believe that He always keeps his promise. I told my little old mother not to worry; that it was all right, and that I was coming back; and I told my brothers and sisters; and I told Pastor Pile, and I prayed with him; and I told everybody else I discussed it with. But it was very hard on my mother, just like it was on all mothers, and she didn't want to see me go.

…

NOVEMBER 17, 1917

...

I had never traveled much before going to camp. I had never been out of the mountains before, and I'm telling you I missed them right smart down there in that flat, sandy country. And my little old mother and Pastor Pile wanted to get me out. Pastor Pile put in a plea to the government that it was against the religion of our church to fight; and that he wanted to get me out on these grounds. And he sent his papers up the War Department, and then filled them out and sent them to me at the camp and asked me to sign them. They told me all I had to do was to sign them. And I refused to sign them, as I couldn't see it the way Pastor Pile did. My mother, too, put in a plea to get me out as her sole support. My father was dead and I was keeping my mother and brothers and sisters. And the papers were fixed up and sent to Camp Gordon and I was asked to sign them. But I didn't sign them. I knew I had plenty of brothers back there that could look after my mother, that I was not the sole support, and I didn't feel I ought to do it. And so I never asked for exemption from service on any grounds at all. I never was a conscientious objector. I am not today. I didn't want to go and fight and kill. But I had to answer the call of my country, and I did. And I believed it was right. I have got no hatred toward the Germans and I never had.

...

MARCH, 1918

Camp Gordon: Well, they gave me a gun, and oh my, that old gun was just full of grease and I had to clean that old gun for inspection. So I had a hard time to get that old gun clean, and oh, those were trying hours for a boy like me, trying to live for God and do His blessed will. So when I got this gun, I began to drill with the gun, and we had to hike once a week.

...

MARCH 29, 1918

Pall Mall, Tennessee: So I had to start back to my company, and that was a heartbreaking time for me, as I knew I had to go to France. But I went back to my company trusting in God and asking Him to keep me although I had many trials and much hardship and temptation. But as I could look up and say:

> O God, in hope that sends a shining ray
> Far down the future broadening way,
> In peace that only Thou can give,
> With Thee, O Master, let me live.

Then it was that the Lord would bless me and I almost felt sure of coming back home for the Lord was with me.

...

APRIL 30, 1918

Boston, Massachusetts: And then we went to Boston. Captain Danforth came around and asked every man in the company if he objected to going across to fight, and if he did what his objections were. He came to me, and I told him I didn't object to fighting, but the only thing that bothered me was, were we in the right or wrong? He and I had a short conversation. Then he asked me again if I objected and I told him I did not. He quoted, "Blessed are the peacemakers," and I replied that if a man can make peace by fighting he is a peacemaker. We thought when we got over there, it would not be very long before peace was made, and it was not very long after we got there that there was peace.

...

JULY 1st 1918

Montsec Sector, France—A few words on Christian witness in war and why a Christian does worry. Yet there is no use worrying about anything except the worry of so many souls who have passed out into the Deep of an unknown world and have left no testimony as to the welfare of their souls. There is no use of worrying about shells, for you can't keep them from busting in your trench, nor you can't stop the rain or prevent a light from agoing up jest as you are half-way over the parapet.

So what is the use of worrying if you can't alter things? Just ask God to help you and accept them and make the best of them by the help of God. Yet some men do worry, and by doing so they effectually destroy their peace of mind without doing anyone any good. Yet it is often the religious man who worries. I have even heard those whose care was for the soldier's soul deplore the fact that he did not worry. I have heard it said that the soldier is so careless, he realizes his position so little.

Oh, yes; I felt before I left home—in fact, I told them when I left—I was coming back, and I felt I was going to get back safely, and I never did doubt it in the least, because I had my assurance that I would return home safely.

I carried a Testament with me. I have the Testament I carried with me during all my fighting at home now. I read it through five times during my stay in the army. I read it everywhere. I read it in dugouts, in fox holes, and on the front line. It was my rock to cling to. It and my diary. I didn't do any cursing, no, not even in the front line. I cut all of that out long ago, at the time I was saved.

...

OCTOBER 5th 1918

Argonne Forest, France—We went out on the main road and lined up and started for the front and the Germans was shelling the road and the airplanes was humming over our heads, and we were stumbling over dead horses and dead men, and the shells were bursting all around us.

And then it was I could see the power of God helped men if they would only trust Him.

Oh, it was there I could look up and say:
"O Jesus, the great rock of foundation
Whereon my feet were set with sovereign grace.
Through shells or death with all their agitation.
Thou wilt protect me if I will only trust in Thy grace.
Bless Thy Holy Name!"

OCTOBER 7th 1918

Argonne Forest, France—We lay in some little holes by the roadside all day. That night we went and stayed a little while and come back to our little holes and the shells busting all around us. I saw men just blown up by the big German shells. So the order came for us to take hills 223 and 240 the 8th.

It was raining a little bit all day, drizzly and very damp. Lots of big shells bursting all around us. We were not up close enough for the machine guns to reach us, but airplanes were buzzing overhead most all the time, just like a lot of hornets. Lots of men were killed by the artillery fire. And lots more wounded.

We saw quite a lot of our machine gun battalion across the road from us blown up by the big shells. The woods were all mussed up and looked as if a terrible cyclone had swept through them.

But God would never be cruel enough to create a cyclone as terrible as that Argonne battle. Only man would ever think of doing an awful thing like that. It looked like "the abomination of desolation" must look like. And all through the long night those big guns flashed and growled just like the lightning and the thunder when it storms in the mountains at home.

And, oh my, we had to pass the wounded. And some of them were on stretchers going back to the dressing stations, and some of them were lying around, moaning and twitching. And the dead were all along the road. And it was wet and cold. And it all made me think of the Bible and the story of the Anti-Christ and Armageddon.

And I'm telling you the little log cabin in Wolf Valley in old Tennessee seemed a long long way off.

That night the orders came for us to take Hill 223. The zero hour was set for 6 o'clock, which was just before daylight. We were to go over the top, take the hill, and advance across the valley to the ridges on the other side, and take them and press on to the Decauville Railroad, which was our objective. It was a very important railroad for the Germans.

And the Lost Battalion was in there somewhere, needing help most awful bad!

"When thou goest out to battle against thine enemies, and seest horses, and chariots, and a people more than thou, be not afraid of them: for the LORD thy God is with thee, which brought thee up out of the land of Egypt."
~Deuteronomy 20:1~

OCTOBER 8th 1918

Argonne Forest, France—So on the morning of the 8th, just before daylight, we started for the hill of Chattel Chehery. So before we got there it got light, and the Germans sent over a heavy barrage and also gas, and we put on our gas masks and just pressed right on [through] those shells and got to the top of Hill 223 to where we was to start over the top at 6:10 A.M.

And they was to give us a barrage. So the time came, and no barrage, and we had to start without one. So as we started over the top at 6:10 A.M., and the Germans was putting their machines guns to work all over the hill in front of us and on our left and right. So I was in support and I could see my pals getting picked off until it almost looked like there was none left.

This was our first offensive battle in the Argonne. My battalion was one of the attacking battalions. My platoon was the second. We were in support of the first. We advanced just a few yards behind them. We got through the shells and the gas all right, and occupied Hill 223, which was to be our jumping off place for the advance on the railroad. When the zero hour came, we went over the top and started our advance.

We had to charge across a valley several hundred yards wide and rush the machine gun emplacements on the ridge on the far side. And there were machine guns on the ridges on our flanks too.

It was kind of [a] triangular shaped valley. So you see we were getting it from the front and both flanks. Well, the first and second waves got about halfway across the valley and then were held up by machine gun fire from the three sides. It was awful. Our loses [sic] were very heavy.

The advancement was stopped and we were ordered to dig in. I don't believe our whole battalion or even our whole division, could have taken those machine guns by a straightforward attack.

The Germans got us, and they got us right smart. They just stopped us dead in our tracks. It was hilly country with plenty of brush, and they had plenty of machine guns entrenched along those commanding ridges. And I'm telling you they were shooting straight. Our boys just went down like the long grass before the mowing machine at home. And, to make matters worse, something had happened to our artillery and we had no barrage.

So our attack just faded out. And there we were, lying down, about halfway across, and no barrage, and those German machine guns and big shells getting us hard.

I just knew that we couldn't go on again until those machine guns were mopped up. So we decided to try and get them by a surprise attack in the rear.

We figured there must have been over thirty of them, and they were hidden on the ridges about 300 yards in front and on the left of us.

So there was 17 of us boys went around on the left flank to see if we couldn't put those guns out of action. So when we went around and fell in behind those guns, we first saw two Germans with Red Cross bands on their arms. So we asked them to stop, and they did not. So one of the boys shot at them and they run back to our right. So we all run after them—

Sergeant Harry Parsons gave the command to what was left of our squads—my squad, Corporal Savage's squad, Corporal Early's, and Corporal Cutting's—to go around through the brush and try and make the surprise attack.

According to orders, we advanced through our front line and on through the brush and up the hill on the left. We went very quietly and quickly. We had to. And we took care to keep well to our left.

Without any loss and in right smart time, we were across the valley and on the hill where the machine guns were emplaced. The brush and the hilly nature of the country hid us from the Germans.

We were nearly 300 yards in front of our own front line. When we figured we were on top of the hill and on their left flank, we had a little conference.

Some of the boys wanted to attack from the flank. But Early and I and some of the others thought it would be best to go right on over the hill and jump them from the rear. We decided on this rear attack.

We opened up in skirmishing order and flitting from brush to brush, quickly crossed over the hill and down into the gully behind. Then we suddenly swung around behind them. The first Germans we saw were two men with Red Cross bands on their arms. They jumped out of the brush in front of us and bolted like two scared rabbits.

We called to them to surrender, and one of our boys fired and missed. And they kept on going. We wanted to capture them before they gave the alarm. We were now well behind the German trench and in the rear of the machine guns that were holding up our big advance.

We were deep in the brush and we couldn't see the Germans and they couldn't see us. But we could hear their machine guns shooting something awful. Savage's squad was leading, and mine, Early's and Cutting's followed.

—And when we jumped across a little stream of water that was there, they was about 15 or 20 Germans jumped up and threw up their hands and said, "Kamerad!" So the one in charge of us boys told us not to shoot: they was going to give up anyway.

It was headquarters. There were orderlies, stretcher bearers and runners, and a major and two other officers, They were just having breakfast and there was a mess of beefsteaks, jellies, jams, and loaf bread around. They were unarmed, all except the major.

We jumped them right smart and covered them, and told them to throw up their hands and to keep them up. And they did. I guess they thought the whole American army was in their rear. And we didn't stop to tell them anything different. No shots were fired, and there was no talking between us except when we told them to "put them up."

So by this time some of the Germans from on the hill was shooting at us. Well I was giving them the best I had, and by this time the Germans had got their machine guns turned around and fired on us. So they killed 6 and wounded 3 of us. So that just left 8, and then we got into it right by this time. So we had a hard battle for a little while—

I don't know whether it was the German major, but one yelled something out in German that we couldn't understand. And then the machine guns on top swung around and opened fire on us. There were about thirty of them. They were commanding us from a hillside less than thirty yards away. They couldn't miss. And they didn't!

They killed all of Savage's squad; they got all of mine but two; they wounded Cutting and killed two of his squad; and Early's squad was well back in the brush on the extreme right and not yet under the direct fire of the machine guns, and so they escaped. All except Early. He went down with three bullets in his body. That left me in command. I was right out there in the open.

And those machine guns were spitting fire and cutting down the undergrowth all around me something awful. And the Germans were yelling orders. You never heard such a racket in all of your life. I didn't have time to dodge behind a tree or dive into the brush, I didn't even have time to kneel or lie down.

I don't know what the other boys were doing. They claim they didn't fire a shot. They said afterwards they were on the right, guarding the prisoners. And the prisoners were lying down and the machine guns had to shoot over them to get me. As soon as the machine guns opened fire on me, I began to exchange shots with them.

I had no time nohow to do nothing but watch them-there German machine gunners and give them the best I had. Every time I seed a German I jes teched him off. At first I was shooting from a prone position; that is lying down; jes like we often shoot at the targets in the shooting matches in the mountains of Tennessee; and it was jes about the same distance. But the targets here were bigger. I jes couldn't miss a German's head or body at that distance. And I didn't. Besides, it weren't no time to miss nohow.

I knowed that in order to shoot me the Germans would have to get their heads up to see where I was lying. And I knowed that my only chance was to keep their heads down. And I done done it. I covered their positions and let fly every time I seed anything to shoot at. Every time a head come up I done knocked it down. Then they would sorter stop for a moment and then another head would come up and I would knock it down, too. I was giving them the best I had.

I was right out in the open and the machine guns [there were over thirty of them in continuous action] were spitting fire and cutting up all around me something awful. But they didn't seem to be able to hit me. All the time the Germans were shouting orders. You never heard such a racket in all of your life. Of course, all of this only took a few minutes. As soon as I was able I stood up and begun to shoot off-hand, which is my favorite position. I was still sharpshooting with that-there old army rifle. I used up several clips. The barrel was getting hot and my rifle ammunition was running low, or was where it was hard for me to get at it quickly. But I had to keep on shooting jes the same.

In the middle of the fight a German officer and five men done jumped out of a trench and charged me with fixed bayonets. They had about twenty-five yards to come and they were coming right smart. I only had about half a clip left in my rifle; but I had my pistol ready. I done flipped it out fast and teched them off, too.

I teched off the sixth man first; then the fifth; then the fourth; then the third; and so on. That's the way we shoot wild turkeys at home. You see we don't want the front ones to know that we're getting the back ones, and then they keep on coming until we get them all. Of course, I hadn't time to think of that. I guess I jes naturally did it. I knowed, too, that if the front ones wavered, or if I stopped them the rear ones would drop down and pump a volley into me and get me.

Then I returned to the rifle, and kept right on after those machine guns. I knowed now that if I done kept my head and didn't run out of ammunition I had them. So I done hollered to them to come down and give up. I didn't want to kill any more'n I had to. I would tech a couple of them off and holler again. But I guess they couldn't understand my language, or else they couldn't hear me in the awful racket that was going on all around. Over twenty Germans were killed by this time.

—and I got hold of the German major. After he seed me stop the six Germans who charged with fixed bayonets he got up off the ground and walked over to me and yelled "English?"

I said, "No, not English."

He said, "What?"

I said, "American."

He said, "Good—!" Then he said, "If you won't shoot any more I will make them give up." I had killed over twenty before the German major said he would make them give up. I covered him with my automatic and told him if he didn't make them stop firing I would take off his head next. And he knew I meant it. He told me if I didn't kill him, and if I stopped shooting the others in the trench, he would make them surrender.

So he blew a little whistle and they came down and began to gather around and throw down their guns and belts. All but one of them came off the hill with their hands up, and just before that one got to me he threw a little hand grenade which burst in the air in front of me.

I had to tech him off. The rest surrendered without any more trouble. There were nearly 100 of them.

So we had about 80 or 90 Germans there disarmed, and had another line of Germans to go through to get out. So I called for my men, and one of them answered from behind a big oak tree, and the others were on my right in the brush.

So I said, "Let's get these Germans out of here."

One of my men said, "It is impossible."

So I said, "No; let's get them out."

So when my man said that, this German major said, "How many *have* you got?" and I said, "I have got a- plenty," and pointed my pistol at him all the time.

In this battle I was using a rifle and a .45 Colt automatic pistol.

So I lined the Germans up in a line of twos, and I got between the ones in front, and I had the German major before me. So I marched them straight into those other machine guns and I got them.

The German major could speak English as well as I could. Before the war he used to work in Chicago. And I told him to keep his hands up and to line up his men in column of twos, and to do it in double time. And he did it. And I lined up my men that were left on either side of the column, and I told one to guard the rear. I ordered the prisoners to pick up and carry our wounded. I wasn't a-goin' to leave any good American boys lying out there to die. So I made the Germans carry them. And they did.

And I takened the major and placed him at the head of the column and I got behind him and used him as a screen. I poked the automatic in his back and told him to hike. And he hiked.

The major suggested we go down a gully, but I knew that was the wrong way. And I told him we were not going down any gully. We were going straight through the German front line trenches back to the American lines.

It was their second line that I had captured. We sure did get a long way behind the German trenches! And so I marched them straight at that old German front line trench. And some more machine guns swung around and began to spit at us. I told the major to blow his whistle or I would take off his head and theirs too. So he blew his whistle and they all surrendered—all except one. I made the major order him to surrender twice. But he wouldn't. And I had to tech him off. I hated to do it. I've been doing a tolerable lot of thinking about it since. He was probably a brave soldier boy. But I couldn't afford to take any chances and so I had to let him have it.

There was considerably over a hundred prisoners now. It was a problem to get them back safely to our own lines. There was so many of them there was danger of our own artillery mistaking us for a German counter-attack and opening up on us. I sure was relieved when we run into the relief squads that had been sent forward through the brush to help us.

On the way back we were constantly under heavy shell fire and I had to double-time them to get them through safely. There was nothing to be gained by having any more of them wounded or killed. They done surrendered to me and it was up to me to look after them. And so I done done it.

So when I got back to my major's p.c. I had 132 prisoners. We marched those German prisoners on back into the American lines to the battalion p.c. (post of command), and there we came to the Intelligence Department. Lieutenant Woods came out and counted 132 prisoners. And when he counted them he said, "York, have you captured the whole German army?" And I told him I had a tolerable few.

We were ordered to take them out to regimental headquarters at Chattel Chehery, and from there all the way back to division headquarters, and turn them over to the military police.

...

I had orders to report to Brigadier General Lindsey, and he said to me, "Well, York, I hear you have captured the whole ——— German army." And I told him I only had 132.

After a short talk he sent us to some artillery kitchens, where we had a good warm meal. And it sure felt good. Then we rejoined our outfits and with them fought through to our objective, the Decauville Railroad.

And the Lost Battalion was able to come out that night. We cut the Germans off from their supplies when we cut that old railroad, and they withdrew and backed up.

So you can see here in this case of mine where God helped me out. I had been living for God and working in the church some time before I come to the army. So I am a witness to the fact that God did help me out of that hard battle; for the bushes were shot up all around me and I never got a scratch.

So you can see that God will be with you if you will only trust Him; and I say that He did save me. Now, He will save you if you will only trust Him.

The next morning Captain Danforth sent me back with some stretcher bearers to see if there were any of our American boys that we had missed. But they were all dead. And there were a lot of German dead. We counted twenty-eight, which is just the number of shots I fired. And there were thirty-five machine guns and a whole mess of equipment and small arms.

The salvage corps was busy packing it up. And I noticed the bushes all around where I stood in my fight with the machine guns were all cut down. The bullets went over my head and on either side. But they never touched me.

...

MAY 22nd

Hoboken, N.J.—At 2 P.M. I landed, and the Tennessee Society had a 5 day furlough for me to see New York City. So I stopped at Waldorf Hotel.

The Tennessee Society met me at the boat with a car. There was quite a number of newspaper men met me and photographed me. And so I was under fire again. Ho ho. and the questions they asked me!

By the time they had finished writing about me in their newspapers I had whipped the whole German army single handed. Ho ho. Those newspaper men! But they were very nice. They gave me a right smart reception on my arrival. They drove me through the streets in an open car, and the streets were crowded and we could only go slow.

It seemed as though most all of the people in the streets knew me and when they began to throw the paper and the ticker tape and the confetti out of the windows of those great big skyscrapers, I wondered what it was at first. It looked just like a blizzard. Ho ho. I didn't know it was for me until the Tennessee Society told me.

I don't know what all they did for me, but they did plenty. They took me to the Waldorf Astoria the night of my arrival and we had a little dinner there. I tried to get my mother over the long distance telephone, but we couldn't get through. I wanted to ride in the subway, and, sure enough, next day they had a special train for me. Ho ho.

It was very nice. But I sure wanted to get back to my people where I belonged, and the little old mother and the little mountain girl who were waiting. And I wanted to be in the mountains again and get out with hounds, and tree a coon or knock over a red fox. And in the midst of the crowds and the dinners and receptions I couldn't help thinking of these things. My thoughts just wouldn't stay hitched.

MAY 23rd

New York City.—I was looking at New York City. On the night of the 23d I took the train for Washington, D.C. Honorable Hull had come to get me.

MAY 25th

Washington, D.C.—So I got to Washington this morning about 6 A.M. So we drove a car all over Washington almost, looking at the city, and I had the honor to meet Secretary of War Baker and shake hands with him.

In Washington, D.C., I went in to meet the President, and he was out. I had a nice talk with Secretary of War Baker. I went to Congress. Both houses came together and met me.

From Washington I returned to New York and went out to Camp Merritt and got my transportation papers to Fort Oglethorpe, Georgia, where I got my discharge and my papers and transportation home.

I came on home to Pall Mall, Tennessee, on the 29th of May. My people from all over the mountains, thousands of them, were there to meet me. And my big red headed brothers were there. And we all had a right smart time. And then I lit out for the old log cabin and the little old mother. And then I went to see Gracie—

I didn't do any hunting for a few days. I'm telling you I went hunting Gracie first.

And then, when it was all over and I had taken off the old uniform of the all American Division and got back into the overalls. I got out with the hounds and the old muzzle loader; and I got to thinking and wondering what it was all about.

And I went back to the place on the mountain where I prayed before the war, and received my assurance from God that I would go and come back. And I just stayed out there and thanked that same God who had taken me through the war.

THE END

"For Thou, LORD, wilt bless the righteous; with favour wilt Thou compass him as with a shield."

~ *Psalm 5:12* ~

WORLD WAR II: AUDIE L. MURPHY

Audie Murphy, a baby-faced, 112-pound, twenty-one-year-old with a fifth grade education, was the most decorated soldier in World War II. The following citation describes the heroic action for which he was awarded the Congressional Medal of Honor. Murphy, who was wounded three times and single-handedly killed 240 of the enemy, was given twenty-nine awards for his selfless, astonishing bravery. The story of his exploits was made into a movie titled *To Hell and Back*, in which he starred as himself.

Was Murphy just a cocky, foolhardy kid trying to prove his manliness? All evidence points to the contrary. For all his bravado and macho carousing in the army and afterward, his letters home revealed that he possessed that essential requisite for real courage—fear. Moreover, the war for him was certainly not a romp, but a deeply scarring experience from which he never recovered. For the rest of his life he was plagued by what later came to be called post-traumatic stress syndrome. He had irrational flashes of terror when he sensed that he was still under fire; he was perpetually tortured by grief for his friends who died; and the battlefield constantly haunted his dreams. The persistence of the war in his postwar life, and the alcoholism to which it contributed, made this hero's life a short, tragic one, despite the accolades he received and his successful movie career.

Murphy stands in sharp contrast to the heroic ideal represented by Odysseus in that he sacrificed himself for his comrades instead of selfishly and deliberately placing them in danger. The loss of companions never seems to be uppermost in Odysseus' mind. By contrast, Murphy seemed to be in anguish for the rest of his life over the death of his fellow soldiers. As a consequence, in a profound psychological sense, Murphy, unlike Odysseus, was never able to return home from the war.

FROM OFFICIAL NARRATIVE FOR MEDAL OF HONOR RECIPIENT MURPHY, AUDIE L. COMMITTEE ON VETERANS' AFFAIRS, U.S. SENATE, MEDAL OF HONOR RECIPIENTS

(Washington, D.C.: U.S. Government Printing Office, 1973)

Rank and organization: Second Lieutenant, U.S. Army, Company B, 15th Infantry, 3d Infantry Division.

Place and date: Near Holtzwihr, France, 26 January 1945.

Entered service at: Dallas, Tex. Birth: Hunt County, near Kingston, Tex.
G.O. No. 65. 9 August 1945.
CITATION: 2d Lt. Murphy commanded Company B, which was attacked by 6 tanks and waves of infantry. 2d Lt. Murphy ordered his men to withdraw to prepared positions in a woods, while he remained forward at his command post and continued to give fire directions to the artillery by telephone. Behind him, to his right, 1 of our tank destroyers received a direct hit and began to burn. Its crew withdrew to the woods. 2d Lt. Murphy continued to direct artillery fire which killed large numbers of the advancing enemy infantry. With the enemy tanks abreast of his position, 2d Lt. Murphy climbed on the burning tank destroyer, which was in danger of blowing up at any moment, and employed its .50 caliber machine gun against the enemy. He was alone and exposed to German fire from 3 sides, but his deadly fire killed dozens of Germans and caused their infantry attack to waver. The enemy tanks, losing infantry support, began to fall back. For an hour the Germans tried every available weapon to eliminate 2d Lt. Murphy, but he continued to hold his position and wiped out a squad which was trying to creep up unnoticed on his right flank. Germans reached as close as 10 yards, only to be mowed down by his fire. He received a leg wound, but ignored it and continued the single-handed fight until his ammunition was exhausted. He then made his way to his company, refused medical attention, and organized the company in a counterattack which forced the Germans to withdraw. His directing of artillery fire wiped out many of the enemy; he killed or wounded about 50. 2d Lt. Murphy's indomitable courage and his refusal to give an inch of ground saved his company from possible encirclement and destruction, and enabled it to hold the woods which had been the enemy's objective.

Reprinted from Committee on Veterans' Affairs, U.S. Senate, *Medal of Honor Recipients: 1963–1973* (Washington, D.C., Government Printing Office, 1973).

THE VIETNAM WAR: THE MY LAI MASSACRE

A vastly different kind of conflict from World Wars I and II and different kinds of heroes emerged during the Vietnam War of the 1960s, sometimes referred to as the United States' longest war. Vietnam was still one of the Asian colonies of France after World War II, but in the 1950s it gained its independence as a divided country, communists under Ho Chi Minh governing the north and pro-Western, anticommunist forces governing the south. The corruption in South Vietnam and the failure of its government to allow elections increased the popularity of Ho Chi Minh throughout all of Vietnam, and led to the rise of a South Vietnamese guerrilla force known as the Vietcong, which was supported by the North's Ho Chi Minh. To stem the tide of communism in Vietnam, the United States increased its military strength in the country, up to 500,000 troops by 1967, to battle the Vietcong and North Vietnam.

By the late 1960s, many soldiers began to suspect that native Vietnamese who supported the invading American forces were few and far between, and that the only way to win the war would be to utterly destroy the entire country and its people.

As fighting escalated in what was known as the Tet Offensive of 1968, there was increasing sentiment among U.S. military leaders in Vietnam to "sanitize" villages where Vietcong and their sympathizers were based. Confusion reigned among soldiers about just what their orders were and who their enemies were. The American soldiers' complete lack of understanding of the language, customs, and terrain; their ill-concealed racial arrogance; and the mounting casualties all contributed to their poor relationship with the populace they were supposedly liberating.

It was in such an atmosphere that a military unit called Charlie Company was sent on March 16, 1968, to engage the enemy in a province known to be sympathetic to the Vietcong, in a village referred to as My Lai 4. Upon landing, however, the men found no Vietcong, only civilians—a few old men, and many women and children. Some members of the company began throwing grenades into houses, raping women they captured, and shooting not only livestock but human beings, killing mothers and their babies indiscriminately. Lt. William Calley, their commander, soon gave the order to round up all the villagers into open areas and into ditches and begin killing them. Some men refused, but others, including Lt. Calley walked around, firing into groups of people, killing first the adults and finally the children. Within four hours of their arrival in the village, they had killed 400 to 450 people as an army photographer snapped pictures without lifting a finger in protest.

In the midst of the slaughter, Warrant Officer Hugh Thompson and his two crew members, Larry Colburn and Glenn Andreotta, arrived on the edge of the scene in a helicopter, confused about what was occurring. Hearing gunfire, they signaled to an old Vietnamese woman huddled in a field to stay down while they investigated. Later, when they returned, they found her shot through the head. They then flew farther into the village, and found a huge ditch filled with hundreds of bodies of women and children, and an American soldier firing into it. At this point they began radioing for help. Eventually, they found Charlie Company soldiers preparing to shoot a small group of villagers racing for a bunker. Thompson landed his helicopter between the Vietnamese and the soldiers, and demanded that the shooting stop. He then got out of his helicopter, telling his crew to open fire on the soldiers if any soldier shot a villager. Then he got other villagers out of their bunkers to prevent the marauding soldiers from killing them. And with Vietnamese survivors huddled around him for protection, he radioed for a helicopter to rescue them, remaining until all were lifted out. It is interesting to note that Thompson was outranked by Lt. Calley, who had ordered the massacre. Flying away from the village, the three men spotted movement in a sea of dead bodies and landed again to rescue a child, whom they took with them to an orphanage.

Hugh Thompson immediately informed his superior of what he had observed. Only when he insisted, did the man agree to take him the next day to report to their commander, a full colonel, next in rank to a general. Other numbers should have immediately corroborated Thompson's story: the single American casualty in what was reported as a massive encounter with the enemy was a man who had shot himself in the foot. And only three weapons had been recovered. But a coverup rather than an investigation was forthcoming. Not until two years later, when another soldier, Ron Ridenhour, hearing of the massacre from friends, reported it to his senator, Mo Udall of Arizona, and thirty other congressmen, was an investigation ordered. It was led by a three-star general, William R. Peers. After the hearings, General Peers called Thompson a hero—the only person who had acted to save innocent civilians. As a result of his investigation, Peers recommended that charges be brought against two generals, four full colonels, four lieutenant colonels, four majors, six captains, and eight lieutenants. Only Lt. Calley, however, was found guilty by the military tribunals trying the cases.

Hugh Thompson had received the Distinguished Flying Cross and the Purple Heart for other service in Vietnam. Many people who heard his testimony before the Peers Commission believed that he should have been honored for his courageous stance at My Lai, and they worked in his behalf to get recognition for him. It took twenty-eight years for the government to cite Hugh

Thompson for his actions there. When the army finally agreed to award him the Soldier's Medal for Heroism, it was only on the condition that he, but none of his crew, be recognized and that the award be made in secret in the Pentagon. Thompson refused to agree to these conditions. For two years the army held its ground until finally, in March 1998, on the grounds of the Vietnam Memorial in Washington. D.C., Thompson and his crew were given their medals.

No person could be further from the heroic ideal of Homer than Hugh Thompson. And the fact that the military considered it essential to cover up the massacre for so many years should show us that our own civilization has progressed beyond the days of ancient Greece when, after the Greek victory over Troy, the Greeks butchered men and boys and raped and kidnapped women. It is now a matter of shame rather than of pride to be a "Sacker of Cities."

We call people heroic when they sacrifice themselves for family and friends. But Thompson, Andreotta, and Colburn went beyond even this. They placed their lives on the line to save—not slaughter—people so different from themselves and whom they did not even know.

Almost three decades after the massacre, Thompson and Colburn returned to My Lai, where they broke into tears recalling what they had seen and were embraced by villagers who remembered these men who had saved them from the soldiers with guns.

The two documents included here are, first, Thompson's testimony before the Peers Commission in 1970, and second, a copy of his Medal for Heroism citation.

FROM HUGH THOMPSON, JR., TESTIMONY, IN *REPORT OF THE DEPARTMENT OF THE ARMY REVIEW OF THE PRELIMINARY INVESTIGATION INTO THE MY LAI INCIDENT* (THE GENERAL WILLIAM R. PEERS COMMISSION)

(Washington, D.C.: U.S. Government Printing Office, 1970)

Q: What happened when you put the chopper down?
A: ... When I saw the bodies in the ditch I came back around and saw that some of them were still alive. So I sat [the helicopter] down on the ground then and talked to—I'm pretty sure it was a sergeant, colored sergeant—and I told them there was women and kids over there that were wounded—could he help them or could they help them? And he made some remark to the effect that the only way he could help them was to kill them. And I thought he was joking. I didn't take him seriously. I said, "Why don't you see if you can help them," and I took off again. And as I took off my

crew chief said that the guy was shooting into the ditch. As I turned around I could see a guy holding a weapon pointing towards the ditch.

... And after that we were still flying recon over the village. The village was smoking pretty good. You couldn't get right over it. And we came around somewhere to the east of the village, and I saw this bunker and either the crew chief or the gunner said that there was a bunch of kids in the bunker, and the Americans were approaching it. There was a little open area, field, shaped sort of like a horseshoe, so I set down in the middle of that horseshoe, got out of the aircraft and talked with this lieutenant, and told him that there was some women and kids in that bunker over there, and could he get them out. He said the only way to get them out was with a hand grenade. I told him to just hold your men right where they are and I'll get the kids out. And I walked over towards the bunker, motioned for them to come out, and they came, out. But there was more than women and kids. There was a couple—one or two—old men in there. I'd say about two or three women and then some kids. I got back in the aircraft, didn't take off, just put my helmet on or just plugged my helmet up and I called Mr. Millians who was flying the low gun cover and told him what I had and asked him if he'd come in and get them out of this immediate area back into an area that had not so much firing going on. And he came in and picked up half of them.

Q: Was he able to land in the same horseshoe-shaped area?

A: No, he landed outside the horseshoe-shaped area. He landed behind me.

Q: Yes.

A: And I walked the people to him. He could only take about half of them, and flew them out going back to Highway 521. He flew them, I would say, back up to the vicinity of Hoa My ... because there was a road going off 521 about where he let them out. He came back and got the rest of them and took them up there also. I followed them back. That's how I know where he landed.

Q: How many people did you pick up all told?

A: ... Sixteen, I don't remember today. ...

Q: Now, let me come back here again. Tell me a little more about your discussion with the lieutenant? Did you ever identify the lieutenant?

A: Yes, sir.

Q: Who was he?

A: Lieutenant Calley. ...

Q: Could you tell us what happened as you best recollect, not from the newspapers, but from the time itself?

A: I just did, sir. I told him to stop his troops after he told me the only way he could get them out, and he stopped them. My crew chief and gunner were outside the aircraft also, and I walked across a rice paddy towards the tree line the bunker was in. I got, oh, I would say within 10 or 15 meters of the tree line and motioned for them to come out. As they came out, I gathered them in a little group, and I called for my low gunship and said: "I got some people down here. Can you come in and take them out for me and get them out of this area?"

Q: And that's all that happened? There were no other words or actions?

A: To the best of my knowledge today, sir, there was no words that I can recall between myself and the man who appeared to be the lieutenant.

Q: Any other actions taken?

A: The gunship came in. The one ship came in, took half of them out, went and dropped them off, and then came back and got the rest of them. And I didn't say anything else to the lieutenant to the best of my knowledge today, sir. . . .

Q: Was there any form of altercation or argument between you and Lieutenant Calley or anybody else there . . . ?

A: When I got out of the helicopter, I told my crew chief and gunner to make sure I was covered real close.

Q: From that, I take it, you expected—you were being covered real close. Were you inferring for protection against VC or protection against something that might have been done to you from the U.S. side?

A: I was worried about getting shot, sir, because when I walked over to where the women and children were if the enemy would have started shooting I would have been in a crossfire from the friendly troops because I was between where the enemy was supposed to have been and where our friendly troops were, sir.

Q: Were you afraid of getting shot by our own forces or by the enemy? What I'm trying to get is when you said this to your doorgunners, were they protecting, would they be covering you from the friendly or the enemy side? Or both?

A: They were covering me from both sides, sir. But I'm not saying they were covering me from our troops. Charlie [Vietcong troops] could have been behind our troops also, sir.

Q: Did Lieutenant Calley threaten you with his M-16 or any other way at this time?

A: No, sir.

Q: Did he point his M-16 at you?

A: No, sir, I didn't have any weapons pointed at me. He might have been standing with the—he didn't have it thrown over his shoulder. I mean, I'm sure he had it in his hand. But it wasn't trained on myself, sir.

Q: Was this PFC Colburn covering you with his M-60?

A: Yes, sir. Both my crew chief and my gunner both had M-60s. (vol. 2, bk. 8, 10–12)

THE SOLDIER'S MEDAL FOR HEROISM AWARDED TO HUGH C. THOMPSON, JR.

(United States Army, March 1998)

For heroism above and beyond the call of duty on 16 March 1968, while saving the lives of at least 10 Vietnamese civilians during the unlawful massacre of noncombatants by American forces at My Lai, Quang Ngai Province, South Vietnam. Warrant Officer Thompson landed his helicopter in the line of fire between fleeing Vietnamese civilians and pursuing American ground troops to prevent their murder.

He then personally confronted the leader of the American ground troops and was prepared to open fire on those American troops should they fire upon the civilians. Warrant Officer Thompson, at the risk of his own personal safety, went forward of the American lines and coaxed the Vietnamese civilians out of the bunker to enable their evacuation. Leaving the area after requesting and overseeing the civilians' air evacuation, his crew spotted movement in a ditch filled with bodies south of My Lai Four. Warrant Officer Thompson again landed his helicopter and covered his crew as they retrieved a wounded child from the pile of bodies. He then flew the child to the safety of a hospital at Quang Ngai. Warrant Officer Thompson's relayed radio reports of the massacre and subsequent report to his section leader and commander resulted in an order for the cease-fire at My Lai and an end to the killing of innocent civilians. Warrant Officer Thompson's heroism exemplifies the highest standards of personal courage and ethical conduct, reflecting distinct credit on him, and the United States Army.

HEROIC FIREFIGHTERS AT THE WORLD TRADE CENTER
SEPTEMBER 11, 2001

For four decades, certainly since the beginning of the war in Vietnam, the public had resisted the impulse to designate heroes within the military or other organizational arms at any level of government. But September 11, 2001, was a bloody cataclysm that necessitated a tragic landmark in the history of heroism as New York City firefighters were embraced worldwide as heroes.

At 8:45 on the morning of September 11, an American Airlines Boeing 767, hijacked by Muslim fanatics, blasted into the North Tower of the World Trade Center, dooming the occupants on the top floors of the 110-story building. Jet fuel exploded like the most powerful of bombs. Fire shot out of rooms, and other rooms and hallways collapsed. As occupants streamed down the stairs, rescue workers rushed to the scene and ran up the stairs, searching for people to evacuate. At 9:06 a second hijacked plane crashed through the World Trade Center's South Tower, and firefighters again mounted the stairs, even as smoke choked the hallways and the steel and concrete in the massive buildings began to explode, and workers trapped in the unstable buildings began to jump to their deaths from the high floors. One firefighter was killed when he was hit by someone jumping from one of the towers. Less than an hour later, the 110-story South Tower collapsed, and at 10:29 the North Tower also crashed down, both crushing thousands of occupants, including hundreds of firefighters and policemen. Concrete and steel debris the size of cars crashed to the pavement, crushing nearby buildings and vehicles and killing many people on the ground below. Another firefighter, rescuing the wounded on the ground, ducked under his truck as one of the buildings came down. When he was able to crawl out, he found that his entire company was dead.

Thousands of people died in the attacks that occurred on September 11; close to 300 of those deaths were firefighters'. What made them heroes was their immediate response to the disaster and their disregard for their own personal safety in rescuing others from gigantic buildings that had become death traps. In their actions we see clear evidence of how far the evolution of the heroic ideal has come. Agamemnon's Greek army became heroes because of their brute strength and courage to destroy and rule. The New York City firefighters became heroes because of their decisions and impulses to save.

The following excerpts document the events of that day involving New York City rescue workers.

FIREFIGHTERS' ACCOUNTS OF SEPTEMBER 11

Jane Fritsch's article is a valuable record, focusing on the firefighters themselves, filed for the *New York Times* at the end of a day that wrenched the United States. Excerpts from the article show the heroism of the firefighters, the dangers inherent in the scene, and the personal devastation suffered by the surviving rescue workers.

FROM JANE FRITSCH, "RESCUE WORKERS RUSH IN, BUT MANY DO NOT RETURN"

(*New York Times*, September 12, 2001, A2)

New York firefighters, impelled by instinct and training, rushed to the World Trade Center yesterday to evacuate victims. Then the buildings fell down. The firefighters never came out.

About 200 firefighters were unaccounted for when the day ended. It was the worst disaster in the New York Fire Department's history, explosions having collapsed the two main towers onto the first wave of rescuers as they snaked through stairwells and hallways.

In the tumult of the morning, the temporary command center set up on a nearby street to deal with the calamity was buried in a rolling wave of concrete chunks.

...

"We will be lucky if we don't lose 200 or 300 guys," said Michael Carter, vice president of the Uniformed Firefighters Association, who was on the scene. "There are entire companies we can't find. At this point, it's less of a firefighting operation and more like a war."

...

By the time the buildings collapsed, more than 400 firefighters were at the scene, many of them racing up stairways to reach people trapped on the upper floors, fire officials said. Many of the rescuers were from six-person units that specialize in building collapses, and many are now missing, presumed to have died when the buildings collapsed.

...

Another firefighter, who declined to give his name, knelt on the asphalt, a towel over his shoulder and his eyes bloodshot.

"I saw at least ten people jump," he said. "I heard even more than that land and crash through the glass ceiling in the atrium." ... He stopped, unable to continue talking.

He said he entered the lobby of 2 World Trade Center with his company, but was immediately blown across the lobby. "We did our best to crawl out," he said. "My company is still missing two guys. They went back in to help people." (A2)

A HERO'S WELCOME

The excerpt from an article by Martin Snapp is an indication of just how widespread and enduring was the public's appreciation of the heroism of New York City firefighters, in that the article was written in California some six months after the attack on the World Trade Center.

It also provides a rare view of the events of September 11 through the eyes of a firefighter who was rushing to duty on that day.

FROM MARTIN SNAPP, "IT'S A HERO'S WELCOME FOR FDNY FIREFIGHTER"

(*The Journal* [Richmond, California], March 8, 2002)

Berkeley has played host over the years to presidents, prime ministers and Nobel laureates. But never was the city more honored than last weekend, when it hosted Kenny King, a New York City firefighter. . . .

Next Tuesday will be the six-month anniversary of the Sept. 11 attacks, but for King it feels like yesterday.

He was at home on Staten Island that day, enjoying his day off. But as soon as he heard that the first tower had been hit, he and his fellow firefighter Marco Silva raced to the Staten Island ferry. They were joined by scores of other firemen, all trying to get to Manhattan.

"My firehouse is just a few blocks away from the World Trade Center, and I knew my guys would be among the first to respond," he told the [*Village*] *Voice*. "By the time our ferry left the terminal, the South Tower was already down. All Marc and I could do was pray for the North Tower because we knew our guys were probably still inside."

As the ferry boat passed the Statue of Liberty, the North Tower began to crumble. King grabbed Silva's arm, "Marc—the guys!" he said in disbelief.

"I know, Kenny, I know," was all Silva could say, as they watched helplessly while their friends were being murdered.

The ferry trip took only 22 minutes, but to King and Silva it felt like an eternity. The boat docked at the terminal, a few blocks from Ground Zero. As the firemen walked down the ramp from the boat, they were greeted by an unbelievable sight: The ramp was lined on both sides by thousands of refugees from the war zone, hoping to take the ferry back to Staten Island. They were dazed, disheveled, covered in dust from the explosion. Some were distraught. Many were in pain. All were frightened and exhausted.

"And yet," said King, "even in their worst hour of despair, these desperate people somehow managed to gradually put their hands together in applause. It kept building and building until it crescendoed to a level that made us feel like we were the New York Yankees and had just won the seventh game of the World Series!"

Seven men from Engine 6 went into the North Tower that day. Only three came out. Lt. Thomas O'Hagan and firefighters Tom O'Holohan, Billy Johnston, and King's best friend, Paul Beyer, perished, leaving many small children without their daddies. "They could have gotten out, they could have saved themselves," said King, "but they didn't. They chose to save others, instead." (A10)

MEMORIAL SERVICE FOR MARK BINGHAM, HERO OF UNITED FLIGHT 93

On September 11, 2001, terrorists hijacked four jet airplanes. Two of them crashed into the World Trade Center; one crashed into the Pentagon; and one, probably intended for the U.S. Capitol, crashed in a field in Pennsylvania instead. All those aboard were killed, but many more lives, which would have been lost had the hijackers reached their target, were saved. Before the plane went down, some of the passengers on that flight were able to call friends or authorities on their cell phones to report that a few of them were going to storm the terrorists in order to abort their plans. Mark Bingham, a young, gung-ho graduate of the University of California, was one of those individuals.

In the following article, Martin Snapp reports on the memorial service to this hero—a service attended by Senator John McCain, a hero of the Vietnam War.

FROM MARTIN SNAPP, "MARK BINGHAM REMEMBERED"

(The Journal [Richmond, California], March 8 2002)

Blue and gold mingled with red, white and blue as they said goodbye to Mark Bingham last Saturday at his beloved UC-Berkeley. As probably the whole world knows by now, he was one of the at least four heroes—there may have been others we don't know about—of United Flight 93, who stormed the hijackers and prevented the plane from crashing into the Capitol, at the cost of their own lives.

The memorial service was held on the Cal campus because Mark has to have been the No. 1 Bear rooter of all time. A rugby star who led the Golden Bears to the '91 and '93 national titles, he never spent a day of his adult life without the words "Go Bears" crossing his lips. He once sent a letter to his mom that read, "Dear Mom, Go Bears! (repeated 100 times) Love, Mark."

His affection for his alma mater was matched only by his contempt for that other school down on the peninsula, which he insisted on calling "Leland Stanford Junior College." He never (ever) wore red. And who can forget the awful Big Game nine years ago, when Stanford was running up the score on the Bears and the Stanford mascot, the Tree, was prancing up and down the sidelines, taunting the Cal fans? Remember how someone jumped out of the stands and—how shall we put it?—"defoliated" the Tree? That was Mark Bingham.

. . .

Mark's friends and family flew in from all over the country for the service. But there were also many people like me, who never knew him but wish they did. The service was held in Wheeler Auditorium. I must admit, it was strange to be sitting in the same room where I had attended so many anti-war meetings back in the '60s. I got there early, so I took a few minutes to duck downstairs to the basement to use the men's room. I was the only one in the room. Then the door opened, and in walked a guy in a dark suit, who stood at the urinal next to me. I looked at him, and I couldn't believe my eyes: It was John McCain. I gaped in astonishment for what seemed like hours until he realized that I was too dumbstruck to speak. He stuck out his hand and said, "Hi. I'm John McCain."

We talked for a few minutes about the anti-war rally at Sproul Plaza earlier in the week, and I told him what I truly believe: that while there are a lot of people in Berkeley who are opposed to fighting, there are also a lot of people in Berkeley who aren't. "I know," he said. "People in Berkeley are just as patriotic as people everywhere else."

. . .

The service began with the Cal Men's Octet singing "The Star-Spangled Banner" and, of course, the Cal Alma Mater, "Hail To California" (with its final words, "Fighting 'neath her standard/We will never fail/California Alma Mater/Hail! Hail! Hail!" having tragic new meaning in the wake of recent events).

Then some of Mark's friends, family and former teachers got up to speak; and the picture they painted was of a vibrant, fun-loving young man who, as his lifelong friend, Cameron Dawson, put it, "drank from the cup of life with both hands on the cup." Another friend described him as "a big Labrador puppy of a man, forever bounding through life."

They talked about his passion for rugby, his love of adventure (last spring he ran with the bulls in Pamplona), his penchant for mischievous pranks, and the tall tales he'd tell to try to get out of trouble for having pulled them. They talked about his open heart, his generosity, his knack for making everyone feel included, and his fierce loyalty to the many, many people he loved—especially his mother, Alice Hoglan. (Over his desk in his office, he hung a sign reading, "Alice Hoglan is a goddess!")

. . .

The speeches were interspersed with two multi-media slide shows, featuring snapshots of Mark that made many in the audience laugh knowingly. Most of the people seated on stage twisted around to look at the screen behind them. But McCain waited until the lights went dark; then he quietly got out of his chair and stood to one side, facing the screen directly. I wondered why for a second, and it hit me: He probably can't turn his neck anymore because of the torture he suffered in North Vietnamese prisons.

. . .

Then Paul Holm, the man with whom Mark had a six-year relationship, spoke. Listening to him, I swelled with pride over the fact that Mark was gay, even though I'm straight myself. I couldn't help thinking, "Take that, Jerry Falwell! Let's see you try to mouth off about gays now!"

The next-to-last speaker was McCain. He made it quite clear why he had flown all the way across the country to be there: He wanted to thank the man who saved his life. McCain was in the Capitol that terrible morning. So was every other Senator and Representative. Plus hundreds of Congressional staffers, many of whom are barely out of college. Plus janitors, plumbers, carpenters, electricians, messengers, restaurant workers, security guards, clerks in the House and Senate post offices, salespeople at the souvenir stands—the list goes on and on. Worst of all, hundreds—perhaps thousands—of schoolchildren visit the Capitol every day. You can see their tour busses stretching for blocks and blocks. Mark Bingham, Todd Beamer, Tom Burnett and Jeremy Glick saved them all. They also saved the Capitol itself, the temple of our democracy. They saved the Rotunda, where martyred presidents from Lincoln to Kennedy have lain in state. They saved priceless paintings and irreplaceable historic artifacts. Without them, the unspeakable horror of Sept. 11 would have been even worse.

McCain quoted the Gospel of John—"Greater love hath no man than this: that he lay down his life for his friends"—adding, "The only way I can thank Mark is to try to be as good an American as he was."

...

McCain's remarks were much appreciated by the audience, and he got a long round of applause. But not a standing ovation. That was reserved for the final speaker, Mark's mom, who got two. The first came when McCain introduced her: Everyone rose as one to thank her for producing and nuturing such a wonderful son. The second came when she sat down again, after she said, "God bless you for coming here, God bless Mark Bingham, and God bless America."

I wish I could tell you what she said in between, but unfortunately I took my notes in water-soluble ink, and now they're so runny I can't decipher them.

...

A final note: There are many great paintings in the Capitol, the building that was saved by Mark Bingham and his band of brothers. They depict the great heroes of every generation. (The most recent one is a group portrait of the Challenger astronauts.) And here's the part that always gives me the shivers: Some of the walls are still blank. They're being reserved for the heroes yet unborn and the great deeds yet to be done. I reminded McCain of this when we were talking in the basement of Wheeler Hall, and I said, "Senator, I think it's time for a new painting."

"Don't worry," he said. "It's already in the works."

Thank you, Mark. Say hi to Nathan Hale. I think you two will have a lot to say to each other. And, of course, Go Bears!

PROJECTS FOR WRITTEN AND ORAL EXPLORATION

1. Write a comprehensive definition of what it takes to be a hero in the modern world, using specific illustrations.

2. Write a paper on someone you consider to be a hero and describe what your choice says about you.

3. With reference to your papers on the definition of the hero and your own choice of a hero, examine the character of Odysseus and show how he does or does not measure up to your definition of "hero."

4. As a class project, plan and conduct a poll asking individuals in a given group (or groups) whom they admire as heroes. Analyze your findings and construct a report.

5. Conduct a class discussion on the subject of the modern hero from the working class. Explore the subject of the working-class hero and why, for example, so many of our twentieth-century war heroes came from the lower ranks instead of the ranks of the generals.

6. Write a serious or funny essay on the most heroic thing you have ever done.

7. Conduct a class debate on the question of whether a hero must be a "good" person.

8. Consider the old saying "It is good and glorious to die for one's country." Conduct a debate on the wisdom of this idea.

SUGGESTED READINGS

Anderson, David L. *Facing My Lai*. Lawrence: University Press of Kansas, 1998.

Bilton, Michael. *Four Hours at My Lai*. New York: Viking Press, 1992.

Carlyle, Thomas. *On Heroes, Hero-Worship and the Heroic in History*. Berkeley: University of California Press, 1991.

French, Peter A., ed. *Individual and Collective Responsibility: Massacre at My Lai*. Cambridge, MA: Schenkman, 1972.

Graham, Don. *No Name on the Bullet: A Biography of Audie Murphy*. New York: Viking Press, 1989.

Lee, David. *Sergeant York: An American Hero*. Lexington: University Press of Kentucky, 1985.

Murphy, Audie. *To Hell and Back*. Blue Ridge Summit, PA: Tab Books, 1988.

Nott, Robert. *Last of the Cowboy Heroes*. Jefferson, NC: McFarland, 2000.

Segal, Charles. *Singers, Heroes, and Gods in The Odyssey*. Ithaca, NY: Cornell University Press, 1994.

Whiting, Charles. *Hero: The Life and Death of Audio Murphy*. Chelsea, MI: Scarborough House, 1990.

Index

Achilles, 109–11; death of, 114; myth of, 25–26
"Administration Considers Broader, More Powerful Options for Potential Retaliation" (Schmitt and Shanker), 160
Adventures of Huckleberry Finn (Twain), 148
Aegean Sea, 61–62
Aelios, 4
Aeschylus, 145–46, 151–52
Agamemnon, 3, 11–12, 109–10, 122, 144; House of Atreus, 23–25
Age of Fable, The (Bulfinch), 28–30
Agora, 101
Ajax, 109, 111
Al-Qaeda, 159
Alcinoos, 3
Ali, Muhammad, 170
An Illustrated History of the Olympics (Schaap), 173–74
Andreotta, Glenn, 206–7
Anticleia, 3
Antinoos, 3
Apple of Discord, 22–23

Archaeological excavations, 71–84; chronology of, 78–81; important archaeologists, 71; major relevant areas, 71
Aristotle, 135, 139–40, 188
Arkadia, 43
"Arsonists Burn 10 Catholic Churches in Ulster" (Clarity), 153–55
Ashe, Arthur, 169
Athena, 37–42
Athlete hero, 165–68; as American hero, 179–80; Homeric athlete hero, 165–68; in modern world, 168–71; Owens as, 174–78; salaries of, 169–70; Thorpe as, 172–73
Aulis, delay at, 111

Basileus or King, 100
Beauty contest, 108
Bennet, James, 157
Billy the Kid, 149
Bingham, Mark, 215–17
Blegen, Carl W., 69, 71, 75, 116–17, 126–27
Bonney, William (Billy the Kid), 149

Bradley, Bill, 170
Bronze Age, 88–89
Bruce, Thomas (Lord Elgin), 73
Bryant, Jacob, 72
Bulfinch, Thomas, 27–30
Bury, John Bagnell, 96, 100–3, 117, 124–25
Bush, George W., 149, 159–60
Butcher, S. H., 92

Calley, William, 205
Calvert, Frank, 73
Calypso, 4, 11
Campbell, Joseph, 7
Carter, Jimmy, 168
Cary, Max, 62–64
Chamberlain, Wilt, 169
Characters, 2–3
Chavez, Cesar, 189
Children's education, myth and, 45–52
Chronology of events, 3–4
Cicones, 3
Circe, 4, 10
Clarity, James F., 153–55
Colburn, Larry, 206–7
Colonization, 61
Contemporary applications, Homeric athlete hero, 165–68
Crete, 77, 91–92
Cyclops, 4, 9

Damos (common people), 131
Dark Ages, 93–96, 102–3
Demodocos, 3
DiMaggio, Joe, 169
Dorians, 94
Dorpfeld, Wilhelm, 69, 71, 74, 116

Early prehistory, 87–90
Elgin, Lord (Thomas Bruce), 73
Eumaeos, 3
Eumenides (Aeschylus), 151–52
Euripides, 115

Eurycleia, 3
Evans, Sir Arthur, 71, 74, 76–79, 91, 124
Evelyn-White, Hugh G., 32, 136

Fagles, Robert, 59
"For Fatah, Only a War Can Bring Peace to the Mideast" (Bennet), 157
"For Many, Sorrow Turns to Anger and Talk of Vengeance" (Harden), 161
Freeman, Charles, 96, 99
Fritsch, Jane, 212
Funeral games, 166

Gandhi, Mohandas, 189
Gehrig, Lou, 169
Geographic Background of Greek and Roman History (Cary), 63
Geography of Mediterranean world: invasion, colonization, and trade, 61; location of Greece, 55–56; sites in *The Odyssey,* 57–58; theories on Odysseus' journey, 59
Geography of Strabo, The (Strabo), 65–66
Gibson, Althea, 169
Gods, 30; family tree of, 18–20, 32; in Greek mythology, 17–18; Homer's use of, 18; mythical narratives, 20–26
"Gold Medal for Jesse Owens" (Hearings), 175–76
Grange, Red, 169
Greece: Aegean and Mediterranean Seas, 61–62; ancient account of geography, 65; invasion, colonization, and trade, 61; location of, 55–56; mountains of, 60–61; natural resources, 60–61; Pausanias' guide to, 43–44; sites in *The Odyssey,* 57–58; territory comprising, 56–59; theories on Odysseus' journey, 57–59
Greece in the Making (Osborne), 102

Greek Army, 110–11
Greek mythology: development of the Gods, 17–18; family tree of Gods, 18–20; Homer and, 15–27; Homer's use of Gods, 18
Green Achievement, The (Freeman), 99
Guide to Greece (Pausanias), 43–44

Harden, Blaine, 161
Harris, Janet C., 179
Hatfields-McCoys feud, 148
Hector: death of, 113–14; funeral of, 115
Helen, 3, 12, 18; abduction of, 23, 118–21; birth of, 20–21; courtship and wedding of, 22; Paris' abduction of, 118–21
Hellas, 97–98
Helmick, Robert H., 177–78
Hero: athlete hero, 165–68; ideal of, 188; war hero, 188–89
Hero with a Thousand Faces, The (Campbell), 7
Herodotus, 27, 30–31, 117–21
"Heroes of Young America" (Lane), 179
Heroic Age, 183; political organizations in, 100–1
Heroic ideal, 183–90; Bingham, Mark, 215–17; Murphy, Audie, 203–4; September 11 heroes, 211–17; Thompson, Hugh, 205–10; York, Sergeant, 191–202
Hesiod, 27, 31–36, 135
Hesiod: The Homeric Hymns and Homerica (Hesiod), 31–36
Hill, G. F., 2
Hissarlik, as site of Trojan War, 126
Historical context, 87–96; Dark Ages, 93–96; early prehistory, 87–90; Minoan Crete, 91–92; Mycenaean age, 92–93; proto-Greek invasions, 90–91; Trojan War, 115–17

Histories, The (Herodotus), 30–31
Histories, The (Thucydides), 67, 97–98, 122–23
History of Greece, A (Bury), 100–3, 124–25
History of Herodotus, The (Herodotus), 118–21
Hitler, Adolf, 169, 174
Ho Chi Minh, 205
Homer: Greek mythology and, 15–27; rage in Trojan War account, 112–13; use of Gods, 18
Homer. The Odyssey (Fagles), 59
Homeric athlete hero, 165–68. *See also* Athlete hero
Honor, concept of, 185
House of Atreus, 23–25

Iliad, The, 112, 133, 166, 185
In Search of the Trojan War (Wood), 91, 138
Initiation and resolution, 1, 5–7
Intifada (Arab holy war), 156
Invasion, 61
Ireland, Vengeance and, 153–55
"Israel Strikes Hard at Gaza Strip" (Schmemann), 157
"It's a Hero's Welcome for FDNY Firefighter" (Snapp), 213–14

Jones, Horace Leonard, 65
Jones, W. H. S., 43
Jordan, Michael, 170
Jowett, Benjamin, 67, 97–98, 122
Joyce, James, 1
Judeo-Christian tradition of vengeance, 146–47
Justice, 151

Kalokairinos, Minos, 71, 74
King, Martin Luther, 189
King's companions, 101
Knossos, 77–79
Knox, Bernard, 59

Kournikova, Anna, 170
Kourouniotis, K., 75

Laertes, 3
Land of the Lotus-Eaters, 3, 8
Lane, H. U., 179
Lang, Andrew, 92
Law of state, revenge and vengeance, 147–48
Leake, William, 73
Lechevalier, Jean Baptiste, 72
Lestrygonians, 4
Literary analysis; chronology of events, 3–4; fundamental themes of, 1; initiation and resolution, 5–7; literary technique of storytelling, 4–5; major characters, 2–3; narrative sequence, 4; resolution and return, 7–12; technique of storytelling, 4–5; time frame of, 2; transformation and return, 1–12
Louis, Joe, 169

McCain, John, 215
Maclaren, Charles, 73
Major characters, 2–3
Manatt, J. Irving, 83
Manhood, 1, 5–7
Manning, Peyton, 170
Manual of Mythology (Murray), 37–42
"Mark Bingham Remembered" (Snapp), 215–17
Marlowe, Christopher, 107
Mediterranean Sea, 61–62
Men servants, 133
Menelaos of Lacdemon, 3
Minoan Crete, 91–92
Modern applications: evolution of heroic ideal, 183–90; problem of revenge, 143–50
Monarchy, 101
Morritt, John, 72
Mountains of Greece, 60–61
Munich Olympic tragedy (1972), 169

Murphy, Audie, 188–90, 203–5
Murray, Alexander S., 27, 37–42
My Lai massacre, 205–10
Mycenae, 80, 99
Mycenae (Schliemann), 80–82
Mycenaean age, 92–93
Mycenaean Age, The (Tsountas), 83–84
Mycenaean palaces, 83–84
Myth: children's education and, 45–52; definition of, 15–17; development of the Gods, 17–18; eternal voyage, 1
Mythical narratives, 20–26; abduction of Helen, 23; Agamemnon and House of Atreus, 23–25; apple of discord, 22–23; birth of Helen, 20–21; birth of Paris Alexander, 21; courtship and wedding of Helen, 22; myth of Achilles, 25–26; Trojan War, 23. See also Greek mythology
Mythological atlas, 28

Narrative sequence, 4
Natural resources, 60–61
Nausicaa, 3
Near East, vengeance in, 156–58
Nestor, 3, 58, 109, 111

Odysseus, 1–3, 58, 68, 109–10, 144, 185–86
"Official Narrative for Medal of Honor Recipient Murphy, Audie L.," 203
Olympic Games, 165, 167–68
Orestes, 109, 144–46
Osborne, Robin, 102
Owens, Jesse, 169, 171, 174–78

Palace of Minos (Evans), 77–79
Palestine Liberation Organization (PLO), 156
Paris, abduction of Helen, 118–21
Paris Alexander, birth of, 21
Patroclus, 113
Pausanias, 43–44

Peers, William R., 206–7
Peers Commission, 207–10
Peisistratos, 3
Penelope, 3, 11, 109, 144
Piracy, 67, 138
Plato, 45–52
Poetics (Aristotle), 188
Political organizations, 100
Political power, 124–25
Politics (Aristotle), 135, 139–40
Polyphemos, 3
Poseidon, 37–42
Posttraumatic stress syndrome, 190, 203
Proto-Greek invasions, 90–91
Psychology and Sociology of Sport: Current Selected Research (Velden), 179

Rackham, Harris, 139
Rage, 112
Rawlinson, George, 118
Report of the Department of the Army Review of the Preliminary Investigation into the My Lai Incident, 207–10
Republic, The (Plato), 45–52
"Rescue Workers Rush In, But Many Do Not Return" (Fritsch), 212
Resolution and return theme, 1, 7–12, 192
Revenge, 143–50; Ireland and, 153–55; Judeo-Christian tradition, 146–47; law of state problems, 147–48; Near East/Middle East and, 156–58; Orestes and Aeschylus, 145–46; post-September 11, 149–50, 159–61; problem of, 143–61; retribution in today's world, 149; vengeance in Near East, 156–58
Ridenhour, Ron, 206
Robinson, Jackie, 169
Ross, Adrian, 169
Ruth, Babe, 169–70

Schaap, Richard, 173
Schliemann, Heinrich, 69, 71, 73–74, 76, 80–83, 115–16
Schmemann, Serge, 157, 159
Schmitt, Eric, 160
September 11th attacks, 156, 190; heroic firefighters, 211–14; United Flight 93 heroes, 215–17; vengeance debate and, 149–50, 159–61
Sergeant York: His Own Life Story and War Diary (Skeyhill), 192–202
Servants, 132–33
Severin, Tim, 59, 62, 68–69
Shanker, Thom, 160
Six-Day War, 156
Skeyhill, Tom, 192
Slaves, 132–34, 139–40
Snapp, Martin, 213
"Soldier's Medal for Heroism Awarded to Hugh C. Thompson, Jr.," 209
Stokes, Louis, 176–77
Storytelling technique, 4–5
Strabo, 62, 65–66

Taliban, 156
Telemachos, 1–8, 109, 134, 144
Telepylos, 3
Tennyson, Alfred, 1
Territorial expansion, 124–25
Tet Offensive, 205
Theogony (Hesiod), 32–36
Thetes (slaves), 132–34
Thompson, Hugh, Jr., 190, 206–10
Thorpe, Jim, 171–73
"Three Catholic Brothers Killed in Fire, Stunning Ulster and Raising Fears" (Clarity), 155
Thucydides, 62, 67, 96–98, 117, 122–23
Time frame, 2
Tiresias, 3
To Hell and Back (movie), 203
Tombs at Mycenae, 80–82

Trade, 61
Trojan Horse, 114, 116
Trojan War, 12, 23; Achilles, 110–11; Agamemnon, 110; Ajax, 111; beauty contest, 108; beginning of war, 108–9; current historical view of, 115–17; death of Achilles, 114; death of Hector, 113–14; death of Patroclus, 113; delay at Aulis, 111; documents, 117; Greek army, 110–12; Hector's funeral, 115; Hissarlik as site of, 126; major characters, 109; major warriors, 112; myth and legend of, 107–8; Nestor, 111; Odysseus, 110; political power, 124–25; rage in Homer's account, 112–13; sacking of Troy, 115; ten-year siege, 112–15; territorial expansion, 124–25; Thucydides on, 122–23; Trojan Horse, 114, 116
Trojan Women, The (Euripides), 115
Troy, 109; sacking of, 115; siege of, 112
Troy and the Trojans (Blegen), 126–27
Tsountas, Chrestos, 71, 74, 76, 83–84
Twain, Mark, 148

Udall, Morris, 206
"Ulster Foes Suspend a Last-Ditch Effort to Avoid a Clash After Slight Progress" (Clarity), 154
Ulysses Voyage, Sea Search for Odysseus, The (Severin), 59
Underclasses (supporting characters), 131–40; Aristotle's *Politics* on slavery, 139–40; life and work in ancient Greece, 136–37; workforce and piracy, 138
United States, history of vengeance and law in, 148–49

Velden, L. Vander, 179
Vellacott, Philip, 151
Ventris, Michael, 71, 75, 138
Vietnam War, My Lai massacre, 205–10

Wace, Alan, 71, 75
"War Against America. An Unfathomable Attack" (*New York Times*), 159–60
War hero, 188–89
Warner, Kurt, 170
White, Byron, 170
Williams, Ted, 169
Women servants, 133
Wood, Michael, 91, 116, 135, 138
Wood, Robert, 72
Woods, Tiger, 169–70
Works and Days (Hesiod), 135–37
World War I, heroism of Sergeant York, 191–201
World War II, heroism of Audie Murphy, 203–5

Yom Kippur War, 156
York, Alvin C., 184, 188, 190–201

Zeus, 32–36

About the Authors

CLAUDIA DURST JOHNSON, former chairperson of English at the University of Alabama, is currently a freelance scholar and writer in Berkeley, California. She is the author of books on American history and literature, as well as theater history. She is also series editor for Greenwood Press's Exploring Social Issues through Literature Series and the Literature in Context Series, for which she has authored several volumes including *Understanding* To Kill a Mockingbird and *Understanding* The Grapes of Wrath.

VERNON JOHNSON has wide experience as an author, theater director, and professor of world literature. He is co-author of *Understanding* The Crucible. He now resides in Berkeley, California, where he continues to write and teach.